Hidden Truth from Prophecy Beyond 2012

Robert B. Scott

WestBow Press books may be ordered through booksellers or by contacting:

WestBow Press
A Division of Thomas Nelson
1663 Liberty Drive
Bloomington, IN 47403
www.westbowpress.com
1-(866) 928-1240

ISBN: 978-1-4497-6840-9 (sc)
ISBN: 978-1-4497-6841-6 (e)

Library of Congress Control Number: 2012917797

Printed in the United States of America

WestBow Press rev. date: 10/25/2012

Contents

Introduction

Many books have been written and movies made about Bible prophecy. While many of them are popular, they are also filled with falseness. The truth about Bible prophecy remains hidden to these writers and moviemakers because they have not discovered the keys to understanding prophecy that this book reveals.

This is more than a book that warns the world of what is about to happen. It is also a book that offers a sure hope for the future. While the winter solstice of 2012 will indeed begin the time of the greatest spiritual darkness the world has ever known, it's not the end. It's not the end of the world; it's not even the end of this age.

December 21, 2012 is the beginning of the end—the end of man's feeble attempt to govern himself under Satan's sway.

"It's always darkest before the dawn" is not a quote from the Bible. God's Book does say, however, that trials may last for the night, but joy comes in the morning (Ps. 30:5). Satan's last-ditch attempt to shroud the earth in darkness means that light is just around the corner. Jesus' return is imminent.

Because He is motivated only by love (1 John 4:8), Jesus is about to come back to clean up the mess we have made of things on this planet. The light of His truth is on the horizon. That truth will dispel the multiple errors of man's religion, including the overwhelming falseness of tradition that permeates even the Christian church, including its unusual ideas about prophecy.

Mind you, some of the hullabaloo about December 21, 2012 is true. The winter solstice of 2012 is indeed an open door to hell—and to spiritual darkness like we've never seen before.

The good news is this: you don't have to be affected by that darkness. And you can receive *now* the light of truth Jesus will soon bring to the whole world.

Such discovery of the truth requires more than a cursory reading of the Scriptures. It requires obedience to certain laws of love God gave us in His Word, an obedience that opens the understanding of the Bible and its prophecies. Jesus Himself said, "If you love Me, you will keep My commandments" (John 14:15).

God may have already called you, or He may be calling you (John 6:44), to be a part of the family that bears the name of our Father God, which is Love (1 John 4:8).

Because God is Love, He gave mankind free will. He won't have to force us to choose His way of love and giving. He knows all things, so He knew Adam would mess up and give Satan the right to rule the world for six days of a thousand years until Jesus returns. At that time, He said He'd come back to rule on His seventh millennial day—or Sabbath—over the earth with His saints (Rev. 5:10).

I pray this book will stir believers to prepare and thus speed up Jesus' glorious coming. This world needs Him.

This is not a manual about how to survive physically in times of catastrophe. Deliverance in the times commencing late 2012 will require supernatural help, the kind promised to those who know they are in the protective arms of Father Love. In His arms, "A thousand may fall at your side and ten thousand at your right hand, but it shall not approach you… No evil will befall you, nor will any plague come near your tent" (Ps. 91:7,10).

Even if God doesn't call you in this age, and you do die in the coming times of trouble and war, you're not going to a fiery hell like the misguided preachers tell you. What most evangelists and prophecy teachers don't know, even though almost seven hundred Bible verses prove it, is that you will be raised to have your first real opportunity to know Jesus in a perfect world.

You probably never heard that before! Yes, you will be raised to live out a full life after Jesus' millennial rule on the earth, to accept Him and be part of the Family of Love when Satan will be long gone! I expound on this truth in Appendix I.

You may be a hardened unbeliever as you read these words. This book will serve as a warning that the sins of our nations, in which you have willingly participated, have direct consequences, and this cause and effect will begin to be felt in late 2012.

The nation that has heretofore led the world in economic and political power chose to legalize the shedding of innocent infant blood (an abomination in God's sight, according to (Proverbs 6:17) forty years before December 21, 2012. For what people consider a harmless abortion to protect women's rights, God uses the term "bloodguiltiness" (Deut. 21:8). Such blood defiles the land, and a defiled land has forfeited the right to God's protection.

God has called us to lift up our voices in an unpopular warning to expose the sins of our people (Isa. 58:1). Our calling or anointing as a church is Isaiah 58 and 59:1–3. We want to be faithful so that the blood is not on our heads (Ezek. 33:4).

Part of my mission is to restore truth that sets people free (John 8:32), including the truth that has enabled me to write this book, unique among books on prophecy.

I have received these revelations because I have been blessed to understand and obey, by God's mercy and empowering grace, the secret revealed in my book *Bible Code Broken: The Truth about the Christian Sabbath* (Isa. 58:13–14).

Adhering to God's laws of love and demonstrating a hunger to understand the Word of God and the conceptual nature of the original Bible languages has led the leadership of Freedom Church of God—notably my colleague, apostolic leader Gerald Budzinski—to have an uncommon grasp of end-time prophetic events.

Scholars who specialize in true ancient Hebrew are amazed at the knowledge revealed by church leadership, especially the Hebrew in the much-misunderstood book of Job.

What you won't read in any other book I know of is that Job is the foundational book of Bible prophecy, laying the groundwork for all the other prophetic verses and books. Job was a major prophet, as was Isaiah, which is also a key book of prophecy.

Jesus (the member of the Godhead that dealt with men in the Hebrew Scriptures, as many verses show) called Job a righteous man three times in the beginning of the book. The words and prayers of a righteous man or woman are some of the most powerful forces in the earth. They make things happen. They change the course of events.

If you are—or become—a believer, you have the same power. In fact, the timing and accomplishment of end-time events prophesied in the Bible depends on *you*. Talk about an interactive book!

Yes, Jesus said that if it weren't for us believers, the elect, and our prayers, the events beginning in 2012 would cause all life to be erased from our planet (Mat. 24:22; Mal. 4:6).

God gave man a body appropriate for living on earth and a voice to speak out and prophesy just as God Himself does (Gen. 1:26–27; John 1:1–18). But God gave the power of the tongue over the earth to *man*. When man speaks, we allow God to act on the earth. Angels perform God's Word when man speaks it (Ps. 103:20).

The words of righteous Job changed the course of history. They prophesied the time of unprecedented spiritual darkness that will begin to envelop the world as early as December 21, 2012.

Some of Job's words allowed Satan to bring darkness, even literal darkness, throughout history and in these last days. But His words also allowed Jesus to come into this world to die for it, and then to return in His glory to rescue mankind from the gathering darkness and bring His marvelous light to this world.

Job's words empowered Satan to bring unprecedented trials upon believers in the end time, allowing all hell to break loose in late 2012 to test the Christians living in the last days. Those words of Job, on the other hand, also opened the door for all *heaven* to break forth in the lives of those who would be drawn by the Father to Jesus in the last days (John 6:44; John 15:16). The glorious light of truth in the Person of Jesus will be made available to those who choose to obey His commandments of love (John 14:15).

Because God gives free will, even to believers, He was obliged to pen numerous and varying last days scenarios regarding events that depend entirely on man's free will. Some dates revealed in the cross-referenced chronologies of Bible prophecy are flexible, but 2012 is not one of them.

Books have been written about the events of September 11, 2001. One of those works, a popular one entitled *The Harbinger*,1 reveals some amazing "coincidences" about that time and relates them to Isaiah 9:10. An actual sycamore tree was found in the rubble near ground zero, and a literal cedar tree was planted near the site years later. Leaders made declarations expressing "arrogance of heart" (Isa. 9:9), asserting that America would rise in her own strength to rebuild.

---

1. *Jonathan Cahn. The Harbinger: The Ancient Mystery that Holds the Secret of America's Future (Laguna Hills, CA: Frontline, 2012).*

Author Jonathan Cahn connects these events with the warning signs given to ancient Israel. The events uncovered in Cahn's book have an uncanny resemblance to what happened millennia ago in Israel, and he sees them as harbingers or warning signs to America. And they are.

The prophetic warnings in Cahn's work are incomplete, however, without this book. These signs show something far more important than a similarity with ancient Israel. They are among the many factors revealing an amazing truth that unlocks the hidden truths of Bible prophecy for these last days.

That truth is a shocker: America *is* Israel!

I will prove that assertion later in this book. It is provable both biblically and historically, and without that truth you cannot understand prophecy.

It is impossible to understand the chronological sequences that involve 2012 without understanding the identity in prophecy of the major Anglo-Saxon players in the last days. Furthermore, only obedience to all God's laws of love, with failings recognized and cleansed by the blood of Jesus, can make sense of the pieces of the prophetic puzzle.

That's why we believe this book presents a unique prophetic scenario. After all, how could you possibly understand what is going to happen in these last days if you don't know the identity of the major players in Bible prophecy, past and present?

It is essential to know the truth that has been much maligned but stands the test of biblical study and history: America *is* Israel.

The little nation of Israel will certainly be an important player in end-time prophecy. It is, after all, the geographic center of end-time prophetic events. God says He will "make Jerusalem a heavy stone for all the peoples" (Zech. 12:3). But if that's all you know, you don't know enough to expound prophecy. Yet virtually none of the famous prophetic teachers know this truth.

It's time someone published a book on prophecy that exposes the truth!

The purpose of this book is twofold. First, it is important to unravel the mysteries of Bible prophecy as a wake-up call for a nonchalant Christian church, awakening those who are willing to receive the revelation. This awakening will help prepare a spotless bride to meet her Bridegroom, as God calls the church and Jesus (2 Cor. 11:2; Eph. 5:27).

The prophecies of Job are not only wake-up calls, however. They explain what believers have gone through and why, giving encouragement and instruction to believers in these last days so they can prepare spiritually. This is indeed a book about important spiritual preparation. It's about how to walk in love and pray in love for our spiritual brothers—not to mention for the world—so God's Kingdom of Love can come to this earth soon.

The second purpose of these words is to be a part of the fulfillment of Matthew 24:14, preaching the gospel of the Kingdom of God as a warning to the world. We must announce the good news that Satan's darkness, soon to engulf the world, will be short-lived. The light of Jesus will quickly dissipate Satan's darkness, crushing his feeble attempt to defeat Jesus and His believers.

Our mission as a church is not always a pleasant one, but we must obey what God has revealed as our task, to cry aloud and show both unbelievers and believers their sins (Isa. 58:1) so they realize that what will begin to happen in December 2012 is a matter of cause and effect. Sin brings consequences.

One of the tasks Jesus gave His disciples, including us, was to teach (or disciple) those God has called, "teaching them to observe all that I commanded you; and lo, I am with you always, even to the end of the age" (Mat. 28:20).

Jesus was the Word who spoke throughout the Bible, even in what men disparagingly call the "Old" Testament, a term God never used. So, teaching believers to obey the whole Bible seems like a daunting task, and of course we can't do it in one book. Nor can we begin to obey in our strength. Jesus is the Grace and Love in us, enabling us to keep His commandments of love (Rom. 13:10). Jesus encouraged us all not to be afraid in these last days, because He is with us and in us.

We can do nothing of ourselves (John 15:5), and whether He holds our hand as we walk through the valley of trial (Ps. 23:4) or He raptures us out of the worst scenario (Ps. 91:14; Isa. 26:20–21; Luke 21:36), He says He will never leave us (Heb. 13:5). If that doesn't give us hope and courage in these dark times, what will?

Some Christians will fail to heed the wake-up call sounded in this book, mirroring the most important Book of all—the Bible. They will have to go through the Great Tribulation, whose beginning date will be determined by how well and how soon the church prepares spiritually. They will be required to give their lives to prove a loyalty they did not show before it was too late, going heavenward the hard way.

For you who seek to obey and understand, whether God draws you to Jesus through this book or whether or not you heed its warning, you will find much spiritual meat in these unique pages.

We must give the warning of what will begin to happen soon, and then it will be your responsibility. We pray that many will heed and be blessed with Jesus' light. That light will protect you from any and all of the darkness Satan is preparing.

For those who have ears to hear, we say with Jesus, "Choose life" (Deut. 30:19). The darkness is about to strike as never before, but we encourage you to choose light—the light and truth of Jesus. His truth is a lifesaver, and it includes some important warnings.

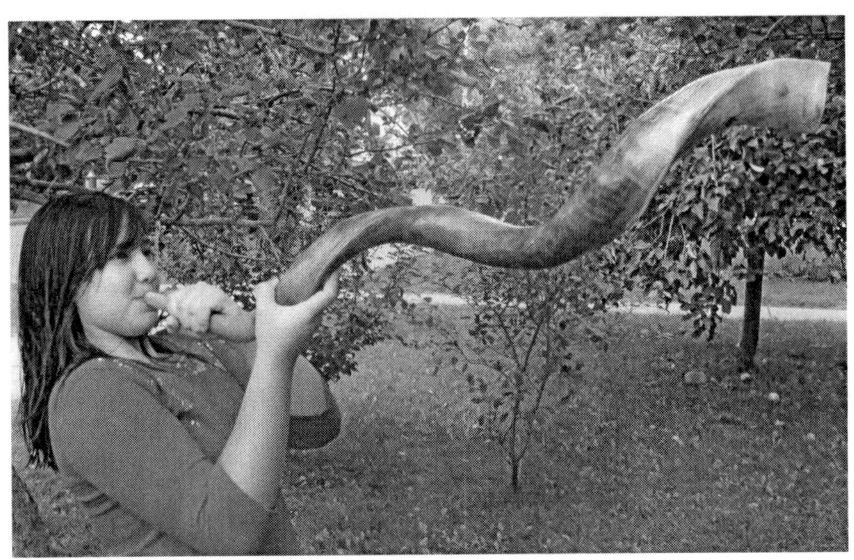

The warning must go out! Freedom Church of God is called to lift up their voice like a trumpet or shofar, showing God's people their sins (Isaiah 58:1) and announcing the good news of a better world to come where Jesus will reign.

Chapter One:

The Warning Must Go Out

So many false warnings have gone out that our world may mock the true warning when it comes. Wild speculations about December 21, 2012 will tend to cloud the issue, but the truth must be told. The truth is that our planet will experience on that date an event that has never occurred since man existed on earth—we will enter the dark part of our galaxy.

This event is not only referred to in the writings of numerous ancient cultures, it is also alluded to in the most important book of prophecy in the Bible, a misunderstood and overlooked book—the book of Job. Translators give virtually no idea of the true meaning of the profound significance of the words Job spoke in the original, conceptual Hebrew language, a tongue in which one word can have up to two hundred meanings—vast and often contrasting meanings.

Certain words Jesus spoke in the First and Second Testaments (commonly known as the Old and New Testaments) give an ominous warning, especially to Western, supposedly Christian nations. We shall see that the judicial legalization of abortion in 1972 is a *harbinger*. This decision portends a cause and effect result that will begin to occur as early as forty years after that ominous event. December 21, 2012 falls within a month of that pivotal ruling.

Our commission as a church is one we must fulfill. While it isn't popular to "cry loudly" and "not hold back," declaring to God's people and unbelievers alike ("the house of Jacob") their sins, which are the cause of the effect about to come upon them (Isa. 58:1), the warning must go out.

The words of the ancient prophets aren't for the ancients. They're for us in these last days. Those words must ring loud and clear for the generation for whom they were mainly intended (Ezek. 33:1–7, 33).

John the Baptist came to prepare Jesus' ministry on earth. A number of groups come today in that same spirit to prepare a people for God (Luke 1:17), to "restore all things" missing in the teachings of the church (Mat. 17:11), and to follow Jesus' own example by declaring, "The time is fulfilled, and the kingdom of God is at hand; repent and believe in the gospel" (Mark 1:15).

God will draw some of those reading this book to Jesus (John 6:44), and Jesus will choose them (John 15:16) so that they will carry His light to the world in a time of unprecedented darkness.

For some of you, this will be a warning of dark times to come and an announcement of the hope that Jesus is returning soon to extinguish Satan's darkness with His glorious light.

For others of you, this will be a wake-up call, a call to repentance or change, a way out of the nonchalant, Laodicean attitude that has characterized the end-time church (Rev. 3:14–22).

Protection Prophesied

For those who have ears to hear and are being called to be part of a great harvest in these last days, you have a promise of protection from the evil to come that will begin to grow strong in late December 2012. We encourage you to look up and read the passages cited in this book, which would take too much space to reproduce textually, to see how they fit in the overall scheme of prophecy. It is your responsibility to prove all things and hold fast to the truth (1 Thes. 5:21).

Whatever category in which you fall, you need to know what is going to happen in the next few years, as well as the glorious outcome in the end. As Daniel stated, "none of the wicked will understand, but those who have insight will understand" (Dan. 12:10). Those who obey Jesus (John 14:15) will understand (Ps. 111:10). God does nothing on this earth without first revealing it to His obedient servants so they can announce it (Amos 3:7).

As servants of God, we must make the call for repentance, showing the causes that will bring the prophesied negative effects, but more importantly announcing the good news that Jesus is coming back to change the darkness to light (Mat. 24:14). That message goes out as a witness, not to save.

Saving is God's job—not ours. He is the One who called us, and He is the One who may be calling you to His Kingdom for such a time as this, the most ominous yet exciting time in mankind's history.

Ignorance has reigned supreme in the Christian world when it comes to prophecy. Weird, unbiblical ideas have been spread abroad, putting a bad taste in the mouths of unbelievers and muddling the minds of believers. Job prophesied it. But he also prophesied the solution.

It's time the truth be told to set God's people free from ridiculous speculations and to tell the unbelieving world in clear terms what they can expect and why.

Keys to Understanding Hidden Truths

It is impossible to make sense of the prophecies for the last days that are unfolding before our eyes without understanding who God's physical people, His nations, are. It is equally impossible to fully grasp the meaning of end-time events without realizing what few know, that the book of Job is the foundational and most important book of Bible prophecy, setting the stage for Jesus' Olivet prophecy, Daniel, Ezekiel, Revelation, and many other prophetic books that most do not consider prophetic.

One mere verse, Job 3:3, opened the door for the revelation of over a thousand specific Bible prophecies.

Jesus told us to ask, and we would receive. My colleague and apostle Gerald Budzinski asked years ago for the Holy Spirit to teach him the meaning of the conceptual, biblical Hebrew. While other pastors scoffed at his childlike request, one of the rare rabbinical authorities on this ancient language exclaimed, "God is with you!"

As you read this book, I believe you will stand in awe of the God who packed so much understanding into the Hebrew words Job was inspired to use. Our God is awesome. He knows the end from the beginning and has caused prophecies to be written that are flexible in their fulfillment, in most cases having numerous possible fulfillments, taking into account all the possibilities involved in respecting man's free will—even yours.

If you're a believer, or become a believer by reading this book, the outcome of world events, beginning in late 2012, which is only the beginning of the end of this age of man's rule on earth, depends on you!

Matthew 24 speaks of a time of Great Tribulation such as has never before been seen in history, not even in 70 A.D. He said, "Unless those days had been cut short, no life would have been saved; but for the sake of the elect [that's you, if you are a true believer] those days will be cut short" (Mat. 24:22). A group must wake up to bring "the hearts of the children [of God] to their fathers [including Father God, whose name is Love (1 John 4:8)], so that [Jesus] will not come and smite the land [the earth] with a curse" (Mal. 4:6).

Some prophecies are set in stone, like the truth that Jesus will return to earth. Other prophecies are conditional. Deuteronomy 28 says, in effect, "If you obey, you get one thing, but if you disobey, you get something else." Prophecies have a personal and a national/global fulfillment. Some prophecies can have many fulfillments.

Multiple Fulfillments of Prophecy

Prophecy teachers have erred, saying, "This verse means one thing, and it can't mean anything else!" What a misunderstanding of God's vast mind and the amazing, original Hebrew in which He wrote virtually three-quarters of the Bible!

We limit our great God by our small-mindedness and by our disobedience to His laws of love. God lamented, "My people are destroyed for lack of knowledge" (Hos. 4:6). He goes on to say that it's the priests (or pastors) who have rejected the knowledge and forgotten God's laws of love.

We won't take much time in exposing the facts of what ancient civilizations saw coming in 2012. After all, you can do an internet search for 2012 and get millions of results. Facts that used to be considered futile speculations of conspiracy theorists are much more in the open, as government realizes its cover-up tactics are futile—the real leaders behind the scenes are preparing a new world order and want some of these facts to be released to cause fear. The History Channel did a twelve-part series, "Ancient Aliens," that exposed what once was available only on certain websites and in certain books.

Respected, highly-placed military men have openly spoken of the government cover-up of the capture of aliens, and some U.S. presidents, including Ronald Reagan, have known and spoken of the alien threat. Even some astronauts broke their forced vow of silence to talk about alien craft that followed their ships.

Countless ancient societies have predicted the return of the "sky gods" and giants that roamed the earth in the days of Noah. Certain Jewish authorities even deduced from Daniel 9 and the book of Enoch (not included in the inspired "canon" of Scripture) that seventy generations (of the longer, Flood-era generations of seventy years) would elapse before the giants could return.

It's easy to calculate: one generation of seventy years times seventy generations equals 4,900 years. Using one starting point of their calculation from the Flood date would bring us to 2012, corroborated by other biblical considerations we will examine.

Is There Any Truth to the 2012 Hype?

While we hope to steer clear of hype, taking God's whole program into account leads us to one solid conclusion: the ensemble of Bible prophecy, including Job, indicates that the winter solstice of 2012 will begin a time of unprecedented spiritual darkness—and eventually the physical kind.

That's why the first statement Jesus made in response to His disciples' questions about the last days was this: "See to it that no one misleads you" (Mat. 24:4).

Two events in particular point to 2012 as the date marking the beginning of the end of this age: the first extraterrestrial landing on Mount Hermon in Israel and the mathematical and longitudinal facts involving the 1947 Roswell crash. David Flynn's studies into these Masonic "secrets" are as fascinating as they are factual.[2] Visiting this website will show you why 2012 is important.

2. *David Flynn. "An Occult Translation of the Roswell Event: Count down to 2012." Accessed: May 28, 2012 (http://www.ahrimangate.com/flynn.htm).*

One flagrant example of misinformation comes to mind: "You better be ready; Jesus may come back tonight!" Those who say this have no understanding of end-time events, even though they see themselves as prophecy experts. We haven't yet seen the two witnesses prophesy in Jerusalem, which they must do for three and a half years before the whole world sees them killed by the beast power[3] and then raised to life (Rev. 11:3–12). What Bible are these "experts" reading?

Those three and a half years occur before Jesus returns. So how can Jesus come back tonight? Too much has to happen in prophecy before He returns. Much of this misunderstanding stems from their confusion about the timing of the rapture (or raptures, when understood properly). We write about this conditional prophecy in this book.

God provides a way of escape from the calamities beginning in late 2012. If you heed the warning, you and your loved ones can be spared. You don't have to buy into Satan's plan of darkness for this world. The light of Jesus can shine in and through you, in a way more glorious than you have ever imagined (Isa. 60:1–3). Not all prophecies are gloomy. Job prophesied days of darkness, but He also prophesied that the light of Jesus would prevail.

Yes, "darkness will cover the earth and deep darkness the peoples" (Isa. 60:2). This book will warn of the darkness, but it will also prophecy the Light, which represents Jesus, returning to throw the prince of darkness into the pit in which he belongs. Stay tuned for the light.

---

3 *"Beast power" is a term I use to describe the coming European superpower that is prophesied to be headed by a dictator who is called the beast. "Beast power" differentiates between the man called the beast and the superpower itself.*

Chapter Two:

Foundations and Purpose of Prophecy

We only know what we know because God has given us, in His mercy and grace, the key to unlocking prophecy, which opens to us the foundation and purpose of prophecy. We start with that foundation.

In Psalm 11:3, the psalmist David, who spoke many prophesies that were fulfilled to the letter, wrote: "If the foundations are destroyed, what can the righteous do?"

The apostle Paul wrote of the importance of the prophets. He said that we are God's household, "having been built on the *foundation* of the apostles and prophets, Christ Jesus Himself [who was both an apostle and a prophet] being the corner stone…" (Eph. 2:20).

God's household, the church, is built on a foundation, and the prophets and their prophecies are an important part of that foundation. Did God give prophecy as a foundation only so we can see how prophesied events were fulfilled, so we could know what's going to happen in the future? Are there other purposes for this foundation of prophecy?

Jesus said, "In everything, therefore, treat people the same way you want them to treat you, for this is the Law and the Prophets" (Mat. 7:12). Jesus includes the teachings of love and the Golden Rule as part of the teachings of the prophets.

So, prophecy isn't simply an exercise in calculating dates, specific timelines, or deciphering complicated prophecies for the future by theologians, Bible buffs, or Hebrew and Greek language geeks who delve into mysteries the common Bible reader never studies. Prophecy is practical. It has a bearing on our daily life.

In a greatly misunderstood parable that Jesus told about Lazarus, Abraham, and a rich man, the rich man, as he approached the flames of the lake of fire to come at the very end, asked Father Abraham if someone could come back from the dead to warn his brothers not to come to the same fate he had. Abraham answered, "If they do not listen to Moses and the Prophets, they will not be persuaded even if someone rises from the dead" (Luke 16:31).

In the end time, great lying signs are prophesied. False leaders will make it look like they are raising the dead when Satan and/or demons inhabit dead bodies and live and speak through them. If Christians are ignorant about what the prophets really say, they will be deceived.

How can you be persuaded of the truth or know which miracles are real and which are false if you don't listen to Moses and the prophets? If the foundations are destroyed, you may be destroyed as well. Your understanding of the First Testament, including its prophecies (even those of Job) could save your life.

Jesus even quoted the prophets to explain the truth about a resurrection for the unsaved, which is revealed in Appendix I but is only known by an extremely small percentage of Christians. He said, "It is written in the prophets, 'AND THEY SHALL *ALL* BE TAUGHT OF GOD'" (John 6:45). Yes, all mankind will one day have an opportunity for salvation in a second general resurrection (Rev. 20:5).

You couldn't know this rarely known truth unless you know what the prophets say about it. When you connect the First Words of Jesus (what men call the Old Testament; in this case, especially the prophets) and the Last Words of Jesus (the New Testament), you can see the pattern and understand the doctrine of the second resurrection.

Without the prophets, you cannot fit together the pieces of the prophecy picture. Finding truth in the Word involves reading a bit here and a bit there (Isa. 28:10), but if you only read the last fourth of the Bible that most Christians read, you won't have any clues to help solve the puzzle of Bible prophecy.

A God of Few Words

In one of our voyages to Africa, we were somewhat amused by a pastor who stood up at a pastors' meeting in a small mud house. He stood and spoke somewhere between thirty and forty-five minutes, if memory serves me. It seemed longer. Near the end of his soliloquy, he made this statement: "I am a man of few words."

Authors can be wordy at times, and that's why we thank God for editors. Sometimes some verbosity can slip through, for which we ask forgiveness. When it comes to God, however, we can truly say He is a God of few words.

Few words.

Words like, "Choose life" (Deut. 30:19).

Words like, "Stop sinning" (1 Cor. 15:34).

Words like, "Remember the sabbath day, to keep it holy" (Ex. 20:8).

He can say so much with a few words. He does not speak a word He doesn't mean, nor does He write anything that's not important, even though men may judge some of His words as unimportant.

The whole of the Bible was written and preserved for us "upon whom the ends of the ages have come" (1 Cor. 10:11). We are at the very end of this age, unlike the early church, which lived in the last two thousand of the six thousand years allotted to man's rule on the earth. God wants His people to understand what's going on and why.

God doesn't use idle words. His prophecies usually have a minimum of four fulfillments.

God speaks volumes with one prophecy, and often with one word containing as many as two hundred meanings. Have you perhaps missed some understanding of the Bible? Have you misunderstood prophecy because you haven't grasped the amplified meanings of Hebrew words, especially those in the prophecies of Job?

Did you even know that Job was a prophet? Most don't. The Jews regard him as a major prophet. James calls Job a prophet (James 5:10–11).

Yet you cannot fully understand and grasp the power of his prophecies unless someone helps you understand the conceptual Hebrew in which his words are written. That's why God gave us the fivefold ministry (Eph. 4:11–12; Rom. 10:14).

No, you don't need to know Hebrew or Greek to be saved. However, God's secrets are revealed to His servants the prophets, as Amos 3:7 tells us, and to the "preachers" without whom you cannot hear the truth (Romans 10:14). Read, see, and test us to prove whether these things we teach are true according to God's Word (Acts 17:11).

Does it all fit? Does it make sense according to the Word? If you test the popular movies according to the Word, will you find the light of truth? (Isa. 8:20)

Have you been "left behind" because of watching prophetic movies and reading books on prophecy without testing what you watch and read in the light of God's Word? Is it possible that you have allowed yourself to leave unheeded the initial warning Jesus gave to His disciples about the last days, "See to it that no one misleads you" (Mat. 24:4)?

We want you to prove to yourself from the Word and the Holy Spirit what you read here as we explain the purposes of prophecy. Many purposes exist, as well as many foundations of prophecy. We give ten.

Why Prophecy?

The first purpose of prophecy is to *bring the elect of God comfort.* Knowing the plan of God and the future fulfillment of that plan (how it plays out) is comforting. When you don't know, you're left to wonder. Fear thus has an easy entry point.

For instance, some prophecy teachers believe that to be good Christians in the last days, you must be a martyr during the Great Tribulation. Some believers who have known as children the horrors the Jews had to suffer during World War II feel they must suffer again and go through the tribulation.

But that's not what God says. He says He has not destined His people for wrath (1 Thes. 5:9; 1:10), either Satan's wrath in the Great Tribulation or God's wrath for a year after that. For those who love Jesus and His name and have kept His Word, God promises that He will keep us "from the hour of testing, that hour which is about to come upon the whole world" (Rev. 3:8–10).

Sure, you can find verses that say believers will be martyred. But for the most part that's because they didn't prepare. They didn't bring extra oil in their flasks (Mat. 25:2–4). The wise virgins told the foolish ones to "go instead to the dealers and buy some for yourselves," but it was too late since the door to the first rapture wedding feast was shut (Mat. 25:9–10).

The dealers are the persecutors of the beast power with the woman or universal church riding it. In other words, these Christians must prove their loyalty, losing their heads in martyrdom because they didn't use their heads while they had the time. They will still have a good reward (Rev. 3:18–21), but it will come the hard way.

When you know what's coming and understand prophecy and your right to "get in the boat," as Noah did, you don't need to be in fear. You can have peace. You may not know every detail as He does, but you can know the overall plan and more details than most.

You may have heard preachers use the phrase, "God comforts the afflicted, and He afflicts the comfortable." He does indeed comfort the afflicted, and at times He allows trials to shake up those who are comfortably lazy in their walk with Jesus. He often uses words to shake and wake them up, even words of prophecy.

The Warning

The second purpose of prophecy is to give a *warning to the world.* When disasters come, where do people look for answers? Whatever the culture, men look to God and use biblical terms like "apocalypse" and "Armageddon" to seek answers to what's going on to upset their comfortable world. They use biblical references to wars, famines, earthquakes, and other disasters of "biblical proportions."

These people have no other way to explain what they see but to use Bible terms. After all, they tend to blame disasters on the Almighty, calling them acts of God when they are instead acts of Satan or the result of cause-and-effect laws.

The wacky weather we see today is often blamed on God, since He made the heavens. But it is rather the "prince of the power of the air" (Eph. 2:2), or his demons, that cause weather upsets, more and more at the behest of witches who can control the weather. Believers could easily oppose their works, but they don't. Mind you, God warned our nations that if we refused to obey Him, curses would be the automatic result, and those include bad weather.

While Americans have forgotten that they are Manasseh (the Israelite tribal name which means "forget"), the Arab world knows who they are, and they know who Israel is. They call America "the great Satan" and are archenemies of both the tiny nation of Israel and the other lost Ten Tribes who were scattered throughout Europe and North America, headed by the birthright nations America and the British Commonwealth.

Our enemies have a better idea of who we are than we do.

At one time, ninety-five percent of the world used the dollar as their reserve currency. That percentage has decreased to less than twenty percent as the prophesied downfall of America takes place before our eyes. The lying politicians (willing puppets in the hands of an evil group whose goal is a one-world government) may deny it, but the world sees it clearly.

The "house of Jacob [the unbelieving world]" (Isa. 58:1) must be warned of what is coming as well as "My people" (same verse), the believing nations (or once-believing nations, such as the U.S. and the Commonwealth), and all individual believers in Jesus.

The time of "Jacob's distress," or Great Tribulation (Jer. 30:7), the time of testing to come upon the whole world of unbelievers—and believers who have not prepared—is at the door. So a warning must go out. Prophecy must be explained, and correctly.

We believe, like the early church before the faith was perverted, that we have the prophetic word made more sure, to which you [all our readers] do well to pay attention as to a lamp shining in a dark place, until the day dawns and the morning star arises in your hearts. (2 Pet. 1:19)

This world is indeed a dark place, and the evil that is abounding makes it darker and darker as "deep darkness [covers] the peoples" (Isa. 60:2). Darkness even covers the Christian world in the realm of prophecy since the truth about prophecy has been hidden from them.

Make no mistake. Prophecy comes from the God who inhabits eternity and knows every detail of the future.

As Peter explains it, "But know this first of all, that no prophecy of Scripture is a matter of one's own interpretation" (2 Pet. 1:20), yet that is what's happening. The Bible is often twisted to fit the paradigm of the teacher rather than the Word of God in its original and inspired form. Teachers are not allowing the Holy Spirit to teach them. And they seem to have forgotten the scripture that says, "A little here, A little there" (Isa. 28:10), which shows that the Bible interprets itself.

Peter continues, "for no prophecy was ever made by an act of human will, but men moved by the Holy Spirit spoke from God" (2 Pet. 1:21). The prophecies we cite in this book are indeed God-breathed, and we should allow God to interpret them through His Spirit and the rest of His Word. Will you allow God to do that?

Jesus: the Only Way Out

The third purpose is to *show the fullness of understanding and provision of and in Jesus and in His name.* Over two hundred names (some cite many more) are given for Jesus in the Bible. God wants us to use the appropriate names of Jesus for the situations we face. In the times of trouble prophesied for our day, believers can only seek refuge in the name of Jesus and in the shadow of His wings: "The name of [Jesus] is a strong tower; the righteous runs into it and is safe" (Prov. 18:10).

In the day of God's wrath against the rebellious ones who want to fight Jesus at the end, Isaiah says they will cast away their idols of gold that cannot save them "to go into the caverns of the rocks and the clefts of the cliffs before the terror of [Jesus] and the splendor of His majesty, when He arises to make the earth tremble" (Isa. 2:21).

The prophet then utters this stern warning in the next verse: "Stop regarding man, whose breath of life is in his nostrils; for why should he be esteemed?"

The day is coming when no security or protection will exist but in the name and power of Jesus. No army will save you. No homeland security system will be in place to protect you. Jesus will be your only way out. This book points you to Him.

Oh, the Depths of Our Awesome God's Wisdom!

The fourth purpose is *to express the wisdom of God by having two to four main fulfillments of all prophecy.* Sometimes you can have two major and two minor fulfillments; at other times you may have four major fulfillments. Those who insist a verse can only mean one thing, usually the understanding they have of that passage, have missed out on understanding the scope of prophecy and the vastness of Scripture in general.

How can those with such myopic vision stand in awe of our great, wise God as Paul did in Romans 11:33? He exclaimed, "Oh, the depth of the riches both of the wisdom and knowledge of God! How unsearchable are His judgments and unfathomable His ways!"

When you grasp the vastness and complexity of prophecy revealed in this book, and especially in God's Book, you can't help but say amen and praise God with exclamation points, as Paul did.

When I was healed of two incurable and devastating illnesses in 1998, I jumped for joy and couldn't help praising Jesus in the dance. It was only shortly thereafter that my heart leaped for joy, for I discovered something else that made me stand in awe of God, something I hadn't fully realized before. I became aware that our great and awesome God doesn't only amaze us by His miracles and healing power, but by what we call the omniscience of God. That means He knows everything. He knows everything about the past, present, and future of every man, woman, and child who ever lived or will live. He knows every detail about every nation in its past, present, or future. Wow! Think about that.

He knows every hair on our head (a little less awesome knowledge in my case), every detail of our lives—past, present, and future—except for the sins which He has promised to cast into the sea of forgetfulness (Micah 7:19). He knows when a sparrow has fallen to the ground and He knows the number and names of all the stars in the vast heavens (Ps. 147:4).

Wow! Is that not awesome? Can we stand in awe of our amazing God?

Our awesome Father always allows for free will, but He knows in advance what we will do and what the nations will do, so He can perfectly predict the course of nations. He has allowed for all these variables in His Word, so it may seem contradictory, but it isn't. The prophetic word allows for the free will of nations and leaders, giving different potential scenarios for each choice.

Not every prophecy is variable. Some events, of course, are fixed by God's covenant promises and cannot be altered. God will not allow them to be changed. No man can change the fulfillment of His promises, even if He has to do it Himself (Isa. 59:16).

That amazing foreknowledge—not to mention His patience, mercy, and love toward us, demonstrated by always encouraging us to make the right choices—makes me stand in awe of our great God. I pray that this book will cause the believers who read it to stand in amazement and adoration of the awesome God we serve, the God who knows the end from the beginning in minute details (Isa. 46:10; 47:3–7). He is the God of wisdom and love.

My Father knows what I'll do with the choices before me at any given time. He prophesies what *could be* even if He knows in advance that I will miss the mark. Yet He always has a powerful, redemptive solution in Jesus, and His mercies never fail.

He sees America going down the tubes, rejecting Him. He is grieved that He has no choice but to allow this nation, who forgot who they were, to be besieged by foreign powers and to see those He loves go into national slavery. But He sees ahead the mercy He will show them when He brings them back into their original Promised Land and shepherds them, binding up their wounds and giving them abundant joy for their many sorrows (Isa. 27:12–13; Ezek. 36:25–38; Jer. 31:1–20).

Our God is Love and His wisdom knows no equal. Bible prophecy, when properly understood, should compel us to look in reverent awe of the infinite wisdom, knowledge, and love of the God no one can outsmart. Don't try.

God Is the Smartest Person in the Universe

The fifth purpose is to show every man, every human, every angel, Satan, and every demon that no matter what they do, *no one can outsmart God the Father.*

They try. God warns the angels, "Don't get caught up in Satan's rebellion." He says to Satan and to all mankind, "You can't outsmart Me. I have a master plan, and it will be fulfilled no matter what you do."

We, upon whom the end of the ages has come (1 Cor. 10:11), are living at a time when over ninety percent of all prophecy is being fulfilled. We are witnesses of God's great foreknowledge. We are blessed to live at the very end, which will become the very beginning of a new world under Jesus. We are living at the apex and turning point of mankind's history.

Are you fearful? Why not be excited?

We are watching the close of the six days of work of man and the imminent coming of the millennial Sabbath (2 Pet. 3:8). As we release all of our weekly burdens to Jesus on Friday evening before Sabbath sunset, mankind is about to release to Jesus the sins and burdens of six one-thousand-year "days" of fruitless toil in the sweat of our brows. While not fully realizing it, the world stands on the threshold of a new world of love, peace, and joy in Jesus.

Preaching the gospel of the Kingdom of God involves announcing that good news: a new world is coming soon!

The six thousand years ended in 1996 (since Jesus was actually born in the year 4 B.C.), and we are nearing the end of the nineteen-year span of time (which has been extended, because the church is not ready). That period is symbolized by the span of Goliath's hand. That hand had a span of nineteen inches, which was added to his six cubits of height, representing the six thousand years of the reign of Satan. God foreknew it all; He has revealed His secrets to His servants and to those who have eyes and ears to see and hear the truth about prophecy.

An Opportunity to Change

The sixth purpose is to *give mankind the opportunity to change and to prosper.* Many Christians are aware of the prophecies of prosperity for the church in the last days, the wealth of the wicked being released to the righteous (Prov. 13:22). But few actually allow Jesus in them to keep His laws of love and prosperity. Prophecy offers a chance to change and repent.

By the way, it would surely help to understand prophecy if we could know the real Jesus, the One who is the Word of John 1, the One who dealt with men in the First Testament. The One who did all the smiting in the first part of the Bible was the One who said, "Oh that they had such a heart in them, that they would [revere] Me and keep all My commandments always, that it may be well with them and with their sons forever!" (Deut. 5:29)

The One who gave Ezekiel a warning message for a people who had already been taken captive and whose descendants would hear the message in the twenty-first century was the One who said He had no pleasure in the death of the wicked. He cried out with compassion in Ezekiel 33:11, "Why then will you die, O house of Israel?"

What few understand is that this Member of the Godhead (the Word, Jesus Himself) was the very One who came to die so that people could have His heart of love living in them. He was the One who took a whip to drive out the moneychangers from His Father's house. Yes, He did some "smiting" in the New Testament as well. Ananias, the man who dropped dead when he lied, can tell you when He's resurrected.

This Jesus was also, on the other hand, the same One in Luke 13:34 who cried over Jerusalem, saying, "How often I wanted to gather your children together, just as a hen gathers her brood under her wings, and you would not have it!"

This is the same One who rejoiced, unlike Jonah, when a whole city repented.

The city of Nineveh actually repented at Jonah's prophecy. America was given ample time to repent, but she chose not to turn toward God. While it's too late for the nation, it's not too late for individuals to repent so they don't have to go through the calamities that are prophesied.

If we don't know that something important is about to take place, we tend not to get ready for it, do we?

What if you knew that if you were to take a certain route today, you would be involved in a fatal automobile accident? God won't force you to take another route, but choosing correctly would save your life.

That knowledge saved one of our bloggers on Freedom Blog. Teea had a dream about being in a snowy accident, yet her boss asked her to leave for Red Deer that day. Our gifted interpreter on the blog gave her this answer: "Teea, your dream is a warning that you should not make that trip. Wait until tomorrow to go there, and don't forget to tell your boss. Such a trip would be tempting God if you moved to go."

Teea responded, "Thank you for your help. When I left for Red Deer, I saw sixteen cars in the ditch with several people waiting for a tow truck. And everything went very well for the meeting this morning."

Prophecy is given for you to change and prosper. God tells you what is going to happen so you can make changes in your life in order to avoid disaster. The purpose of prophecy is to turn your heart to the Father (Mal. 4:6). God wants a heart change, not a just-in-case religion.

We're talking about a real change of heart to the way of love and forgiveness. The hearts of the fathers will be turned to forgiving and loving their sons and daughters, and the hearts of the children will be turned in forgiveness to their fathers and to Father God Himself. Otherwise He may have to smite the whole earth with a curse and be obliged to bring in the Kingdom of Love by Himself (Mal. 4:6). I plan to publish a book on this crucial subject soon.

A Way of Escape

The seventh purpose is *to show the world that every direction that is taken away from God's purpose and plan has already been thought out and found to be faulty, yet a way of escape has been provided.*

Anything that's not based on God's way of love and truth creates false prophecies. You may go through some of the consequences because of your wrong choice, but Jesus is merciful and provides a way of escape.

Jesus tells us that when we turn to Him in obedience, He quickly subdues our enemies (Ps. 81:13–14). The name *Yashua* signifies, among many other concepts, the aspect of deliverance. The faithful who reject the ways of the coming beast power will be spared from its infliction of persecution and martyrdom.

This important passage in Luke 21:36 should encourage us: "But keep on the alert at all times, praying that you may have strength [from Jesus] to escape all these things that are about to take place, and to stand before the Son of Man."

Daniel spoke of that time of Great Tribulation, "a time of distress such as never occurred since there was a nation until that time" (Dan. 12:1). He also speaks in the same verse of supernatural deliverance: "… and at that time your people, everyone who is found written in the book, will be rescued."

When you keep Jesus' Word and refuse to deny His name, He promises to "keep you from the hour of testing, that hour which is about to come upon the whole world, to test those who dwell on the earth" (Rev. 3:10). Will you escape?

Jesus Is Redeemer

The eighth purpose is that *Jesus (Yashua) is the Savior and Redeemer of every wrong choice and every disaster that can come upon the earth.*

We must turn the wrong choice and its consequences over to Him so He can turn it around for good. We turn over the bad choices on the new moon[4] so the sad prophecy we have created can fail, and the good prophecy God has for us can replace it (Jer. 29:11). We become accustomed to speaking prophecies over ourselves that are in harmony with God's Word. We turn Satan's prophecies of condemnation for our sins into God's prophecies to work things out for the good (Gen. 50:20; Rom. 8:28).

4 *The Bible speaks of bowing down to Jesus in surrender at the new moon (Isa. 66:23). More information is available at www.freedomchurchofgod.com and in my book* God's Fruit of Forgiveness, *as well as in the ebook* New Moons, New Lives!

Yashua Gaal is Jesus the Redeemer. We can claim His name and the covenant of redemption (the ninth or New Covenant) in Jesus' blood and we have the assurance of "abundant redemption" from all our sins and bad choices (Ps. 130:7–8).

You may have had personal prophecies spoken over you that failed to come to pass. This means your free will choices kept them from being fulfilled. But be encouraged: as with Bible prophecy, Jesus the Redeemer has a plan of redemption for the sin to be turned over and a new and good fulfillment of the prophecy to take place. Expect good things.

Aren't we blessed to have a Savior and Redeemer who takes our sins and mistakes and turns them into future good for us? These are the lessons that prophecy teaches us.

Its Not Law *Versus* Grace!

The ninth purpose is that *peace, rest, and prosperity comes from keeping God's laws.* This has become a controversial point because of the deception with which Satan has attacked Christian churches.

Some say only two laws exist—loving God and loving neighbor. Jesus gave these two laws as a reminder and a template explaining the first four and the last six of the Ten Commandments, respectively.

Christian leaders, and thus Christians in general, misunderstand law, grace, and faith. They try to separate law and grace, not understanding that Jesus is the One who gave the law in the First Testament.

The Hebrew letters in the word for law, *torah*, tell an intriguing story. Here is their meaning: that which comes from the man nailed to the cross.

After giving the law, Jesus came as the Son of Man to die for us so He, Grace personified (1 Cor. 1:4), could live in us to keep His laws of love, laws which would be impossible to keep in our own strength. It's His power (or grace), not ours, that enables us to keep the laws of love (Eph. 3:16). He is the Love that fulfills the law through us (Rom. 13:10).

Teachers quote some of Paul's words out of context. The law only brings death when we break the law. God's laws of love were meant to bring blessings when obeyed.

Keeping the commandments is not a burden (1 John 5:3).

It takes faith to keep the law, and it takes the grace or empowerment of God, which is Jesus in us, to do the same. Even the faith we need to keep the law comes from Jesus (Eph. 2:8). It is part of the fruit of the Spirit (Gal. 5:22).

It is a mystery to me how people can take Jesus' words that He didn't come to destroy the law and then say that He did just that (Mat. 5:17–19). When did the word "fulfill" become synonymous with "destroy"? Only those who "turn the grace of our God into licentiousness" (Jude 4), or license to ignore or disobey the law, can come up with such distortions of the truth.

People think that the God of the First Testament was unfair. He gave strict laws and stern commands without mercy. Where do they get that? Jesus was that God, the Word who spoke to men (John 1:1–18). He showed great mercy—for example, by not destroying Israel when they complained. He endured their rebellions ten times before He had to keep the older ones from entering the Promised Land. That's mercy.

He forgave David of adultery and murder. That's mercy.

Jesus is the same yesterday, today, and forever (Heb. 13:8), but many Christians don't know who He is. They have not seen Him in the first three-quarters of the Bible, so how can they know Him only as the wise Master and suffering Savior in the New Testament? They can't. They don't see the full picture.

If you went to a movie about Jesus and only saw the last quarter of the story, would you say you got to know the main character? You must know Him as the strong Lawgiver as He reveals Himself early in the Bible (Isa. 33:22). Otherwise you don't really know Him.

Pastors preach law *versus* grace, not law-keeping *through* grace. They can't fathom a God who would visit "the iniquity of the fathers on the children, on the third and the fourth generations of those who hate [Jesus]" (Ex. 20:5).

What's so cruel about that? Witchcraft curses are forever. Jesus has produced a law that enacts a penalty (or curse) upon the children for only three or four generations. And those curses come because the father speaks evil words that actually change his DNA for the worse, thus affecting the DNA of his progeny. These curses are words of failure that cause the generations to see that things are going bad, thereby motivating them to change.

Why do people have to see God as the bad guy? He is Love. He does nothing outside the motivation of love.

Jesus gave the law, and then He came to die for those who couldn't keep the law. He didn't die for them so they could say they didn't need to keep the law. Keeping the law brings the blessing (Deut. 5:29; 28:1–14). Doing away with the law does away with the blessing (Isa. 1:19–20). Why would Jesus do that?

When you read the prophecies of the Bible, you begin to understand this simple but overlooked and misunderstood truth: bad things happen when we disobey and ignore God's laws and prophetic warnings.

That's why Jesus said in Matthew 5:17, "Do not think that I came to abolish the Law *or the Prophets*; I did not come to abolish but to *abolish*." No, wait. It doesn't say that, does it? Indeed not. Jesus said, "I did not come to abolish but to *fulfill*."

When you read the verses that follow, you cannot possibly have any justification for saying that Jesus came to keep the law so we wouldn't have to keep that hard, harsh, old law. He came to magnify the law, amplifying and making it more glorious by showing how demanding it really is (Isa. 42:41; Matthew 5,6, and 7), all the while showing us that without Him we can't keep it.

He says that our righteousness must surpass the legalistic law-keeping of the self-righteous Pharisees. In other words, it's not our righteousness He wants, which is like filthy rags to Him (Isa. 64:6).

He paid for our sins and our self-righteousness by His blood, meaning that only the blood or sacrificial laws He gave in the First Testament are no longer binding. All the other laws are, and 613 of them exist. In addition, 613 more dos and don'ts are enumerated in the New Testament.

The truth is, law-keeping is a lot stricter than you have imagined, but it's a lot easier than it was thousands of years ago, because most of the people then didn't have grace—Jesus in them to keep the law.

When will the Christian world understand that prophecy teaches that the law of God must be kept if we are to be blessed? But we can't keep it without Grace with a capital G—Jesus. We can't keep it unless we have Love living inside us, because "love is the fulfillment of the law" (Rom. 13:10).

The apostle whom Jesus loved, John, the man who kept the laws of love and the days of love of Leviticus 23 (attested by history since his disciple Polycarp kept those days), put this concept in a few words: "For this is the love of God [not merely the love of the Jesus of the New Testament], that we keep His commandments; and His commandments are not burdensome" (1 John 5:3). That is the teaching of the Law and the Prophets.

The Sabbath Door to Intimacy and Revelation

The tenth foundation of prophecy is that the *Sabbath is the doorway to Jesus and the Father, and that no other day will do.* One of the main reasons the church has not understood prophecy is that they've been deceived since the fourth century about which day is the Sabbath.

The Sabbath opens the door to intimacy with Jesus the Revelator, allowing us to understand prophecy. The seventh day mirrors the seventh millennium of mankind's history when Jesus returns to rule on the seventh day of a thousand years. The Sabbath is a recurring theme in this book.[5]

We must understand, however, why we preceded this foundation with the one on grace. Mercy is only a small part of the meaning of the Hebrew words for grace. Jesus shows great mercy to the majority who has been deceived about the Sabbath.

Mercy is not receiving what you deserve. Treating mercy and grace as synonyms is a huge mistake. Breaking one of the Ten Commandments would normally carry a heavy penalty, but when you are sincerely deceived, God extends mercy. You simply miss out on the blessing. He doesn't condemn you.

The problem is that most Christians see grace only as the initial unmerited pardon they receive from God because Jesus paid the price for them. We all need mercy at times. However, God wants us to come to the point of tapping the immense riches of His grace, which is much, much more than unmerited favor. Grace is power. Grace is the empowerment to do what we cannot do ourselves—keep the commandments of love.

Grace is Jesus in us!

---

5 *A search on our website (www.freedomchurchofgod.com) for the Sabbath will yield numerous results, and our book* Bible Code Broken! *gives complete proof of our need to receive the blessings of Sabbath-keeping.*

Rather than believing that grace means we don't have to keep the laws of God, including the fourth or Sabbath commandment, Jesus wants us to look to Him for the power.

Jesus doesn't condemn you for being misled by teachers who have almost universally kept and taught Sunday-keeping. He simply wants you to seek His help to understand and enter into the Sabbath blessing.

We give you here a brief synopsis of the overwhelming biblical evidence that the fourth commandment has not been done away. It is an important doorway. The Hebrew word for fourth, *dalet*, as in the fourth commandment, signifies a door. It is a door of understanding, a door of great prophetic revelation. We pray that more and more Christians will enter that door of blessing.

We know that God is a God of mercy who overlooks the deception that has covered the Christian world since Constantine brought his pagan ways and holidays into the organized church. We stress, however, that obedience to any of the commandments comes only through Grace with a big G and a big J—Jesus.

Jesus offers us supernatural power to obey His commandments, which are impossible to obey in our own strength. But we must make a choice. When we make the choice to obey, Jesus even promises us the desire and will to obey (Phil. 2:13). His grace overpowers our weakness, and His grace is sufficient to empower us to obey, not to excuse our disobedience. Oh yes, He will pick us up when we fail; however, He says we can do all things in Him, by His grace or empowerment (Phil. 4:13; 2 Cor. 12:9).

We will always need mercy, yet we must grow in grace and knowledge as we walk in obedience (2 Pet. 3:18).

Consequently, please understand that as soon as you make the choice to obey the Sabbath commandment, your eyes will open to the profound revelation you read here.

Proof of the Sabbath Blessing in Brief

The Sabbath is both the open door to the unraveling of the rapture mystery, the mystery of Bible prophecy, and the day for preparing us spiritually to meet Jesus. Have you ever asked yourself why you're not keeping this holy day, if that is the case?

Religious people in general have swallowed so many absurd excuses for not keeping the Sabbath that they have a hard time accepting it. They make you wonder if those who make them have ever read the Bible and believe what it says.

That being said, I can nevertheless have compassion since I once gobbled up some of the same excuses as a Sunday-keeper. So please, don't take offense. Take instead your Bible. Read it—not the commentaries of men with highfalutin words and arguments that don't hold any weight with God.

It's really quite simple. It's the only day you can find as a commanded day of rest and corporate worship in the Bible. Jesus blessed the day in Genesis 2:2, confirmed it before Sinai with the manna miracle in Exodus 16, and wrote it with His own finger on tablets of stone in Exodus 20.

He called Himself Divine Master of that day, declaring that He made it for all mankind, not only the Jew (Mark 2:27–28). He never did away with it on the cross, as some say, since His most faithful disciples kept observing it after the cross (Luke 23:54). He prophesied it would still be a day of rest to be respected in the last days (Mat. 24:20) and that it would be observed when He returns to make all things right (Isa. 66:23).

The Holy Spirit confirmed that it would remain under the New Covenant as a day of rest for God's people, who would rest as Jesus did by keeping the Sabbath day (Heb. 4:9–10; 8:10; Jer. 31:33; Mat. 5:17–20; 19:17; 1 Cor. 7:19). More verses confirm that Jesus kept the Sabbath, the fourth commandment, than any other commandment in the gospels.

At least the universal church is more honest than her protesting daughters. She told her daughters that they didn't get Sunday from the Bible but from her tradition (which you can confirm by doing a web search for "Rome's challenge").

The evidence for the Sabbath is overwhelming. The ignorance and/or resistance of the churches to keeping it are also overwhelming.

People know that the Jews kept the day that begins on Friday sunset and ends at Saturday sunset. And since Jesus had to keep perfectly the law, He Himself gave in order to be our sinless Savior, He would have had to keep the Sabbath on the right day. We see that the Jews of His day kept the same day, which they have continued to keep throughout their history up to today.

It is easy to conclude that the day we are to keep is the same day the perfect Jesus kept two thousand years ago. How else can we obey both the spirit *and the letter* of one of those famous Ten Commandments that Christians say we are supposed to observe? After all, Jesus didn't command us to keep the first day of the week, but the seventh (Ex. 20:8–10).

It's really quite simple, so alarmingly simple that you have to wonder how theologians and pastors can get around such a simple truth. Oh, but they do, with such unbiblical and convoluted arguments that make you shake your head. They fear change.

How about you? Are you willing to change?

If your fervent desire is to understand prophecy and escape the events ahead of us that will shock the world, we invite you to enter into the special presence of Jesus on the Sabbath day. It is Jesus' day of love, peace, and joy. In His presence is fullness of joy (Ps. 16:11).6

---

6 *One of our blog posts on Freedom Blog, "Jesus' Day of Joy," drew much attention. We're not fully sure why this post got so many comments, but perhaps it's because people live in a world of sadness today and they're reaching out for joy. Jesus wants His people to meet with Him on His Sabbath day to express their joy and thanks, and to receive a fresh infilling of His abundant joy and peace. You can see the post for yourself by going to our blog entry on Freedom Blog (www.freedomchurchofgod.com), dated April*

Tis the Season to Be Alert

As Jesus instructed us, we must know the times and seasons. The world can tell the difference between summer and winter. As God made four seasons, so He has established four seasons in prophecy, or four fulfillments of each prophecy. Events are fulfilled in their season. While at this point we cannot tell the exact time of Jesus' return, we can discern that we are in the last season of mankind's journey on earth as ruled by Satan.

Prophecies too long to go into here indicate that we can also be sure that this world mess will not last past 2028 A.D. But we don't want it to last that long since that would mean the earth would be cursed. The ideal time for Jesus' return, in the years 2015 or 2016, is no longer possible because the church was not ready as Jesus predicted.

The truth is, we cannot predict the timing of Jesus' return at this point. At a certain point in time it will be possible, but at that time we will hope to be raptured. It is not a major consideration, even though people don't understand the verse about not knowing the day or the hour (a long explanation I hope to provide in a future book about the rapture). The important thing is to be ready.

When we understand these foundations and purposes of prophecy, we will be able to understand Bible prophecy and learn valuable lessons independent of the knowledge of what is going to happen in our future. We pray that God will enlighten us with greater understanding so that we can be secure and full of faith in this exciting time.

8, 2011. We published another post, challenging those who were not yet Sabbath-keepers to read what we think is a brief, convincing proof of the Sabbath. It's entitled, "Sabbath Keepers, Arise!" It was published on December 29, 2011, on the same site.

Chapter Three:

Good News and Bad News

You may remember the story of the pilot who comes on the loudspeaker to announce the following message to the passengers: "This is your pilot speaking. I have good news and bad news. The good news is, we're making excellent time. The bad news is, we don't know where we are. We're lost!"

I also have good news and bad news. I want to share mostly the good news in this chapter. After all, the gospel means good news—and we're called not only to publish the gospel as a witness, testimony, and warning to the world (Mat. 24:14), but also to preach the good news of the establishment, or should we say reestablishment, of the Kingdom of God on this earth.

One aspect of the good news is that you can escape the really bad news of famine, war, and destruction coming in the Great Tribulation and the subsequent wrath of God.

Another important aspect of the good news is that Jesus is coming back soon to transform this world and bring lasting peace. Love will rule—not hate, competition, sadness, and strife. Joy will burst forth as the world recovers from six thousand years of Satan's rule.

A good place to start this good news is in Paul's letter to the church at Thessalonica. The members there had asked questions about a rapture. Would the faithful be raptured up to heaven out of the calamities they saw as imminent? What requirements would exist for being rescued "from the wrath to come" (1 Thes. 1:10), which Paul promised them on God's behalf?

These words of Paul were written for us at this exciting but troubling time of the end. We shall begin in Chapter Five of Paul's first letter to this church. Consider it as a letter to you personally:

> Now as to the times and the epochs, brethren, you have no need of anything to be written to you. For you yourselves know full well that the day of the [Eternal][7] will come just like a thief in the night. While they are saying, "Peace and safety!" then destruction will come upon them suddenly like labor pains upon a woman with child, and they will not escape. (1 Thes. 5:1–3)

Those who are not under God's protection, the majority of this world, will not escape this time of trial that will "come upon the whole world" (Rev. 3:10). But Paul has good news for you if you choose to walk in the light of Jesus, if you choose to obey Him in these last days.

Paul continues, "But *you*, brethren, are not in darkness, that the day would overtake you like a thief" (1 Thes. 5:4). *You*, readers, are being warned. This day doesn't have to come upon you. You have been called to come out of this world, symbolized by ancient Babylon (Rev. 18:4), so you won't receive the plagues coming upon this devilish system.

When we walk in the light and consistently confess our sins to our Father, knowing we are forgiven (1 John 1:9–10), we walk in the light and righteousness of One who is perfect, Jesus: "…for you are all sons of light and sons of day. We are not of night nor darkness…" (1 Thes. 5:5).

---

7 I have written whole chapters in other books, including Why Doesn't God Heal Me?, about the wrong translation of "LORD" beginning with the King James Version. The correct translation of Yahweh (or Yahovah, in Hebrew) should be "the Eternal" or "the Eternal One." The word "Lord," in lowercase, appears only about four per cent of the time in the First Testament and should be translated "Divine Master," from the Hebrew Adonai.

We may stumble temporarily, but we get up and keep going. We sin, but we are not sinners. We are saints who sometimes sin, but we quickly confess and are washed clean by Jesus' blood.

Paul continues: "...for you are all sons of light and sons of day. We are not of night nor of darkness; so then let us not sleep as others do, but let us be alert and sober" (1 Thes. 5:5–6). The sleeping virgins of Matthew 25 must awake and be about the work of God, for the night comes when no man can work.

Great Rewards for Those Who Walk in the Light

Jesus said, "We must work the works of Him who sent Me as long as it is day; night is coming when no one can work" (John 9:4). We who are of the day, who walk in the light of Jesus, must get His message of warning and good news out before it's too late to work. That's what we're endeavoring to do by God's grace, and Jesus asked us to call for more laborers into the harvest. You may be part of that great end-time harvest, but you are also called to be a harvester.

The spiritual coasters, the lazy believers, will say, "'My master is not coming for a long time,' and begins to beat his fellow slaves and eat and drink with the drunkards" (Mat. 24:48–49). You have the choice of many addictions today in which to drown your sorrows instead of giving them to Jesus. Will you escape in fantasy, or will you be that faithful servant who is counted worthy to escape the coming time of turmoil? (Luke 21:36)

Paul warns us not to be of those who get drunk and carouse at night, but instead to walk in the light of Jesus (1 Thes. 5:7–8). If you do, God gives you a great promise. Those of the night, the sinners of this world and the coasters who talk the talk of Jesus but don't walk His walk in the light, cannot claim this promise. You are not destined for end-time wrath but for salvation from it (1 Thes. 1:10; 5:9).

Salvation includes physical deliverance and protection, as evidenced throughout the Bible, and, as we have seen, from God's and Satan's wrath. The best way God provides is the rapture to heaven to be with Jesus before returning to rule with Him.

Here's the way to be ready:

> Rejoice always; pray without ceasing; in everything give thanks... Do not quench the Spirit; do not despise prophetic utterances [including inspired teaching]. But examine everything [thoughtfully and prayerfully]; hold fast to that which is good; abstain from every form of evil. (1 Thes. 5:16–22)

If we are faithful in these things, relying on Jesus when we miss the mark of perfection, we have the attitude of a rapture-ready believer. Thus, we have this further promise in the following verses:

> Now may the God of peace [*shalom*, wholeness and oneness] Himself sanctify [perfect you in His holiness] you entirely; and may your spirit and soul and body be preserved complete, without blame at the coming of our [Divine Master] Jesus Christ. Faithful is He who calls you, and *He* also will bring it to pass. (1 Thes. 5:23–24)

Look to Jesus!

That's right. Jesus will do it. Paul often calls forth the blessing of the grace of Jesus, the grace or empowerment who *is* Jesus (1 Thes. 5:28). We can't qualify for these inestimable blessings by ourselves. We must stay close to Jesus, the author and finisher of our faith (Heb. 12:2), taking His hand to lead us through any end-time valleys (Ps. 23:4) without any fear. He will get us ready.

We don't have to be literally perfect, only perfect in Jesus' mercy and grace, because whenever we fall short, we go quickly to the Father's throne room to ask forgiveness (Heb. 4:16). He then cleanses us immediately by the precious blood of Jesus (1 John 1:9–10). Then we can say, "I am blameless. I am washed clean from all sin, guilt, and shame, because my Father loves me and has redeemed me by Jesus' blood."

When we stay in that attitude, obeying by God's grace what He reveals to us, we will escape these terrible events soon to come upon all the inhabitants of the world. But there's more.

If we stay in God's circle of love, keeping His Word and not denying the name of Jesus in a world that's trying to forbid us from using His name, a world which instead allows and encourages the use of the powerless term "the Lord," we have a greater promise. It's a promise to those who do the above and who allow Jesus in them to make them "overcomers," believers who truly change, overcoming sin and bad habits so they can be a light of love to the world.

The church who dwells in brotherly love is given this promise: "He who overcomes, I will make him a pillar in the temple of My God…" (Rev. 3:12). He will be a priest in the very temple of God in Jerusalem, part of the church headed by Jesus that will serve as the team for the earth and the expanding Family of God throughout the universe (Isa. 9:7).

Isn't that good news?

You'll be reading lots of bad news in this book, since we are called to tell you what is coming in the world, giving you the truth about the coming events, truth you won't get from the prophecy books and movies currently out there.

We wanted to start, however, by showing you how it's all going to end—or rather, how a new world is going to begin.

The new world Jesus will bring will feature abundant crops.

Chapter Four:

The New World Jesus Will Bring

Those who keep the Sabbath day have experienced the wonderful sigh of relief that comes Friday sunset after having been through some of the pressures this world can bring during the week. Satan has put pressure on the world's inhabitants for six days of one thousand years, but his time is almost up.

The prophet Isaiah, who preached the good news of the Kingdom of God, described the glorious day when the world will finally shout for joy as they enter into Jesus' one-thousand-year day of joy. When the Christian world understands and appreciates the rest and joy of the biblical, seventh-day Sabbath, they will begin to look forward with greater eagerness and pray more fervently for God's Kingdom of love and joy to come quickly.

Isaiah speaks of that day, the day when Jesus will give you "rest from your pain and turmoil and harsh service in which you have been enslaved…" (Isa. 14:3). The whole world has been in bondage to Satan since Adam sinned and turned over his authority on the earth to the devil.

"The Gospel According to Isaiah," as Isaiah's book could be called, speaks of the end of Satan's rule of and the time when Jesus will take over. Isaiah rejoices that the day will come soon when Satan the oppressor will see Jesus put him away (Isa. 14:5–6). The inhabitants of this world, who have toiled for six days under the yoke of the devil, will then finally find peace and rest in Jesus. What a day that will be!

Here's the way Isaiah puts it: "The whole earth is at rest and is quiet" (Isa. 14:7).

People will finally know Sabbath rest in two ways. One, they will be keeping the Sabbath day (Isa. 66:23) and thus resting in Jesus on His day. Since they live in the seventh millennial day, they will begin to enjoy peace, love, and joy for a Sabbath of a thousand years. What will be the result? It will be the same result those who keep the Sabbath day now experience: "They break forth into shouts of joy" (Isa. 14:7).

Those who seek the real Jesus on His day of joy experience what the world will know in a few short years. They will break forth into shouts of joy. They will finally be free from the slavery into which Satan has put them.

Furthermore, as more and more Christians discover that they've been lied to about the Sabbath day and again they keep it, the prayer "Your Kingdom come" will echo more strongly in the throne room of heaven. Jesus will hear and come back quickly to save this world.

A Glimpse into a Much Better World

We often meditate on the Sabbath day on the concept of eternity. We also like to ponder on the Sabbath what the day represents—the transformation of this evil world by our Savior Jesus. Would you like to have a glimpse of that much better world Jesus has prophesied in His Sabbath day?

Don't you think that would be good news?

It is indeed good news. It is the gospel (good news) of the coming Kingdom of God, whose name is Love.

Can you imagine a world where hatred no longer exists, where men learn war no more, where babies don't starve to death as so many do today, where no lies are told and the truth abounds? That is the world Jesus has in store for us. And if we respond to the exhortations of this book, we will rule with Jesus in helping people to understand the ways of love and joy that will change their lives.

Think about it. A world of no poverty, no famine and starvation, no crime, no rapes or murders, no stealing other people's property, no sexual immorality, and no sickness.

Isaiah says, "And no resident will say, 'I am sick'; the people who dwell there will be forgiven their iniquity" (Isa. 33:24). What would happen today if we had no hospitals? Many would die. But Jesus and His co-rulers will do as He did and say to the sick, "All your sins are forgiven. Rise and be healed!"

Here's the way Isaiah expresses this good news: "Then the eyes of the blind will be opened and the ears of the deaf will be unstopped. Then the lame will leap like a deer, and the tongue of the mute will shout for joy" (Isa. 35:5–6).

Healing will spring forth quickly and dramatically. Great rejoicing will break forth as Jesus and the glorified saints call for healing of soul and body. Legs will grow suddenly from severed limbs. *Shalom*, meaning peace and wholeness, will describe the new world. It will literally be a *Shabbat shalom* ("day of peace and wholeness") since the seventh "day" of a thousand years will begin.

In the world Jesus will bring you will see no deserts anymore. The desert will blossom like the rose!

We Need Jesus

One of our bloggers on Freedom Blog once posted a comment asking, "Why would you want Jesus to come back?" He wrote, "I think that everything is going so good on the earth, why would we need Jesus to return?"

What kind of dream world are some people living in? They must be reveling in the temporary pleasures of sin, like the story of the man who was supposedly falling twenty-five stories from a building and commented just before smashing on the hard sidewalk, "Everything's going well so far."

The truth is, this world is in sad shape and getting sadder and sadder as we plummet to the fall of over six thousand years of man's and Satan's rule. The world is in danger of radical nations and people who are about to get their hands on weapons of mass destruction, which they will use without hesitation.

Even a half-century ago, a leading American newsweekly related that among government officials, the prevailing view was gaining acceptance that world problems could not be solved "except by a strong hand from someplace."

That's exactly what powerful men behind the scenes, and now even more in the open, are plotting—a one-world government. The beast power, headed by a nation whose ancestral counterpart is Assyria (Isa. 10:5), will answer that call, although they will rule one-third of the world rather than its entirety.

The powers that be on earth will busily try to rule the world Satan's way by eliminating most of the population so they can easily rule when Jesus returns to put a stop to human and demonic efforts for world government. Most will not welcome the King of kings. They will fight God and His rule as many are fighting Him today.

The situation will require a strong hand indeed—the hand of God. He will be obliged by the rebellious attitude of those who resist Him to bring His wrath upon this world for a day of reckoning that will last one long year. When Jesus raptures those who are faithful, and afterward those who are martyred, few true believers will be left.

Satan is conditioning the people of this world to fight against Jesus and His ways of love, to hate Him so fiercely that they will fight Him at His coming. Their fierce hatred of the One who died for them will be so strong that severe judgment from Jesus will have to come. The world will have become so evil that Jesus will have to rule with a strong hand when He returns. He has allowed Christians to go their own way, to keep their own days mixed with paganism, and to deceive people into believing Satan's lies—lies which look so good.

Jesus' ways and days of love may be unfamiliar to most Christians today, so what you read in the Bible may seem strange:

> Then it will come about that any who are left of all the nations who went against Jerusalem will go up from year to year to worship the King, [Jesus, the Eternal] of hosts, and to celebrate the Feast of Booths [Tabernacles]. (Zech. 14:16)

How could Jesus be so serious about a feast that Christians today neither observe nor know anything about? Why would He dare bring back "those awful Old Testament things"? That's the way many Christians look at these verses.

It doesn't stop there. Jesus will smite the nations who don't keep His feast with the plague of no rain (Zech. 14:17–18).

"Wait a minute," you may say. "I thought it was that mean old Father God who who did all that smiting in the Old Testament? Here we see Jesus doing the smiting."

That's right. It was Jesus, not the Father, who was the God of the First Testament, the Word who did the speaking on behalf of the God Family (John 1:1–18). He is the One who will rule in the Millennium soon to come.

He won't be ruling with you, however, if you don't agree with Him. How can you rule with Jesus if you're not in harmony with His ways and days of love?

If you have been deceived, our God is merciful. He understands. He will give you time to see things clearly. And if you ask Him, He will help you grasp the truth. Jesus meets us where we are, but we need to seek Him earnestly.

Yes, we truly need Jesus. He is the Truth we need to understand and obey.

Pastor and Author Robert B. Scott pastors Freedom Church of God in Edmonton, Alberta, Canada, a church of healing in Jesus called to announce the truth that sets people free.

Chapter Five:

A World of Lies Transformed by the Truth

As I was preparing to write this chapter, I answered the phone for one of the many interruptions that make it difficult to be a pastor, writer for two websites, and author.

The call started with a voice that said, "Don't hang up! I am not a telemarketer trying to sell you something. A burglar has been spotted in your neighborhood..." And then the recording began to do exactly what they said they wouldn't do: try to sell me on a home security system.

Talk about lies! This world is full of lies.

A funny and somewhat weird movie came out recently about a dramatic change in a world of liars. All of a sudden everyone began to tell the truth, no matter how untactful and unloving. They missed the part about telling the truth in love, which the Bible teaches.

Can you imagine a world without lies and liars? A world where everyone speaks the truth—in love?

You may remember the quip asking how you know when a politician is lying. The answer, of course, was when he moves his lips. Press secretaries avoid tough questions about their president that would force them to tell the truth, and they often speak outright lies, as does their boss.

The sad thing is that most people—oh yes, even Christians—love to be lied to. They are lovers of lies, not truth.

We've become accustomed to hearing lies and calling them truth. Our parents told us, and many of us have told our children, a blatant lie. We told them about a man dressed in red who you see in department stores at Christmas time, a man who can appear in all kinds of sizes and faces and voices, a man who can travel to every house in the world on a single night, somehow sliding down a soot-filled chimney without sullying his red outfit, and leave toys for every child on earth, except for those who come from poor families.

What a pile of horse manure!

Oh, but we believed it at one time, and even when we knew it was a "white lie," we spoke it out to those we love, making them feel enormously betrayed when they found out their parents, who they looked up to as gods when they were young, had told them a gigantic fib.

We've been fed a lot of lies about Jesus and the Bible that come direct from the pit of hell—over nine thousand, in fact!

We've been the victims of many lies about Bible prophecy. Hey, since most prophecy "experts" teach them, they must be true, right? Sorry. The popular books, the ones on the bestseller list, the ones written by those who are well-known and whose names sell books, are full of twisted truth and outright lies. Perhaps we should say untruths, since they for the most part don't know they're speaking lies.

Like many of us in our lifetimes, they have been deceived, like Eve. They don't know that they've been sold a set of lies. They believe them and teach them with zeal.

We hope to dispel those lies in this book. But first, let's look at the world the way it will be under the rule of the One who calls Himself, because He is, the Way, the Life, and the Truth. He is the Truth, and He always tells the truth. He is the greatest Prophet of all time.

Yes, Jesus always speaks truth, so we ask you to examine all that we write in the light of His Word of truth, the Bible (1 Thes. 5:21). We also ask you to pray about what you read, so that our Teacher, the Holy Spirit, can confirm the truth to you in areas that require more understanding.

Why don't we start our advanced view of a world without lies?

A World Where Truth Will Reign Supreme

Let's start with a minor prophet. Here is Micah's inspired view of the coming world: "And it will come about in the last days that the mountain of house of [Jesus] will be established as the chief of the mountains" (Micah 4:1). As we see in Daniel and other passages, mountains symbolize many things, including, in this case, governments. Micah is talking about the government—the Kingdom, or the ruling Family of God, who is Love.

Hate will be eradicated. Love will reign supreme. Those who know the joy of keeping the Sabbath day as they experience the joy of Jesus will see joy explode around them as never before.

God must think Micah's prophecy is important because He spoke almost exactly the same words in Isaiah 2. We repeat what Micah prophesies: "And it will come about in the last days…" We repeat these words to explain that one prophecy can have a number of meanings and fulfillments. The phrase "the last days" applies both to the return of Jesus and to the very last days leading up to His coming.

While not every word of this prophecy will be fulfilled as it will be in the Millennium, the Kingdom of God has come since Jesus came in the last days, or the last two thousand years of a six-thousand-year rule of man. God is ruling His Family on the earth even though that Family is presently small. A great harvest is prophesied to come into God's Kingdom in these very last days.

If those in the God Family called in the last days do their part, they will exercise authority over the "mountains" (or governments) of this world. They will expose the errors of the "hills" (or high places) of religiosity with the effect of "pulverizing" their power and authority (Micah 4:13). Truth from the Word of God of God's government will flow from centers of reformation and revival as truth will flow out of Jerusalem when Jesus returns.

Now, back to the future, Jesus reigning from Jerusalem. His government will be established as chief among all governments and His law will be indisputable (Micah 4:1–2). Jesus will not allow any government or church to interfere with the powerful proclamation of truth that will come forth from His headquarters at Jerusalem. There He will sit on the throne of David to rule in power and love. Having been humbled by the disasters they will experience in the last days, the small number of survivors of the Great Tribulation and the wrath of God will finally submit to the ways of the real Jesus.

Religious Lies Versus the Real Jesus

In the prophecies, Jesus continually says, paraphrased, "You will know that I am the Eternal. You will know that I am the 'I Am' who made you and who died for you." Even those from the "hills" (or religions) of this world, including Christianity, will find out that most of what they were taught was a pack of lies. In their humble state, they will finally be willing to know the true ways of Jesus and keep His days.

By the way, keeping those days holy as Jesus commanded throughout the Bible is the key to understanding what this book reveals about prophecy. These truths have been hidden from those who have been deceived by the many false doctrines of Christianity.

Jesus will make true disciples in the new world coming soon. And you may be or could become one now.

Jesus said to the believing Jews, "If you continue in My word, then you are truly disciples of Mine; and you will know the truth, and the truth will make you free" (John 8:31–32).

Yes, you will be free from all the errors that have kept today's church in bondage. You don't have to be a slave to Satan and his popular lies.

The Christian world teaches that you are a sinner saved by grace. God tells you that you are a saint who sometimes stumbles into sin but who confesses the sin, is cleansed by the blood of Jesus, and gets up and goes forward without guilt or shame.

Religion says that Jesus died on a Friday afternoon and rose on a Sunday in the early morning. Yet the only sign Jesus gave that He was the Messiah was that He would be in the grave for seventy-two hours, three full days and nights (Mat. 12:40).

Somebody's lying. Who is it—Jesus or religion?

The Christian world, including me, has a desire to celebrate Jesus' coming into the world and the glorious truth expressed in the phrase, "He is risen!" I believe only one method, however, stands up to biblical scrutiny.

Religion says we should observe Christmas, Easter, and even Halloween. God says not to mix pagan days with true worship (Deut. 12:29–31), but to worship Him in spirit and in truth (John 4:24).

Lies abound in the world of Christianity. Religion lies. God tells us the truth in His Word. God wants us to be shining examples of knowing, speaking, and living truth. We can thus be a light to the world and give the world hope that truth will one day reign supreme. We want to fill this book with truth. Truth liberates.

Chapter Six:

Forget Baby Jesus—The Lion of Judah Comes Roaring Back!

I want to prepare you for the reality of the bad news that is prophesied for the years to come. We want you to fully understand that a great hope lies in the soon-coming return of Jesus Christ to rule this earth in love, joy, and peace.

After all, Jesus lives in us, so we have the same anointing God gave him, to "bring good news to be afflicted… To proclaim the favorable year of the [Eternal]" (Isa. 61:1–2). Unlike Jesus, of course, we are called to read further in the scroll of Isaiah 61 than He did. He stopped before it was written, "And the day of vengeance of our God" (Isa. 61:2).

Yes, a day of reckoning is coming soon (Isa. 2:12). The law of cause and effect must inevitably run its course. Not only that, but Jesus must intervene powerfully to bring His day (or year) of wrath that will bring repentance and prepare the people of the world who survive to submit under His strong hand.

Jesus is no pansy, as some portray Him. He is no longer a baby in a manger, nor was He an effeminate weakling when he walked this earth. In His glorified form as the mighty Lion of Judah, He is coming with power to rule in love.

Nevertheless, His main message was that of the good news of the coming Kingdom of God (Mark 1:14–15). And that should also be our focus. I'm talking about a world ruled by Jesus, who will smash the puny efforts of power-hungry men who seek to establish a new world order. Jesus will pulverize the new world order. His government will, in fact, be the old world order, the one established by Adam before he sinned. That order will come back in power, ruled by Jesus Christ.

Whether you like it or not, you are living in a historic moment, the major turning point of mankind's history. It's also the most calamitous time we have ever faced. Nevertheless, for those who know Jesus this is the most exciting time ever in which to live.

All creation is poised, eagerly awaiting with bated breath the manifestation of the true sons of God in these last days and for the "period of restoration of all things about which God spoke by the mouth of His holy prophets from ancient time" (Acts 3:21).

Acts 3:22 quotes Moses with some strong words that serve as a warning for this end time. If we don't heed the words of the greatest Prophet who ever lived, Jesus Christ of Nazareth, we will be destroyed in the coming calamities.

On the other hand, if we heed His words, including the words of the prophets of old, which are in reality His own words, we will be saved. That salvation includes physical deliverance from the times ahead. These coming calamities will frighten the world, but they should not frighten those who trust in Jesus and have His joy and love in which no fear exists.

We want you to overflow with joy at the good news of God's coming Kingdom on earth, so full of joy that the bad news only makes you more fervent in your prayers for the Kingdom of Love to come.

A wonderful, new world is coming soon. Read all about it!

A New World Tomorrow

People respect power. Jesus will have to show His power to humble humankind[8] as He comes to squash their rebellion and force His government on this world. Did I say "force"? Yes, you got that right. Jesus gave mankind over six thousand years to do it his own way. He's about to show us His way in no uncertain, politically correct terms.

In a strange movie my wife and I saw on one of our first dates, a father prayed at the dinner table to the baby Jesus. Can you imagine praying to a helpless baby in a manger and getting results?

No way. We pray to our Father in heaven in Jesus' name, as He commanded. Governments are trying to outlaw prayers in the name of Jesus. I hope you'll join me in following Jesus' own directive. He never said to pray to "the Lord." He said to pray to the Father in His name, the name of Jesus (John 16:23).

We follow the prayer example of Matthew 6, calling for God's Kingdom to come. We pray that His Kingdom will come soon, and we know that He has answered us, that He is indeed coming soon—not as a baby, but as the powerful Lion of Judah.

Yes, Jesus will "rule all the nations with a rod of iron" (Rev. 12:5).

No more political correctness, hallelujah! No more compromising, weak-kneed tolerance of false religions. Jesus' law will go forth from Jerusalem and He will accept no compromise. His Word is law, and it will be the law for the whole world, whether they like it or not. They will still have free choice to obey or not obey, but the choice will be clear and unequivocal.

8 *Humankind represents a mixture of mankind DNA and giant DNA introduced by Satan. Being free from this polluted giant DNA is a process that begins with accepting Jesus, being baptized, and taking communion regularly.*

Beware of Chrislam!

One of the latest heresies we see in the Christian world is the rise of the deceptive heresy of Chrislam. Don't fall for it!

You can't combine light and darkness. You can't make the God of the Bible, who is named Love and always acts in love (even when He disciplines), agree with the demon of cruelty, which is the spiritual force behind the name of the false god Allah. Jesus said we would know people and ideologies by their fruits (Mat. 7:20).

While not every Christian is a strong believer who walks according to the name of Father Love, those who are strong in the faith do indeed walk in love and forgiveness, especially those who read and practice my book, *God's Fruit of Forgiveness.*

The book Islam goes by advocates hatred and murder of infidels or non-Muslims. Jesus is only mentioned as a prophet who eventually makes people worship Mohammed. The God of love has nothing in common with the god of cruelty. Loving Muslims is one thing. Extending the hand of fellowship to a false religion is quite another. And putting Allah into God's Word, as some translators have done, is a grave error.

Chrislam is idolatry. It's the spirit of compromise that characterizes the last era of the church, Laodicea (Rev. 3:15). Don't be deceived. Don't allow the spells of witches to lull you into compromising everything you believed from the Bible.

We have strong believers in Jesus on Freedom Blog who have not always known Jesus. Some have previously practiced the dark arts for as much as fifty years. They know the workings of darkness and the schemes of the devil (Eph. 6:11). One of them answered questions about Chrislam.

The blogger explained that Chrislam and the writings justifying it were

> designed and orchestrated by three hundred warlocks and sorcerers from a variety of faiths. They are ready to make their final move to unite the world under the new world order. The Christian world has fallen asleep and into chaos. They have no idea who they are in Jesus and what authority they have; therefore, they are ready to fall under the final set of spells that will start to be issued at the next full moon [April 2012]. The so-called Christian world will then reject all that they know in favor of the false Jesus who will unite the beast and destroy North America… The final set of spells represents spells that put people into a dreamlike state that allows them to shout "Peace, peace in our time" just before major wars break out. It also causes our leaders to fail to see the schemes behind the covenant of death.[9]

Satan's strategy is to use many leaders of Christianity—or more correctly said, "churchianity"—leaders who are warlocks, to establish this worldwide heresy. The idea is to declare "peace, peace," as the Bible prophesies, and if you don't want this perfect solution to peace, as they see it, you need to be eliminated so peace can be produced. If you call yourself a believer and embrace this doctrine, you are eating at the table of demons and trying to combine the darkness with the light (1 Cor. 10:21). It will tear you apart.

We prefer to be biblically correct rather than politically correct. We love all people; however, we want to agree with God in saying no to tolerating evil of any kind.

---

9 *While the "covenant of death" (Isa. 28:15) can be understood more generally, it can refer specifically to a pact the tiny nation of Israel will make with the European beast power at the end, a covenant of betrayal that will end in death.*

Only the prayers of strong believers can wake the Christian world, especially those in North America, who could come against this heresy. Whether the European beast is angered by America's resistance to Chrislam or by the rising number of Sabbath-keepers, the beast will find whatever excuse it needs to destroy North America, as evidenced by the devil's end-time ire against commandment-keepers (Rev. 12:17). The fake peace the beast establishes with Chrislam will turn quickly to war, even pitting the Arab Mahdi (or Antichrist, the King of the South) against the church-led European beast, the King of the North.

As the power of deception increases and ominous prophetic events unfold, we must be on the alert to avoid all forms of heresy and stay strong in Jesus. Those who truly know Him will not be deceived by these false ideas. And we thank God for Jesus' return, which will put an end to the efforts to blend paganism with the true worship of God.

Jesus Will Enforce *His* Days

Jesus will not tolerate pagan mixtures in the worship of Him. He will enforce the days He Himself gave in Leviticus 23, the days He and His apostles kept while on this earth (Luke 23:56; Acts 13:42–44; 18:3–4; 20:6; 24:14; 1 Cor. 5:7–8).

No pussyfooting. No diplomacy. No tolerance. Jesus will lay down the law. It will not be a democracy or a republic. It will not be sharia law, nor will it be a case where the candidate who has the most money wins. Jesus wins because He has earned the right to rule. Will we earn the right to rule with Him by relying on His grace or empowerment to make the changes in our lives we need to make?

What a day that will be! No more evil kingmakers behind the scenes buying victory for the man they want to carry out their evil plans. No more vicious, mud-slinging political campaigns. People will lay down their "mud," their dirty problems, and their sins to Jesus as they bow down to Him weekly on the Sabbath day, laying down their long-term problems at the new moon (Isa. 66:23).

All mankind will seek the King of peace on His Sabbath day, not on Sunday. This truth is so strange to our Christian world today that the above verse should be repeatedly emphasized so it can sink in: "And it shall be from new moon to new moon and from sabbath to sabbath, all mankind will come to bow down before Me" (Isa. 66:23).

That's Jesus speaking these words—the Jesus who is the same yesterday, today, and forever (Heb. 13:8). Sabbath peace (or *shalom*) will come to the whole world on the seventh period or "day" of one thousand years, a millennial Sabbath of peace and joy (2 Pet. 3:8–9).

We've seen that Jesus will bring about a world where men learn war no more. But for that to happen, Jesus will have to quell initial rebellions to His rule, rebellions that prophecy teachers misunderstand. They fail to see that the war described in Ezekiel 38 speaks of a land of Israel that's not like the land we see today or the land we'll see before Jesus returns. It will be a land "restored from the sword" (Ezek. 38:8), a phenomenon that doesn't exist today and won't exist before Jesus brings real peace to that turbulent area of the world.

This chapter of Ezekiel, and the following one, speaks of a time of which Jesus says, "And I will set My glory among the nations" (Ezek 39:21), a time that will not come before Jesus returns. Israel, in the last days, will not be a "land of unwalled villages," a people who "are at rest, that live securely, all of them living without walls and having no bars or gates" (Ezek. 38:11). You have to twist the Word of God to see this war as a battle waged before the return of Jesus.

You would be best to disregard teachings that twist the Word of God, no matter how popular they may be or how famous those who bring these teachings may be. This is the good news of a time when truth will be restored. The Kingdom of truth can come for you right now as you prove all things and hold fast to the truths verified by the Word of God.

Peace will finally come, but not by the hand or mouth of those who curse the nation of Israel and appease Arab terrorists. Peace can only come by the mighty hand of Jesus.

Ezekiel 34:28–29 describes that day:

> They will no longer be a prey to the nations, and the beasts of the earth will not devour them; but they will live securely, and no one will make them afraid… they will not endure the insults of the nations anymore.

The nations of Israel, America (Manasseh), and modern Israel (Judah) will be blessed, not cursed.

What a world it will be when neither beasts nor their spiritual counterparts (demons) will trouble mankind. David will be king over Israel, and Jesus, who will rule over David, prophesies a time of peace: "I will make a covenant of peace with them and eliminate harmful beasts from the land so that they may live securely in the wilderness and sleep in the woods" (Ezek. 34:25).

Today you can get killed in the woods, attacked by man or beast. Tomorrow you will be able to sleep in the woods and camp out under the stars. In a world of peace, we will be able to be close to God, taking time to think and meditate on Him and His Word. The mad rushing and stressful society that pressures us today will be a thing of the past.

When you keep the Sabbath day, you get a small foretaste of what that world peace will be like. As you keep that day, you do more than pray for God's Kingdom to come. You act out the faith of that coming Kingdom every week.

Joy Will Abound

As a student in 1970, I had the pleasure of stepping on the hills near Salzburg, Austria, where Julie Andrews sang the beautiful theme song from *The Sound of Music*. In the 1980s, I delivered a sermon in French on that theme at the Feast of Tabernacles in Quebec, since I had found a verse in one of the French translations that used the exact phrase of the movie title.

Singing is an expression of joy, and those expressions will abound in the world to come:

> Indeed, [Jesus] will comfort Zion; He will comfort all her waste places. And her wilderness He will make like Eden [a return to the perfect world ruled by Jesus before Adam and Eve sinned], and her desert like the garden of [Jesus]; joy and gladness was found in her, thanksgiving and sound of a melody. (Isa. 51:3)

The sound of music was a happy sound in the movie. The French title would be literally translated as "The melody of happiness (or joy)." In the world tomorrow, joy will explode in songs of exaltation. Our Sabbath praise and worship songs look forward to that glorious time.

Jeremiah foresaw in that wonderful world to come

> the voice of joy and the voice of gladness, the voice of the bridegroom and the voice of the bride, the voice of those who say, "Give thanks to the [Eternal One, Jesus] of hosts, for [Jesus] is good, for His lovingkindness is everlasting…" (Jer. 33:11)

Those songs will be sung, and all words will be spoken in a new, pure language, most probably the original, conceptual Hebrew language God gave to Adam to speak: "For then I will give to the peoples purified lips ['a pure language' (NKJV)], that all of them may call on the name of

[Jesus], to serve Him shoulder to shoulder ['with one accord' (NKJV])" (Zeph. 3:9).

Our languages today are filled with bad words, words that cause us to curse ourselves and to speak negatively of ourselves and others. We have borrowed words from paganism and witchcraft that should not be in the mouth of believers. We hear lyrics in worldly songs and even Christian songs that speak falsehood rather than truth. In this new world, we will no longer live in a world of "unclean lips," as Isaiah expressed it (Isa. 6:5). A pure language will allow all men to speak and worship "in spirit and in truth" (John 4:24).

The world will rejoice in a universal Sabbath rest, a rest from sorrow, fear, pain, turmoil, and from the bondage of Satan's ways (Isa. 14:3).

Jeremiah gives encouraging words from Jesus that should express hope: "There is hope for your future… and your children will return to their own territory" (Jer. 31:17).

Idolatry will be a thing of the past (Isa. 31:7). No more false gods. No more addictions to drugs, alcohol, prescription drugs, or sex. This glorious freedom will be reason to sing and shout for joy. Jesus will turn the mourning of this world into joy. He will change the poverty to abundance (Jer. 31:12–14).

Wow! What a world! Jesus will bring prosperity plus, and the veil of lies will be removed (Isa. 25:6). While almost everything we hear today is a lie, such evil is going to stop soon: no more lies, no more deception, and no more twisted stories about the Bible or Jesus.

In this world of starving children, untimely deaths, and tragedies, it may be hard to imagine a scenario that isn't too good to be true: "He will swallow up death for all time, and [Jesus] will wipe tears away from all faces, and He will remove the reproach of His people from all the earth; for [Jesus] has spoken" (Isa. 25:8).

Jesus has spoken. He has spoken out His Sabbath covenant promise: He will bring about a wonderful world tomorrow on the seventh millennial day—even if He has to do it Himself (Isa. 59:16–20).

Health and Well-being—A True *Shabbat Shalom*

Shalom is a greeting of multiple blessings (over seventy!) we give to each other along with enthusiastic hugs of love at Freedom Church of God on Jesus' day of joy, peace, and love. On the Sabbath day, we say, "*Shabbat shalom!*" By doing so, we prophesy the glorious time when wholeness, health, and total well-being will be the order of the day—the millennial Sabbath day.

Sickness will be a thing of the past (Isa. 33:24). Food will no longer be polluted by dishonest industrial giants and by food and drug associations who only want to push pharmaceuticals, unjustly penalizing natural foods and supplements. In this coming world, we won't even need to supplement our foods; they will no longer be depleted of nutrients because of bad farming practices.

Communism will not be the solution. Private ownership and honest practices will bring abundance, and God's love will cast out fear (Micah 4:4). Showers of God's blessings will bring abundant crops. People will dwell in security, and then "they will know that I am [Jesus]" (Ezek. 34:26–27).

We know that it is Jesus, not the Father, who will rule in the coming Millennium of peace (Rev. 20:6). Jesus is the real "I am," the One who spoke to Moses as the "I am" in *The Ten Commandments*, a movie I saw as a boy when it first came out. My young mind was impressed by the powerful, mysterious voice of Yahweh. I only discovered when I was sixteen that the voice Moses heard was the voice of the real Jesus who few know today. In the new world Jesus will rule over, all will know the real Jesus and His voice.

Rain in due season and abundant crops will be the norm (Isa. 30:23) as "the plowman will overtake the reaper" (Amos 9:13–14). That's what God wants for us here and now, if we would only obey him, so we could "eat the best of the land" (Isa. 1:19).

Better Than in Your Dreams!

Picture this: a movie preview of the wonderful world where Jesus will be King. It's in Zechariah 8. Jesus says He will return to Jerusalem, which "will be called the City of Truth, and the mountain of the [Eternal] of hosts will be called the Holy Mountain… And the streets of the city will be filled with boys and girls playing in its streets" (Zech. 8:3,5). And they won't be trying to avoid filth, drug needles, or gangs.

Our children will be healthy and happy, not cooped up in some ghetto. No more traffic snarls in rush hour madness, no more drug dealers, homelessness, street gangs, criminals, thieves, rapists, murderers, abortionists who think they're doing God and women a service, and no more "adult" trash to watch on television. And our children will play safely in the streets.

At my church's Sabbath services, we can hear the joyful sound of children laughing and playing (Ps. 8:2). It's a beautiful and powerful sound that chases evil away.

Jesus is about to transform this sad, sordid world into a Garden of Eden better than Adam and Eve enjoyed. He will judge righteously and strongly (Isa. 11:4), transforming even the genetic structures of the violent animals that Satan had a right to change for the worse because of Adam's sin.

The result, written in Isaiah 11:6–9, will be glorious:

> And the wolf will dwell with the lamb, and the leopard will lie down with the young goat, and the calf and the young lion and the fatling together; and a little boy will lead them. Also the cow and the bear will graze, their young will lie down together, and the lion will eat straw like the ox. The nursing child will play by the hole of the cobra, and the weaned child will put his hand on the viper's den. They will not hurt or destroy in all My holy mountain, for the earth will be full of the knowledge of [Jesus] as the waters cover the sea.

Satan's cacophony will end, replaced by the glorious sounds of celebration. Jesus will turn the mourning of this world into exuberant joy. He will even transform the physical earth, which has become desert in many places because of the ravages of sin.

Here's the good news from Isaiah 35:1–2:

> The wilderness and the desert will be glad, and the Arabah will rejoice and blossom; like the crocus it will blossom profusely and rejoice with rejoicing and shout of joy. The glory of Lebanon will be given to it, the majesty of Carmel and Sharon. They will see the glory of [Jesus], the majesty of our God.

The next words should encourage those who have decided to believe and obey Jesus in these last days:

> Encourage the exhausted, and strengthen the feeble. Say to those with anxious heart, "Take courage, fear not. Behold, your God will come with vengeance [for the rebellious sinners who will fight against Him]; the recompense of God will come, *but He will save you.*" (Isa. 35:3–4)

Yes, Jesus will save you. The good news is that if you choose to obey Jesus, you and those you love can be protected and prosper in the turbulent times ahead. Don't allow Satan's deceptions to keep you from that protection and prosperity.

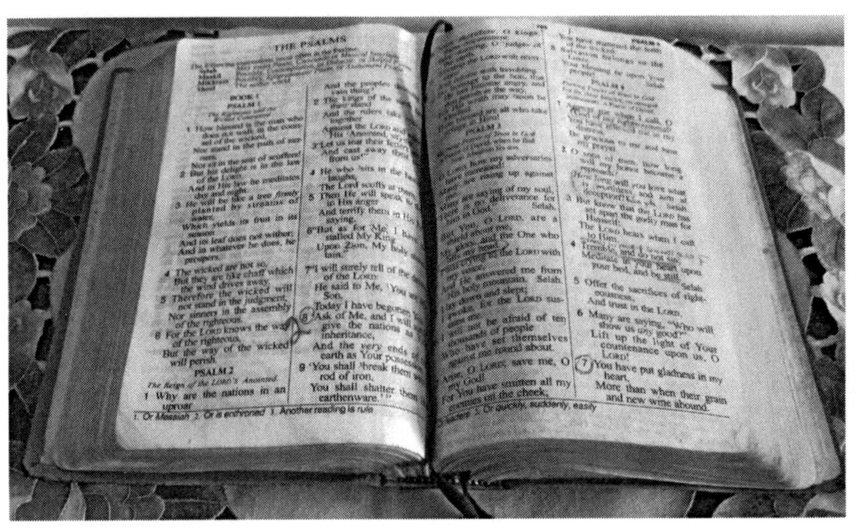

God commands us to prove all things on the basis of His Word so we won't be hoodwinked (1 Thes. 5:21; Isa. 8:20).

Chapter Seven:

Don't Be Hoodwinked!

Jesus' first warning to His disciples who asked about the prophetic signs of His coming was to guard against being deceived (Mat. 24:4). Modern-day disciples can have many roots of deception.

One is being bored with Jesus. The world has turned sour to hearing the words of Jesus, His name, His teaching and the good news He came to give us. Have you joined the world's rejection of truth and become bored with Jesus? Have you joined the walking dead who don't know Jesus—or His message of love, hope, and purpose?

Jesus came and gave us the gospel (good news), which has become perverted over the years. Christians and believers have either never heard the good news or never bothered to study its true meaning. What is the good news Jesus brought?

The good news or gospel is that…

- the Kingdom of God (or the Kingdom of Love) has been reintroduced to the earth so that it may reclaim the earth and the universe from the power of death (Heb. 2:14).
- in Jesus, the Kingdom of Love is established in your heart, will, and mind (Rom. 5:5).

- the empowerment of change, authority, and strength in receiving the graces of God is released in you so that nothing is impossible (Mat. 19:26).
- in accepting Jesus as the God of your life, you are righteous and have the righteousness of Jesus as your shield (Rom. 5:17).
- you can use the blood of Jesus as a weapon of warfare against Satan and his accusations (Rev. 12:11).
- Jesus came to reveal the Father, whom no one had seen or talked to before (John 5:37).
- we are called for a purpose and are given a vision of the end of Satan and his rule of pain and death (Rev. 21:4).
- all the power of sin and its curse is broken (Gal. 3:13). You are forgiven of every sin you have ever committed (Isa. 1:18).
- you have been called to live forever (John 3:16).
- you can speak what will be, not in "I guess" speculations (Rom. 4:17; 1 Cor. 1:20).
- no one will have to learn war anymore (Isa. 2:4).
- no one will live in poverty (Isa. 25:6).
- no one will have to suffer loss (Isa. 35:10).
- no one will be homeless (Amos 9:14).
- no one will have to learn sickness and death (Isa. 33:24).

Yet it's this good news that brings in boredom. The world is expecting bad news, not good news. What you are expecting becomes all that you look forward to and become emotionally involved with, not to mention what draws your energy and interest.

It Feels Good so it Must Be True

Another root of deception is the "it feels good so it must be true" lie. It's not about feelings. It's about truth. God says in His Word to prove all things according to the Bible (1 Thes. 5:21), and He says that if someone isn't speaking according to the Word, they do not have the light of truth (Isa. 8:20).

They may be charismatic. They may be popular and sell millions of books. That does not mean they speak truth. They may soon come on the scene displaying amazing signs and wonders that make you either wonder if they are from God or convince you that they are.

Believing them may seem good and feel good, but that doesn't mean they're speaking the truth. God says some ways seem right to a man, but the end of those ways is death (Prov. 14:12).

Because the heart is so deceitful, we must understand what makes it tick. We must examine the foundations of this "feels good, must be true" lie.

Your Physical Senses

The first foundation involves the *five physical senses*, which everyone possesses and that can develop in us to varying degrees of proficiency. Science has recognized sight, touch, hearing, taste, and smell as the basic senses. Scientists are also beginning to acknowledge "time expanded" as a sense, since some people even under sensory deprivation can still sense how much time has lapsed.

The basic five senses cannot begin to explain all the mystery senses that have been found yet remain unexplainable by what science is willing to accept. How do people know when they're walking down a street and sense someone's eyes upon them? They will turn and look right into the eyes of their watcher. How is that possible?

A person will be driving and suddenly stop, thereby avoiding an accident that should not have been avoidable. How does this happen? It involves sensing something from the soul and spirit realm, and that's why science refuses to acknowledge it.

The Heart

The second foundation is *the heart*—the seat of emotions for the soul. It's also the filter for hearing from the spirit man guided by the Holy Spirit. The heart is the director of the *will*, so when the heart and will come into agreement to think along certain paradigms, they enable the mind to handle new information along the guidelines of that paradigm.

When we put our spirits before our heart or feelings, we guarantee God's blessings, including long life. When feelings, deceptions, and lies lead us rather than the Holy Spirit in us, early death is inevitable.

Worldly people have this wrong foundation of feelings as their basis for determining truth and their course of action. Truth becomes what they feel it to be, irrespective of what God says in His Word. The good news is, we don't have to live that way.

The Brain Versus the Mind

The third foundation involves the *brain versus the mind*. Those with the "feels good, must be true" mentality believe everything that the mind relays to the brain. Even voices in their head are believed above evidence, truth, laws, and facts. Everyone is affected in some way by this foundation for establishing his or her own truth.

When sexual abuse occurs in childhood, the brain and the mind have a hard time communicating with each other.

Many believe the brain and the mind are one and the same. Not true. The brain is a physical organ with certain powers. However, the mind is a part of the spiritual makeup of mankind called the soul, which includes mind, heart, and will. Special cameras that capture what some would describe as an aura extending several inches away from the body have photographed the soul. That spiritual element outside the body is the soul, and thus it is also the mind. It has amazing abilities far above the functioning capacity of the brain. We have not begun to tap its powers, even less the enormous potential of that mind as supernaturally empowered by the Holy Spirit.

Lust and Lies

The fourth foundation revolves around *lust, lying, and the learning of lies*. These are enemies of the mind and produce the voice of the enemy in your head. These enemies cause the brain to react in anger when you don't get your own way. Lust activates the agents of "get," Lying activates the agents of fear, and the learning of lies (deception) produces a willingness to reject the Word of God in order to accept the pain of restlessness and guilt.

The fourth foundation has become the way of life, especially the political life, for the end of this age. Deceitfulness has touched the whole world so thoroughly that no one can stand to hear the truth (Isa. 59:13–15).

Did You Hear That?

The fifth foundation is expressed in the question, "*Did you hear that?*" It causes the brain to seek out and speak gossip, innuendo, and tattling. And the demons make the flesh feel a high in doing so. Each time an adrenaline rush comes, the flesh feels good and seeks to hear more gossip, innuendo, and tattling so that it has more to talk about and feel good about.

"I am so good and they are so bad" becomes a new goal, vision, and purpose for life. This is so common that Jesus warned about getting caught in this trap in Matthew 7:1–2, stating that we would be judged with the same measure by which we judge others.

Jesus asks in the next verse why we see the speck in others' eyes but not the log in our own. The answer is, "I feel good doing it, so it must be good to do, and I must be true to how I feel."

The "did you hear that?" condition creates a veil over the ears and eyes so that the clear warning of mercy versus judgment in Luke 6:36–37 cannot be heard. Sowing the seed of no mercy will mean no mercy will come to you (Mat. 5:7). Love, joy, and freedom will be stolen from your life.

I've Read That

The sixth foundation of the "feel good, must be true" lie applies specifically to understanding prophecy. It is embodied in the phrase, "*I've read that.*" People read something that feels good or sounds good without checking with our Father. They say, "I will accept this as true. I will trust whoever wrote it to have researched it, proven it, or validated the truth of what they said."

The danger of quoting man is in its quickness to take you back into error or repeat the same mistakes. The Word of God corrects errors; the word of man embellishes errors into doctrines. The word of Satan turns errors into religions.

The "I've read that" syndrome creates self-satisfaction, self-justification, and legalism. Especially if one is quoting oneself, the syndrome is unchallengeable. And with the rise of electronic communication, the "I've read it, so it must be true" argument has made stupidity a god.

Do you believe every word in a book about prophecy because so-and-so wrote it? Do you believe every part of a prophetic movie because you saw it and it seems true and plausible? Do you believe all that a man writes because he's "an anointed man of God"?

In Your Dreams

The seventh foundation for falseness is, "*I had a dream about that, therefore it must be true.*" Most people rely on non-thought processes, and some use tangential thought processes to arrive at what they consider to be truth. These are the sort of people who are locked into watching soap operas and sick comedies in order to establish their foundation for judging what's true. They become so caught up in their show or enraptured by their movie heroes that what happens in their hero's show becomes an active part of their life and identity. If their hero went out and committed adultery, it would also be acceptable for them to do so. If their hero's wife or husband is cheating or stealing, then their mate must also be involved with such activities. They become so out of sync with reality that they begin to talk like their hero, idol, or god—perhaps even dressing like them, judging what is truth by the standards set by their heroes.

Before Jesus became my hero, Yankee baseball slugger Mickey Mantle was mine. When I saw a commercial showing him showering without a washrag, I discarded my washrag and lathered up with my hands like my hero.

God says to imitate Him, not the idols we worship. Some people hang on every word a prophetic teacher may say because he is who he is and he couldn't make a mistake.

The "I had a dream" foundation affects over ninety percent of all mankind. Dream heroes, dream idols (music world), or false gods established a person's identity, their foundation for truth, their will, the way they evaluate right or wrong, and their purpose of life. *And the majority must be right.*

This means that unscrupulous people can pollute the will of ninety percent of the people so that their choices are always directed to error. What God has declared wrong in His Word can become accepted as the norm because of the ability to adjust the will of the majority. The great American dream has been adjusted and adjusted so that the vision and purpose of the founding fathers has been totally lost. A people kept ignorant by a false dream will avoid the truth at all costs.

False dreams, signs, and the misleading phrases we have seen build a *paradigm of errors.* Here are a few of its components:

1. "I am a good person. My goodness means that what makes me feel good has to be true."

2. Error plus error equals truth. A lie protects you and supports a secondary lie as truth. Two wrongs make a right.

3. "I believe that God wants me to enjoy both sides of life."

4. "It's not my fault. If something goes wrong, I follow my feel-good feelings, so it has to be someone else's fault.

5. Regarding diving into the deep end: "You've got to try it at least once before you can judge it."

6. Regarding demonic doctrines: "You cannot understand the Word or will of God, so you need to follow your feelings or heart to find happiness, love, and truth."

7. "They need to be punished. If they do not approve of my feelings about what is right or wrong in my eyes, punish them."

8. "The traditions of the past must be right. If the traditions have been around for a long period of time, they are time-tested truth. We have always done things this way." A flagrant example is the keeping of Sunday. "Because a pagan emperor imposed it on the organized church, and we've been keeping Sunday for seventeen hundred years, we cannot be wrong."

9. "The law is done away with. It was nailed to Jesus' cross. I live by grace now."

10. "Everything I do pleases God. I keep the feasts of the world, so God knows my heart is pure."

This paradigm of errors repeats itself over and over again, and it is deepened with each disaster. The idea is, "False security makes one feel good, so it must be the true way to go."

We pray that as you read this book, you will see past your feelings and seek the truth of Jesus in the whole, living Word of God. We bless you with the grace to prove and understand the truth that will set you free.

As you read the next chapter, you will need that grace.

Chapter Eight:
Surprise! America Is at the Center of Bible Prophecy

We have seen the good news of the coming Kingdom. If we're going to understand the bad news of prophecy, we must understand who the players are. We must know who Israel is in Bible prophecy.

A book by Messianic pastor Jonathan Cahn, *The Harbinger: The Ancient Mystery That Holds the Secret of America's Future*, made the New York Times bestseller list in early 2012.[10] The book links nine specific warnings of destructions that hit ancient Israel to modern-day America by citing Isaiah 9:10 in its relation to the infamous occurrence on September 11, 2001.

Two major political figures read the Isaiah 9:10 passage after the 9/11 attacks. Arrogance colored their statements, with the emphasis on the word "we." "We will rebuild," not "We ask forgiveness for the sins which opened the door for this destruction."

Whether the phrase "The bricks have fallen down" refers to the leveling of the twin towers is debatable. The important thing to note is that those towers symbolized the economic might of America, while

---

10 *Jonathan Cahn. The Harbinger: The Ancient Mystery that Holds the Secret of America's Future (Laguna Hills, CA: Frontline, 2012).*

the Pentagon attack signified an assault on the symbol of America's once-mighty military.

The Leaven Behind Nine Eleven

Jesus has not started directly punishing the nations, as He must when His wrath begins a year before His return. He does, however, withdraw His blessings from nations that had it when the leaven of sin starts to leaven the whole lump, when sin starts to infiltrate the whole society (1 Cor. 5:6). When a nation is sick from top to bottom, God's protection cannot continue.

God did not cause the 9/11 attacks, but He had to allow it because of America's rebellion. Since 1972, her courts decided to allow the shedding of innocent, young blood in the form of abortion, an abomination in God's sight that brought "bloodguiltiness" on the land and made it indefensible.

America has repeatedly shown God that she wants no part of God. The way governments and people talk and act, you would believe they think God is dead. Officials took the Bible out of the schools, forbade the display of the Ten Commandments, and have tried to wipe out the name of Jesus from our public prayers—and indeed our whole land. The government has encouraged sexual deviation and called what God calls abominations the norm. Elected officials have bowed to foreign religions, protecting their rights while stealing the rights of true believers in Jesus.

The people of America condoned the lying under oath of a president in a sex scandal and they have thus reaped lies and liars in high places on a much more serious scale. We have become a nation of liars that loves lies. God hates lies, and He will allow the consequences of our love for lies to fall upon us.

Reaping the Whirlwind

An effect stems from every cause that creates it. We cannot go on thumbing our national nose at the Almighty without consequences. As I write this, a wave of unprecedented tornados is ravaging the American heartland in a season where usually no tornados are spawned. Satan, "the prince of the power of the air" (Eph. 2:2), is the author of these storms, not God.

God, however, has taken His hand of protection away from the nation as a whole. Only true believers have the authority to calm these storms, but most Christians are too scared by Satan's attacks that they don't take their God-given authority. Jesus spoke peace to the storm, and He said we would or should do greater works than He did (John 14:12).

God allowed 9/11 to happen. He has allowed the government behind the government to continue their plan for their one world order, a part of which is the destruction of America. While it was Arab terrorists who willingly cooperated, the attack was clearly allowed by insiders who are intent on seeing America go down.

Go down it will. It has passed the point of no return. America has shown Jesus it does not want to return to Him. Some will repent in a great harvest in these last days, but the nation and its leadership, even its spiritual leadership, have encouraged foreign religions to dominate a people called to be a believing nation. They have bowed to a religion of cruelty whose God is not named Love like the God of the Bible (1 John 4:8).

These verses are indeed warnings to Israel. The events of Isaiah 9 were part of a limited attack by Assyria against the northern ten tribes of Israel, whose tribes were later led off into captivity into Assyria. Where they subsequently migrated is historically documented, but few have made an effort to trace their steps to determine where these lost tribes went.

It is significant that just as Israel's leaders boasted they would rebuild the symbols of strength of the nation in defiance of God, America has also made its boast instead of humbling itself before the Almighty. And just as America has been warned by the 9/11 attacks before an imminent national captivity, so ancient Israel was warned by the limited attack in Isaiah 9 before they were carried away by Assyria into captivity.

This is eerily similar to what will happen to the same nation thousands of years later. That nation is not the tiny nation the world calls Israel today.

Cahn makes the case in his fictional account based on facts that Isaiah 9:10 applies to America, that all the divine incidences mentioned are definite harbingers (signs of warning) to America. What the author and most of today's prophetic teachers do not grasp is much more shocking, however, than the meaning of Isaiah 9:10. The truth is, virtually all of the first three-quarters of the Bible is addressed to America. This statement may astound you, but I will prove it.

America *Is* Israel!

I better say that again: America is Israel!

That's a shocking statement to most. This is not some theory advanced only by cultists or "British Israelite" groups. We are not a cult. Cults think they are the only true church and worship men.

The story I am about to tell you is most probably a story you have never heard. It's more than a story; it's the gospel truth. While this truth may not be the foundation of the gospel of the Kingdom, you can't understand how the Kingdom of God will come about on earth if you don't understand who Israel is in prophecy.

The story I am about to tell you, in resume form, can be found on the internet by typing certain keywords into search engines, like, "U.S. and British Commonwealth in prophecy." You'll find much on the subject. However, since some who teach this truth are cults, you may find some falseness in their teaching. That's why I give a brief synopsis of this astounding truth, which has been overlooked and/or ridiculed by prophecy teachers.

What you're about to read isn't necessary for salvation, but it's essential knowledge in many ways. It's stranger than any manmade plot, yet it is true. If it weren't true, God's promise to Abraham and afterwards to Jacob, who was renamed Israel, was not fulfilled.

America Is Israel, or God's a Liar!

If America isn't Israel, God would have to be a liar, but we know He cannot lie. This is a powerful lesson in God's faithfulness to His promises. Sometimes those promises must be delayed, but they are always fulfilled. God will watch over His Word to perform it, even in the minutest detail.

Without this understanding, it is impossible—yes, impossible!—to understand end-time Bible prophecy. Yet none of the major, respected expositors of Bible prophecy have any inkling of this important truth—at least not yet. They speak of Russia and China and the tiny, modern Jewish nation of Israel, but they ignore the two brother-like nations that were once the most powerful nations on the face of the earth.

Is it possible that the God who knows the end from the beginning could ignore these nations? Could the Bible ignore a nation and a commonwealth of nations who, beginning in the early 1800s, came into great prominence?

At their zenith of power, the United States and the British Commonwealth possessed together almost three-quarters of the world's wealth and resources.

As we shall see, God promised unconditionally to Abraham that he would be the father of many nations. The promise was elaborated on and reconfirmed to Jacob. But the promise of national wealth and influence didn't involve all the tribes of Israel, of which there were twelve. Judah was only one of the twelve tribes.

Judah became the modern nation of Israel while others, in comparatively small numbers, scattered throughout the world becoming nations of little to no influence. The promise of national greatness, known as the birthright blessing, was given only to the birthright brothers Ephraim and Manasseh, who were sons of Joseph (1 Chron. 5:1–2).

God prophesied that they would become a nation and a multitude, company, or commonwealth of nations (Gen. 48:15–16, 19; 17:4). While the apostle Paul was speaking of spiritual Israel in Ephesians 2:12, it is no coincidence that he referred to Israel as the "commonwealth of Israel."

Consider thoughtfully this important fact: until several centuries ago, never had there appeared in history a nation and a company of nations joined in a commonwealth that could have fulfilled the promises of national prosperity and greatness given to Ephraim and Manasseh. No such nations other than the brother-like nations of America and the British Commonwealth nations of Anglo-Saxon origin could have fulfilled this prophecy.

Prophecies can indeed fail because of free will (1 Cor. 13:8). The prophecy about Nineveh failed because they repented.

Jesus, however, swore by Himself when He saw Abraham give up his only son as His Father would do, and said,

> *because* you have done this thing and have not withheld your son, your only son, indeed I will greatly bless you, and I will greatly multiply your seed as the stars of the heavens and as the sand which is on the seashore; and your seed shall possess the gate of their enemies. (Gen. 22:16–17)

By these words, Jesus made the promise absolutely unconditional. It couldn't fail. The prophecy, while delayed by disobedience, would have to come to pass, or Jesus was saying that what He swore by Himself was a lie. But Jesus doesn't ever lie. Numbers 23:19 states this: "God is not a man, that He should lie… Has He said, and will He not do it? Or has He spoken, and will He not make it good?"

Jesus swore to Abraham, "Because you have done this, indeed I will do this." Do we realize the importance of these words? Do we realize that unless we find who fulfilled these promises, we cannot believe any other word that God has spoken?

A Story of Race, Grace, and Gates

While the prophecy about the gates of the enemies has multiple fulfillments among God's physical and spiritual people, one accomplishment of that prophecy is undeniable.

Britain and America possessed for many years the most important sea gates of the world. Because of their disobedience, according to the prophecies of Deuteronomy 28 and Leviticus 26, they are losing those gates. The Strait of Hormuz, a choking point for the flow of the world's oil, has become a major gate that the Gentile nations use as a weapon. Israel has lost these gates, and we're not talking about the tiny nation named Israel. Tiny Israel, or Judah, never had such power.

We're talking about what Britain and America at one time controlled. We're speaking of the promises of national greatness, the promises of race versus grace.

The promise of grace, the coming of Jesus the Messiah, was called the scepter promise, and it came through Judah (Gen. 12:3; 49:10). However, the promise of race, of undeserved national prosperity, could only have come through the brother-like nations of the U.S. and the British Commonwealth (Gen. 12:2).

It is impossible to cite any such nations in all of history who could ever have fulfilled these promises.

Rome didn't.

Greece didn't.

Babylon didn't.

Yet these promises were fulfilled exactly on time seven biblical, prophetic times (or 2,520 years) after these believing nations were sent into captivity by Assyria between 721 and 718 B.C. (Lev. 26:24)

Jesus foreknew the rebellion of the Anglo-Saxon nations, so He said He would strike them seven times (*shibah*, in the Hebrew) for their sins. That Hebrew word has several meanings, including a punishment that was seven times more intense and seven times more chronological punishments. It is not the same word used in Daniel 3:19 in referring to the furnace being heated seven times hotter. Seven times also implies duration or continuation of punishment.

The punishment was originally pronounced on the ancient northern tribes of Israel, headed by the birthright sons Ephraim and Manasseh. So the duration of punishment for their sins would be for whatever period the seven times signifies.

2,520 Years from 718 BC to 1803 A.D. Is God on Time or What?

It is evident that this duration of punishment is one of the meanings here since God doesn't lie, and since He began to bring the Anglo-Saxons into unprecedented global power and wealth beginning with the acquisition of the Louisiana Purchase in 1803. The promise was withheld because of the disobedience of the children, but finally fulfilled because of the faithfulness of the forefather. God could not lie to Abraham. He swore by Himself. He had to come through, and He did.

This is a prophecy and these are seven prophetic times. The day-for-a-year prophetic principle is explained in Ezekiel 4:6 and Numbers 14:34, and the biblical definition of a "time" is found in comparing Revelation 12:6, 14, and 13:5. It is one year. When you take 360 days for a biblical year and multiply that by seven times (or years), you come up with 2,520 days.

When each day, according to the day-for-a-year principle, is considered, that makes 2,520 years in fulfillment. The punishment due to ancient Israel would last for 2,520 years, at which time the punishment would end and another opportunity would be given them. At that time, Jesus would be obliged to deliver on His promise of national greatness to Abraham. That promise never came to Judah, who was scattered throughout the world and who came back according to other prophecies to become the small nation of Israel in 1948.

The year 1948 was indeed an important year prophetically, but the year 1803 has been overlooked in its significance. When you add 2,520 to 718 B.C., compensating for the fact no year 0 existed, you come amazingly and exactly to 1803 A.D. That is no coincidence.

Also beginning in the 1800s, England began to dominate the seas while the fledgling United States suddenly acquired, for virtually nothing, a significant part of its landmass. The Louisiana Purchase would bring it the greatest prosperity. Also not coincidentally, America obtained it from none other than France, ancient Reuben who lost his birthright to Joseph.

I lived in France for almost five years, where they say, "Vive la France!" Looks like they were saying in 1803, "Vive les États-Unis (Long live the United States)!" Once again, they were reminded that they had to surrender their ticket to national greatness to Ephraim and Manasseh.

As numerous historical documents attest (including *The Light and the Glory* by Peter Marshall11—fascinating reading!), those who first came to the New World, including Columbus and the early settlers in America, knew they were coming to a promised land. They had been expelled for various reasons, including Sabbath-breaking (See Ezekiel 20 and 22), from the original Promised Land. Only Judah and Benjamin stayed in that land and came back to it in 1948 in fulfillment of certain prophecies I will explain in this book.

The Anglo-Saxon nations will only return to the Promised Land of Israel after their time of judgment and captivity, the time of Jesus' return to rule the earth in the Millennium.

Jacob, once a cheat, scoundrel, and unbeliever, was renamed Israel, which means "overcomer with God" or "believer." Jesus repeated, in resume form, the promise He had given to Abraham: "May God Almighty bless you and make you fruitful and multiply you, that you may become a *company* of peoples" (Gen. 28:3).

Notice this: "Your descendants will also be like the dust of the earth, and you will spread out to the west and to the east and to the north and to the south" (Gen. 28:14). The Anglo-Saxon nations and the British

---

11 *Peter Marshall & David Manuel. The Light and the Glory: Does God Have a Plan for America? (Grand Rapids, MI: Revell, 1980).*

Commonwealth spread far and wide around the world. At one time, the sun never set on the British Empire.

What Jesus told Israel in Genesis 35:11 could only apply to United States and the British Commonwealth: "A nation and a *company* of nations shall come from you..." Rome may have had its empire, but it was never allied with a brother-like nation as in the case of America and the Commonwealth. No other nations in world history could have fulfilled this amazing prophecy.

Blessings of Oil, But Betrayals

I would like to take a few pages to discuss the blessings of Joseph. Genesis 49:22 calls him a fruitful bough whose "branches run over a wall." His influence extends beyond his territory. Britain, America, and Canada have had a far-reaching influence all over the world, even sending missionaries to spread a sincere yet tainted gospel message.

They received "blessings of the deep that lies beneath" (49:25), wealth from resources in the sea, and wealth from valuable resources in the ground, such as precious metals and oil.

The Harbinger makes a case for how Isaiah 9:10 applies to America, but it ignores the quite specific prophecy of Isaiah 9:21 that is being fulfilled before our eyes today.

The Ephraimite nation to the north of the America, Canada, is blessed with valuable oil resources. Yet America, once a closely-knit brother to Ephraim, has recently become a betrayer of that brother. One betrayal, a major one, was a secret one never exposed in the media. A public betrayal of importance came later.

In early 2012, America publicly betrayed its northern brother Canada, as well as a majority of its people who are in need of jobs. The Keystone Pipeline copout forced Canada to ally itself with China rather than with its southern, brother-like nation. This was only one small fulfillment of Isaiah 9:21, in which God prophesied: "Manasseh devours Ephraim, and Ephraim Manasseh, and together they are against Judah."

This verse is coming alive in news reports these days. The American administration has on a number of occasions insulted both Britain and Israel. America has betrayed its northern brother Canada, the United Kingdom, and Judah (the modern nation of Israel).

America has treated Israel and its prime minister, once solid friends, as its enemy, showing obvious favor to the Muslim world and turning its back on the nation God said to bless—in this case, the tiny nation of Israel (our brother, ancient Judah, also a part of the tribes of Israel). Of course, America and Britain are included in Genesis 12:3: "And I will bless those who bless you, and the one who curses you I will curse."

We have bowed to Muslim leaders and thrown God completely out of the picture. We have declared, sadly but rightly so, that America is no longer a Christian nation. We have tried to force Christian medical institutions to pay, against their godly consciences, for their employees to shed more innocent blood in abortions, which further pollute the land and call for judgment upon the nation.

As prophesied, America has become a byword among the nations. In other words, she is hated. She has lost the pride of her power. She has not won a war since World War II, and defense cuts promise to make her only a regional power, no longer the strongest single nation in the world.

Nations curse the United States. And most Christians make the mistake of only emphasizing the importance of blessing the tiny nation of Israel rather than those God says should wear the name Israel (Gen. 48:16).

America is among the most hated of nations today, and people don't realize that when they curse the United States and the Anglo-Saxon nations, they receive a curse as well. America has already received from God the curses of Deuteronomy 28 and Leviticus 26, but she is further cursed when she curses her brother Judah, who is part of Israel.

Blessings, Then Curses

While believers will be either blessed or cursed by the above verses as they choose to obey or disobey, these verses have specific applications to America and the Commonwealth, as do the other prophecies of both the major and minor prophets. Even Genesis and Exodus are full of prophecies that affect these peoples.

Maybe that's why North American Christians don't like to read the "Old Testament" prophecies. Those prophecies target North America! They are solemn warnings to our peoples.

For emphasis, let's quote Genesis 48:16:

> The angel [this should actually be capitalized since it refers to the Messenger Jesus] who has redeemed me from all evil, bless the lads; and may *my name* [Israel] live on in *them,* and the names of my fathers Abraham and *Isaac.*

When I first studied this verse forty-five years ago, I used the large-print King James Bible that I still have today. As I look at it now, it looms even larger than it did when I was sixteen: "my name be named on them" (KJV).

Notice what God isn't saying here. He isn't saying that the name Israel should apply principally to Judah, the tiny nation we recognize as Israel today. He is saying that the name of Israel should rightly be named on Ephraim and Manasseh, the sons of the birthright promises of national wealth. Judah never received those prophesied promises.

When it comes to prophecy, the name Israel belongs to America and the British Commonwealth. That statement is as surprising as it is true. It's the doorway to understanding prophecy.

Christians tend to disregard the curses in these chapters because they believe the lie that causes them to undermine and disregard what they disparagingly call "the Old Testament," a name given by man, not God. When they accept these verses, they tend to pick and choose what they receive and quote.

It's easy to see how the great United States of America, who once wielded a big stick in the world that no one would dare challenge, has seen the pride of its power broken, as Leviticus 26:19 prophesied. Since Korea, Vietnam, its sellout in Iraq, and the winless war in Afghanistan, the United States is the laughingstock of the world. They even apologize for the role God gave His imperfect but chosen nation to be a strong force in the world.

Gutless, Winless Wars

Even in the Gulf War, in which some of my high school classmates were involved (one of them as commander of all air operations), the United States did not follow through. A former classmate of mine was with the troops near Baghdad who were ready to take care of a ruthless dictator for good, but the weak top brass vetoed a general's strong plan. My macho friends were still mad about it at our thirtieth anniversary class reunion in 1999.

I'm not condoning war, but rather recognizing that this prophecy has been and is being fulfilled. The U.S. has lost its will to win, and ridiculous rules of engagement (particularly in Afghanistan) left our troops as targets. No matter how the military and the administration like to lie diplomatically about success, America has become the loser. Thousands of America's brave young soldiers die, but for what?

Jesus delayed the blessings promised to Abraham, and He gave America and the Commonwealth nations an opportunity to continue to receive those blessings. Conditions applied, however. They would have to obey the laws of God—*all* the laws of God, not simply those they felt like keeping. If they chose not to obey, they would soon see their blessings stripped from them in a major way, receiving instead all the curses written in Deuteronomy 28 and Leviticus 26.

Those passages are sobering. I encourage you to read them, this time with the stark realization that they are talking about America, Canada, and the Commonwealth nations. They are describing our downfall! They reflect the headlines we read.

Those curses are coming upon the Anglo-Saxon nations in ever-increasing intensity, leading to the perishing of two-thirds of their inhabitants, and the remaining third being taken as slaves into a harsh captivity similar to the concentration camps of the Nazis.

Ezekiel 5:12 describes what's going to happen to our modern Israelite nations, symbolized by the city of Jerusalem, capital of Israel. The descendants of ancient Assyria (Isa. 10:5) will head a European superpower that will inflict a threefold series of tragedies principally upon America and Canada.

The same Assyria that took the northern tribes of Israel captive in 721 B.C. will once again take them captive. Historical evidence points to Germany as modern Assyria. God will use "a nation of fierce countenance who will have no respect for the old, nor show favor to the young [as was the case in the concentration camps of the Nazis]" (Deut. 28:50) to punish His people.

We are among those charged with crying aloud and lifting up a warning to God's people physically and spiritually (Isa. 58:1; Ezekiel 33). We must deliver the message in order to be faithful to God and His calling upon our lives. It's your choice what to do with the warning.

The recent royal wedding of Prince William and Kate Middleton brought forth another interesting aspect of this truth about the Anglo-Saxons (which sounds curiously like Isaac's sons). I publish here a slightly edited version of an article on prophecy I wrote for the Freedom Church of God website.[12]

Royal Wedding: What You Havent Heard!

One-seventh of the world's population of seven billion is expected to watch it. The coming royal wedding will likely eclipse the impact of the wedding of Charles and Diana. But there is a story behind this wedding that you haven't heard and will probably only hear at www.freedomchurchofgod.com. Were you aware of an ominous event that may involve the throne of England? The time is so short before Jesus' return that Prince William may not see the day that he inherits the throne. But did you know that Jesus Christ will sit on that very throne? While that fact isn't ominous, it might stir your interest to find out about the evil that could be committed by one soon to sit on that throne before Jesus does. Knowing could help you avoid being deceived in these last days. Jesus' main warning for the end time was to keep from being deceived. Read more...

On the day of the crowing of Queen Victoria, the *London Sun* published an article featuring the "stone of destiny" under the throne of England.[13] The article states: "History relates that it is the stone whereon the patriarch Jacob laid his head in the plains of Luz." The paper added that Jacob's pillar stone was brought to "Ireland by way of Spain about 700 years before Christ. From there it was taken into Scotland by King

12 *Freedom Church of God (www.freedomchurchofgod.com). In the archives, you can find there other short articles about prophecy being fulfilled before our eyes.*

13 *Thanks to www.thetrumpet.com for uncovering this article.*

Fergus, about 370 years later; and in the year 350 b.c., it was placed in the abbey of Scone..."[14]

Critics like to treat with contempt the teaching that the Anglo-Saxon nations are the descendants of Joseph's sons who inherited the birthright blessings of national greatness. We have explained these truths for hours on www.freedomtruthseekers.com, showing that the U.S. and the Commonwealth nations are not the "The Lost Tribes," but only two of what became thirteen tribes that lost their identity... Just as America started with thirteen colonies, the nation that became at one point the greatest nation on Earth was once one of thirteen tribes, as was the modern nation of Israel descended from the son of Jacob named Judah.

Those same critics laugh at this idea, and they often attack this truth as a theory based on oral tradition and fables. Yet notice that this British newspaper on June 28, 1837 referred to Jacob's pillar stone being under the throne of England as a fact of history...

As a nineteen-year-old in 1970, I was privileged to visit England and to see the throne and the stone. Some say the real stone was stolen by the Masons and is reserved for future evil purposes. So I'm not absolutely sure I saw the real stone.

We won't get into conspiracy theories, but we will examine what the Bible prophesies about a future evil leader who will be an expert counterfeiter, not of money but of prophesied events of a godly nature.

The Bible plainly states that Jesus is going to rule the earth from Jerusalem (Isa. 2:3). The Word also says that He will sit on the throne of David (Luke 1:32; Isa. 9:7).

A few generations back, the royalty of England knew that the throne of David was transported to Ireland and later England, as the Bible

---

14 *The "Stone of Scone" was later transferred to England.*

shows for those who understand it. It would be too long to treat properly in this article, but search engines can help to show how Jeremiah was commissioned by God to move the throne out of Israel until a later time (Jer. 1:10).

Jesus warned that even the elect would be highly tempted to be deceived by the coming despots who falsely represent Jesus or even claim to be Him (Mat. 24:24). We know they will perform, by Satan's power, unusual signs and wonders that will make the world stand in awe (2 Thes. 2:9). But they may have another tactic to deceive.

We know that Lucifer rebelled and tried to take over God's throne (Isa. 14:13). What could convince even Christians that the son of perdition is indeed Jesus returning to earth to rule? Daniel tells us that the beast, with his contingent (the false Jesus and the false prophet), after having done away with the Antichrist (or Arab *Mahdi*) will "pitch the tents of his royal pavilion between the seas and the beautiful Holy Mountain" (Dan. 11:45).

If the throne of David, verified as authentic by the Stone of Destiny, were to fall into the wrong hands (which some believe is already the case), what better evidence would the false Jesus need to convince the world (even some Christians) that he is Jesus than to move David's throne to Jerusalem?

Such an event is likely to happen, and the counterfeit would be foiled since the real Jesus would already have the throne of David installed in Jerusalem when He returns to reign.

God tells us to be alert to the schemes of the devil (2 Cor. 2:11; Eph. 6:10), especially in these last days (Mat. 24:4). Few people would consider this interesting possibility as they watch the royal wedding. But even amidst the great pomp surrounding potential inheritors of the throne of England, we want our readers to focus on the throne itself and consider a likely scenario. This knowledge could one day save you from a deadly deception.

David's Dynasty

God made a surprising promise to David: the establishment of his throne *forever* (2 Sam. 7:13). That's because Jesus would sit eternally on the same exact throne.

What most people fail to realize is that David and Solomon's kingdom was divided into two, with two "houses"—the house of Israel (the ten northern tribes) and the house of Judah (composed of Judah and Benjamin) (1 Kings 12:20–21).

You can see the difference between the two houses in a passage that is a shock to most people. It is the first time *Yehudi*, the word for Jews, is used in the Bible, and you can see it written out in the King James Version. Yes, in 2 Kings 16:5–6, Israel is *at war with the Jews!*

All Jews are Israelites, but all Israelites are not Jews! To demonstrate this point, I was born in South Carolina, even though most can't tell it by my accent. I am an American, a landed immigrant in Canada. All South Carolinians are American, but not all Americans are South Carolinians. Modern Israel or Judah was only a small part of Israel.

Israel was later scattered beyond the Euphrates for their idolatry (1 Kings 14:15–16). We see the distinction clearly in 2 Kings 17:18: "So [Jesus] was very angry with *Israel* and removed them from His sight [and from the world's sight as well]; none was left but the tribe of *Judah*." Israel "was carried away into exile from their own land to Assyria until this day [about 620 B.C.]" (2 Kings 17:23).

Psalm 89:29 repeats the scepter promise: "So I will establish his descendants forever and his throne as the days of heaven."

Jeremiah confirmed the promise of the continuation of David's dynasty (Jer. 33:17), and he was instrumental in the planting of that throne in Ireland, it being transferred later to England (Jer. 1:10). Jesus Himself will sit on David's throne, which will be moved to Jerusalem before His return.

You can research the fascinating story of how Jeremiah traveled to Ireland to fulfill the prophecy of Ezekiel 17:22–23. As with the many legends of the universal Flood, legends often reflect actual history.

Such is the case of an Irish legend which states that around 569 B.C. an elderly, white-haired patriarch arrived in Ireland accompanied by a princess (the "tender one" of Ezek. 17:22) and an assistant named Simon Brach (Berach or Baruch) along with the son of the King of Ireland (who had married the princess), undoubtedly of the Zerah line for the healing of the breach.[15]

15 *The promise of the scepter (or the royal line that would lead to Jesus) came through Judah. A mysterious "breach" was recorded in Genesis 38:27–30, and it had to be written down for a reason. Twins were born to Judah, but the first baby to appear by putting out his hand was Zerah, to whom a scarlet thread was attached. It was the other baby, however, who was actually born first. His name was Perez or Pharez, meaning breach. The mention of this breach prophesies that the breach would be healed someday—and it was, in dramatic fashion!*
David, Zedekiah, and Jesus were all of the Perez line, and it was David's line that God promised the Messiah would come through to sit on David's throne forever. Since David's line (Perez) is to remain on the throne throughout all generations, the transfer of the throne and the uniting of the Zerah line with the Perez line could only occur at an overturn of the throne by a marriage between a Perez heir and one of the Zerah line, thus healing the breach.
History shows the descendants of Zerah journeyed to the north within the confines of the Scythian nations, their descendants later migrating to Ireland in the days of King David. So Zerah was the lower line that aspired to its rightful place. The lowly was to be set on high (Ezek. 21:25) by the overturning of the throne to the proper line by intermarriage. This was part of Jeremiah's mission (Jer. 1:10).
The rest of the puzzle is revealed in Ezekiel 17:21–24. God would take a "sprig," a "tender one" (a princess, a king's daughter) from "the top of the cedar" (King Zedekiah of Judah) and plant it, as Jeremiah was told to do. She would "bear fruit," or have children who would carry on the royal line and establish the throne on which Jesus would sit. The "dry tree" of Zerah would see the throne moved from Ireland to England, flourishing in the prosperous British Commonwealth until the throne on which the Queen sits ended up in Jerusalem so Jesus could sit on it.
According to Irish tradition and legend, one of the two daughters of King Zedekiah, Tea Tephi, married Prince Eochaidh of Ireland who was himself descended from Zerah (the breach baby with the scarlet thread tied around his wrist in Genesis 38). They went on to become the Irish King and Queen, from which the Irish monarchy descended. Queen Tea Tephi was one of the so-called Princesses of the Harp, who may have carried the Stone of

This patriarch was Jeremiah, who brought along a special stone—the *lia-fail*, or stone of destiny. Many kings of Ireland and England have been crowned sitting over this stone, including Elizabeth II. The stone sat under the coronation chair in Westminster Abbey when I viewed it in 1970. The sign beside it read "Jacob's Pillar Stone."

Now, the crown worn by the Irish had twelve points. Some say it is coincidental and that these twelve points don't refer to either the twelve tribes of Israel or America's thirteen colonies (thirteen being the number of the tribes when Ephraim and Manasseh were substituted for their father, Joseph). I prefer to see these so-called "coincidence" as divine incidences that are evidence of a greater biblical truth.

In somewhat cryptic language, Ezekiel prophesied that Zedekiah would fall, and the dynasty would "no longer be the same" (Ezek. 21:26). It would not cease, but simply change. The Zerah line and the house of Israel would be exalted and the Pharez line and Judah would be abased. The throne would be "ruined" (or overturned) three times, and then given to Jesus (21:27).

We get more confirmation of these truths when we ask, "Where did the apostles go?"

Destiny, Jacob's pillow (see Genesis 28:18, and 2 Kings 11:12–14), over to Ireland. This stone has been used in the coronation of Irish, Scottish, and British monarchs for centuries. God's promise to David was unalterable, no matter what God had to do to make his line continue. The throne involving the scepter promise was transferred to Britain, the holder of the birthright promise. God's prophecies are fulfilled in fascinating ways!
–We have only given a brief summary here due to lack of space. You can further explore this fascinating story either on the internet or from the following source: Geoffrey Keating. The History of Ireland from the Earliest Times to the English Invasion (1629). Translated and annotated by John O'Mahony in 1857 by the Irish Genealogical Foundation.

The Apostles Preached in Israel (Britain!)

The apostle Paul was sent to the Gentiles, but Peter and the other apostles were sent first to the lost sheep of the house of Israel (Mat. 10:5–6). Among many works I could cite, Eusebius, bishop of Caesarea in the early 300s, wrote that "the apostles passed beyond the ocean to the Isles called the British Isles."[16]

William Camden wrote in 1674 that even Paul went to Britain: "The true Christian Religion was planted here most anciently by Joseph of Arimathea, Simon Zelotes, Aristobulus, by St Peter, and St Paul, as may be proved by Dorotheus, Theodoretus and Sophronius."[17] No surprise there: Paul's commission included "the sons of Israel" (Acts 9:15).

Both famed Archbishop Ussher of Ireland and Vatican librarian Cardinal Baroneous in the seventeenth century presented evidence that the apostles James, Peter, and Simon Zelotes, along with Joseph of Arimathea, preached the gospel in the British Isles.[18] They simply obeyed Jesus' command to "go to the lost sheep of the house of Israel" (Mat. 10:6).

Some like to throw extraneous arguments into the picture, dismissing evidence in writings throughout history that attest to what the Bible says about who Israel is. Yet the Scottish Declaration of Independence, issued at Arbroath in 1320 A.D., connects the Scots to Israel, declaring, "Thence they came, twelve hundred years after the people of Israel crossed the Red Sea, to their home in the west where they live today."

The British historian Bede, writing five hundred years earlier, also states that the people of Scotland came from Scythia,[19] between the

---

16 Eusebius. Demonstratio Evangelica (Book 3, Chapter 5).

17 William Camden. Remains of Britain, p. 5.

18 Ussher. The Whole Works of James Ussher (Volume 5, Chapter 1).

19 Bede. The Ecclesiastical History of the English Nation, p. 5.

Black and Caspian Seas, where Israel was dispersed. Herodotus called the Scythians the "Sacae,"[20] which comes from the name Isaac, one of the names that Jacob (Israel) said would live on among Ephraim and Manasseh (Gen. 48:16).

In the year 656, Pope Vitalian decided the universal church was not interested in the remains of the apostles Peter and Paul. The pope therefore ordered them sent to King Oswy of Britain! Here is part of his letter to the British king:

> However, we have ordered the blessed gifts of the holy martyrs, that is, the relics of the blessed apostles, Peter and Paul, and of the holy martyrs Laurentius, John, and Paul, and Gregory, and Pancratius, to be delivered to the bearers of these our letters, to be by them delivered to you.[21]

Other parts of this letter show that the universal church wanted nothing to do with the true apostles or Britain. They recognized Britain as God's covenant people Israel, which is not difficult to ascertain historically.

Migrations, Etymology, History, and the Bible Tell the Story

Indeed, the migrations of the Israelite people through Europe are no secret; they are widely known. The traces Dan left with names like the Danube and the Dardanelles, as well as Denmark, are the most widely known of the etymological connections (Judges 18:12; Jer. 31:21, "roadmarks"). And is it coincidence that the word British has a strange

20 *The Histories of Herodotus 4:76.*

21 *Bede. The Ecclesiastical History of the English Nation (Book 3, Chapter 29).*

correlation to the Hebrew words for "covenant" and "man"? They are truly God's covenant men, or people.

The proof is found elsewhere, if naysayers want to poke holes at what they call a theory. These etymological facts are only evidence of a greater truth attested to by history and by the Word of God. But if you refuse to see it, you won't.

The facts don't lie. They are backed up by biblical truth. Constantius of Lyons earlier took the relics of all the apostles and martyrs from Gaul and buried them in a special tomb at St. Albans in Britain.22 No evidence exists in any of the Bible writings or works of history that Peter was ever in Rome. He was buried along with the other apostles in the land of Israel—Britain!

Bede even wrote that the Scottish bishops refused to adopt the Roman Easter in 664 A.D., observing an ancient practice [the Passover], "the same which St. John the Evangelist... with all the churches over which he presided, is recorded to have observed."[23]

Did you catch that? This book isn't directly about the Sabbath and holy days, but we can see we have more than the overwhelming biblical evidence we should be keeping these days. History records the "truth once delivered" (Jude 3, KJV) and the clever apostates who twisted it.

These Scottish bishops showed by their stance in 664 A.D. that they had repented of one of the main reasons Jesus sent Israel into captivity, revealed in Ezekiel 20 and 22: the breaking of God's Sabbath days. Idolatry and Sabbath-breaking will also be the major reasons for the coming destruction and captivity.

Forty years is the period of judgment of man, and the American president celebrated in early 2012 the judicial decision almost forty years earlier to begin legalizing the spilling of innocent blood, the blood of

---

22 *Constantius of Lyon, Life of St Germanus.*

23 *Bede. Ecclesiastical History (Book 2, Chapter 25).*

aborted babies, that would defile the land and bring judgment. Murder was openly celebrated, confirming this nation's imminent destruction. God cannot bless America until Jesus returns.

What may be slightly esteemed, or not esteemed at all, in the eyes of man holds great importance for God, whose ways are far above ours (Isa. 55:8–9). God is not mocked; we reap what we sow (Gal. 5:6). Our sins will find us out (Num. 32:23).

America thinks it can get away with killing innocent babies in the name of women's rights. No right to murder exists in God's laws. Officials think they can get away with denouncing the biblical principles on which the nation was founded, throwing Jesus out of the country and allowing unrighteous judges to rewrite the law and deprive believers of their freedom.

No. Reaping time is coming.

A minority of faithful believers will escape the disasters coming on our modern Anglo-Saxons. But the nations God brought out of slavery in Egypt will receive the wrath of Satan in the Great Tribulation and go back into slavery. A day of rebuke is near.

The Day of Rebuke

Among those in a "great multitude… from every nation" (Rev. 7:9) will be those from America, Canada, and the other Anglo-Saxon, Israelite nations. They will be part of a great end-time harvest of those who will be raptured out of the Great Tribulation. If you heed the warnings of this book, you can be of that blessed number. Or you will face judgment.

God's warning to Ephraim (the Commonwealth nations) also apply to Manasseh (the United States): "Ephraim will become a *desolation* in the day of rebuke [the Great Tribulation]" (Hos. 5:9). The idols and the cities of these nations will be destroyed (Mic.

5:14), which has become quite easy with our modern weapons of mass destruction. Parents will even eat their children (Ezek. 5:10) for lack of food.

Jesus rightly calls America "a godless nation" (Isa. 10:6). The Muslims have more rights and better press than Christians.

Judgment is coming, but it's not always directly from God. He allows the laws of cause and effect to run their course. He set in motion the curses that come from disobedience, so they arrive automatically. Only in some cases does Jesus intervene directly to bring discipline.

You and your family don't have to be among those who receive the severe correction to come. God is allowing you in His mercy to hear this warning message. He says in Ezekiel 18:31–32:

> "Cast away from you all your transgressions which you have committed and make yourselves a new heart and a new spirit! For why will you die, O house of Israel? For I have no pleasure in the death of anyone who dies," declares the [Divine Master] God. "Therefore, repent and live."

America and the Anglo-Saxon world have chosen disobedience, rebellion, idolatry, sexual depravity, perversion, lying, cheating, stealing, and various other forms of sin their evil hearts have devised. They have chosen death. You don't have to die. Repent, obey, and live.

Jesus prophesied the church would fall asleep in the last days, but He called some to give a wake-up call. Here is your warning to "wake up and smell the coffee"!

Chapter Nine:
Sleepy Christians, Wake Up and Smell the Coffee!

God has given free will to the Bride of Jesus, the church. Jesus wanted His bride, symbolized by the ten virgins of Matthew 25, to be ready to be raptured according to God's perfect will, at the preferred time. In this parable, however, we see that the bride wasn't ready, and Jesus foreknew this delay. That's why He said, "Now while the bridegroom was delaying, they all got drowsy and began to sleep" (Mat. 25:5).

The parable speaks in general terms. When it speaks of all the virgins falling asleep, we cannot conclude that all fall asleep at the same time, nor can we conclude that all will wake up at the same time. The preaching of the gospel of the Kingdom by those few who did not fall asleep awakens some. Obviously, for a wake-up call to go out, someone in the church must still be awake.

We also read of a time when only angels announce the message of warning. This tells us that some may not wake up until just before the wrath of God is ready to be poured out in the last, extended year of that wrath period. The foolish ones who awake will have to prove their loyalty by "buying" oil from the persecutors, either those of the Great Tribulation or those who persecute believers during the time of Jesus' wrath.

God the Father gave this parable to Jesus. The Father knew that Jesus would have to delay His coming, since the Father knows the end from the beginning. Jesus was the Word who was with God the Father before time began (John 1:1–18), and He is now with the Father with the same foreknowledge that the Father possesses, as does the Holy Spirit, since they all compose the Godhead. When He was on the earth, He was the Son of Man who had to have special revelation from the Holy Spirit and the Father.

That's why He said, "But of the day and hour no one knows, not even the angels of heaven, nor the Son, but the Father alone" (Mat. 24:36). Religious people are quick to condemn anyone who gives a biblical timeframe leading up to Jesus' return, giving possible dates of Jesus' return. That's because they don't understand the signs of the times Jesus said to watch for, and they don't grasp the truths stated above.

We Can Know the Timing, Yet Jesus Has Delayed

We could have known the timing only the Father knew at the time Jesus spoke His much-misunderstood words in Matthew 24:36. After all, God said He would do nothing unless He revealed His secret counsel to His servants, the prophets (Amos 3:7). Truthfully, God did reveal the timing to His servants. Because the church wasn't ready, however, as was prophesied in the parable of Matthew 25, the timing of Jesus' return is presently unknown. The time of tribulation has been extended because the Bride of Jesus wasn't ready to be raptured.

Those who keep Jesus' feast days know that the Day of Trumpets signals the coming of King Jesus, His birth, and the return of the King. We know He will return on that day. We simply don't know which year He will return, so indeed, we don't know the day or the hour.

God's Sabbath and His feast days, overlooked by the Christian world, give us a good idea of the events to come and their timing.

In the parable of the sleeping virgins in Matthew 25, Jesus warns us to be ready to marry Him and enter into the marriage feast. He even tells us He would have to delay His return to earth because of a drowsy church that fell asleep as they saw Him delay.

Parable of the Ten Virgins

Jesus compares His church to a group of virgins who go out to meet the Bridegroom, Jesus Himself. We should consider what virgins normally have in common:

1. They are eager to meet with their coming mate.

2. They put a high value on every opportunity to communicate with their mate.

3. They have a hope and a trust that a good life with their mate is going to follow them.

4. They study their future mate to know their likes and dislikes.

5. They prioritize everything around their mate and waiting on them.

6. They want to be as acceptable as possible to their mate.

7. They want to share everything they have with each other. They look at what they can bring into the marriage.

We should also ask why Jesus referred to ten virgins. Ten represents law (as in the Ten Commandments) and government in the Kingdom of God. It also signifies a perfect completion. When Jesus gave those ten laws, it is written, "and He added no more" (Deut. 5:22). It is a perfected completion. The bride has made itself ready to be complete in the Bridegroom.

Ten also represents steadfastness. The bride has stayed the course, no matter what was trying to distract it or pull it away. Israel in the desert did not stay the course, so Jesus had to tell them, "You shall not enter the Promised Land. You did not make yourselves ready to enter the Promised Land with Me."

Instead, they tested Jesus ten times. And thus ten is also a number of tests. Jesus was tested ten times before He was put on the cross.

Ten also signifies a final sealing. When children reach the age of ten, they want to expand and test their wings. An individual usually begins to come into his own after ten years as a member of the Body of Christ.

This number also represents a perfect gift or perfect faith, trust, and love. God has ordained ten levels of faith and love.

The First Steps of Faith

Most Christians are still in levels one and two of faith. It is important to understand how we enter and grow in the levels of faith.

Every man, believer or not, has a measure of faith (Rom. 12:3), which is the first level. And the first thing everyone learns about faith is that limitations to that faith exist. Those limitations cannot be overcome unless God gives us grace to grow in the levels of faith as we accept that ability. Often the prayers of others allow us to begin to move into level two.

What is it that allows this move to the second level?

Joel Osteen, who God has anointed especially for this purpose, practices this key. His first greeting on his TV program finds him warmly welcoming anyone who tunes in or wants to visit the church he pastors. It's basically the typical welcome of Southern hospitality magnified by the Holy Spirit: "Y'all come! You'll be right at home with us."

The key mover is seeing yourself as part of something bigger than yourself, a sense of belonging. Sadly, however, religiosity, judgmentalism, and betrayal rule so many churches that members have a hard time growing in faith. Churches and pastors reject them, often forcing them to hop from church to church, feeling homeless.

One of the bloggers at Freedom Blog made an inspired observation in this regard: "From what I have seen, people who cannot forgive themselves are unable to feel like they belong. They therefore attack the weaker among their church." Rejection and betrayal reign.

We have compassion on our African brethren, since we see so many of them under extreme rejection, which opens the door for betrayal. They don't feel trusted because of this, and they tend to distrust those who try to teach them God's Word. Consequently, they are severely challenged in their growth in faith. The white man in Africa has made many promises of help they never followed through on, so the locals have become accustomed to rejection and betrayal. The spiritual ministries of the *wusungu* (or white man) have often been based in legalism and betrayal, thus compounding the problem. Even those ministries that walk in love have challenges being trusted.

I have learned that when you tell a person in faith level one that God loves them, it's only a hurtful cliché since they cannot receive and believe it in their hearts. You have to show, not tell, them that you and God love them. As they feel they are made a part of something bigger than themselves, they can pass to level two.

But a major blockage exists to keep the level two believers from getting to level three. Those in level two are like the man in the parable who hid his talent, seeing his master (God) as a cruel tyrant who reaped without sowing. They see God as not having sown any good seed into their lives, so they choose not to spiritually sow good seed or give. This would explain why only three percent of North American Christians tithe. These believers want to see a harvest without a seed.

The key to overcoming this blockage is the key to turning our hearts to Father Love. This is the key that allowed Peter to be the only disciple to get out of the boat and walk to Jesus (Mat. 14:29). He was the only one focused on Jesus. He kept his eyes on his Master. The eyes of the others were on the waves and the storm, but Peter had gotten to know and trust Jesus more than the others.

Level two is the place where we get to know Jesus and trust Him so that He can reveal the Father to us. As we do, limitations lose their power. Spiritual slumber can come when we take our eyes off Jesus, which explains the state of spiritual sleep of the virgins in these last days.

As we fix our eyes on Jesus, we learn to turn over our problems to Him and receive from Him in thanksgiving, a powerful builder of faith. We can see why Satan personally stepped in to block the understanding and practice of the Sabbath, the feast days, and the new moon turnover. These truths open doors to growth in faith that Satan doesn't want. He doesn't want Jesus to find faith on earth in these last days.

Jesus' days of joy and love enable us to meet with Him, the Word, personally and corporately. Since faith works by love and faith comes by the Word (Rom. 10:17), what better way is there to grow in faith? We meet with the Word Himself, fixing our eyes every week in a special way on Him (Heb. 12:2; 4:9), the Author and Perfecter of our faith.

Are You a Foolish or Wise Virgin?

Matthew 25:2–3 speaks of the foolish and wise virgins. The foolish virgins took no extra oil with them. What constitutes a foolish virgin?

1. They didn't take every opportunity to grow in Jesus.

2. They spent much of their time coasting. If they attended church, their mind was elsewhere.

3. They never developed a prayer life with the Father.

4. They didn't move to get free or stay free from Satan's weapons, traps, and deceptions. They found excuses for not obeying God even though God offered His grace (empowerment) to do so.

5. They couldn't develop the joy of giving. They weren't sowing for receiving but sowing for loss.

6. They never put the blessings of others, especially their enemies, in their mouths.

7. They wanted to accumulate blessings for themselves and had no desire to use their blessings and talents to help others. Hoarding is not a Kingdom spirit.

The oil represents the power or fuel of the Holy Spirit to change facts into the truth that matches God's Word. The wise or prudent virgins "took oil in flasks along with their lamps…" (Mat. 25:4). They were prepared for a long wait in case the Bridegroom decided to delay His coming.

What constitutes a wise virgin?

1. They built up their treasure in heaven. They didn't have their heart set on building up treasures on earth. They did have treasures available to them, but in their use of those funds they put the Kingdom first, making the work of the Kingdom their highest priority. They didn't hoard those funds but used them in giving and serving.

2. They acquired a high level of faith, above the fourth level. The majority gets stuck at level two.

3. They had become full of the Word. They studied and meditated on it. They spoke it aloud into their heart. They loved the Word.

4. They had become so accustomed to speaking the Word that they expected immediate results. They knew God's Word wouldn't come back void.

5. They had grown strong in Jesus.

6. They knew when to rest and when to move. Some get a word from God but aren't yet ready to move on it, yet they move without God's backing.

7. They had developed a strong prayer life with the Father, waiting on His counsel before proceeding.

8. They stood steadfast against Satan and his weapons.

9. They weren't deceived by flattery or deception. They made their commitment to their Bridegroom and chose to stay committed no matter what.

10. They experienced joy by giving and helping people.

11. They blessed everyone and everything.

12. They were sharers, givers, helpers, and teachers of the ways of light.

Why the Delay?

In Matthew 25:5, we see the purpose of the parable: "Now while the bridegroom was delaying, they all got drowsy and began to sleep." Some fell asleep quite soon, while others simply got drowsy first. But in the end, they all fell asleep.

Did you notice that Jesus was delaying His return? He didn't come when His bride thought He would. In the same way, Jesus deliberately didn't come to resurrect Lazarus when His disciples thought He would. He delayed. He didn't come when they thought He should. Jesus is deliberately delaying His return, His calling for the raptures, and the setting up of His Kingdom.

Why? The reason is that the church isn't ready. The bride is not prepared. Jesus is giving us time to repent and get ourselves ready. As He said to the Thyatira era, "I gave her time to repent, and she does not want to repent of her immorality" (Rev. 2:21). Jesus is calling for His virgins to wake up and, for those who choose to do so, prepare for His return.

But what purpose does Jesus have in this delay, caused by the bride's lack of readiness?

1. He wants to test the steadfastness of those called and chosen.

2. It's a test of our levels of love.

3. He is testing the levels of prudence and wisdom we are willing to exercise through the Holy Spirit.

4. He is establishing the very elect. He wants to see who will be the coasters and who will want Him with all their hearts, who want to grow. Who will value their sleep more than they value God?

5. He wants to see who will rejoice at His coming. The foolish were in a tizzy trying to do things at the last minute, while the wise rejoiced at Jesus' coming.

The Perils of Drowsiness

Notice Matthew 25:5: "they all got drowsy and began to sleep." Was it exhaustion? Was it fear? Was it the lack of refreshing? Or was it a loss of faith and trust in God's Word that put them to sleep?

All the virgins fell asleep while gathered, waiting for the Bridegroom, who delayed His reunion with the bride He expectantly wanted. He deeply wanted to be with her, but He deliberately delayed His coming.

The virgins grew tired of waiting. "Maybe Jesus isn't coming back," they may have mused. They all talked themselves into a drowsy state.

A drowsy state means a compromising, lazy, and/or over-busy state of existence, trying to get too much done in our own strength. Affairs of the world kept them from doing all that Jesus had called them to do.

A drowsy state also means that hidden fears are draining our strength, and we have allowed it. We have spoken into our hearts that these fears have a right to be there.

Spiritual drowsiness signifies a love of the sin of the world. No love exists in such a person for resting in Jesus and in His Sabbath days.

Drowsiness comes by not speaking the words of life into your soul consistently. Furthermore, a drowsy state always leads to sleep, which in turn leads to death. We must say no to drowsiness. Teens aren't drowsy when they prepare to see their favorite rock star. But Christians can't get excited about Jesus.

Matthew 25:6 states, "But at midnight there was a shout, 'Behold, the bridegroom! Come out to meet him.'" This is a warning that change was about to occur, a warning issued in the middle of the night. It represents the sounding of the trumpet blast that will warn of the coming of the Kingdom of God (Mat. 24:14). For those who take sleep too long, it may take an angelic message to wake them.

Will You Be In or Out?

Matthew 25:7 states, "Then all those virgins rose and trimmed their lamps." Not only does this refer to trimming the lamps, but also to clearing your eyes so you can see well. After all, we often get mucus in our eyes while we sleep; we need to wipe our eyes clear in order to see properly upon waking.

"The foolish said to the prudent, 'Give us some of your oil, for our lamps are going out'" (Mat. 25:8). The key word here is "give." The foolish were not givers, but selfish takers. They didn't spend any time praying for others. They were self-focused. One of the purposes of having surplus oil is so we can give for the work of the Kingdom and give of our wealth to bless others.

"But the prudent answered, 'No, there will not be enough for us and you too; go instead to the dealers and buy some for yourselves'" (Mat. 25:9). The wise were willing to do the work in the day while there was still light. They were givers, sowers, and light-bringers… the "salt of the earth" who chose to live as ambassadors of the Kingdom, not only consumers of the Kingdom.

Most Christians don't tithe, but they're happy to partake of what the church they attend offers them. They consume. They are selfish.

The wise told the foolish to "go" and "buy" for themselves. In other words, you can't make it into the marriage feast on someone else's merits. You must go and do something yourself. Only your light will carry you into the Kingdom, not the light of someone else. To "go" means it's time for you to act, to go and do what you know you should have done in the first place.

If you don't put your money to work in time, you have to pay for the harvest ("buy"). If you pay for the harvest, you won't be paid for harvesting. You cannot reap what you didn't sow. This is the way to shut the door to the Kingdom, at least to the first and better resurrection, or to enter into it the hard way as a martyr.

"And while they were going away to make the purchase, the bridegroom came, and those who were ready went in with him to the wedding feast; and the door was shut" (Mat. 25:10). Everything we value above Jesus is a door closer that creates a final test for us. Even if you have on Jesus' robe of righteousness, if you have not sown love, you're not yet ready to lead anyone else into the Kingdom, which is the calling of the very elect who qualify for the first rapture.

Those who made themselves ready were already in with Jesus when He shut the door. The pillars (or wise ones) were strong in the Word. The others were not. The pillars were strong in obedience and in giving to Jesus all He had paid for on the occasion of the eve of the Sabbath and the new moon. The pillars were strong because they allowed Jesus to refine them. Because they employed the graces God gave them to help others, the pillars reaped what they sowed. They were prayer warriors, strong in spiritual warfare.

"Later the other virgins also came, saying '[Master, Master], open up for us'" (Mat. 25:11). They didn't accept that the time of change was now. Last-minute repentance doesn't get you into the wedding feast. You must have prepared. Jesus is saying that if you're counting on this last-minute repentance, you're not getting into the marriage feast. You simply don't have the oil to get you through the door before it's shut.

In the time of Noah, when the door to the ark was shut, it was game over for those who didn't qualify. And Jesus said that the last days would be like the days of Noah (Mat. 24:37).

Some Christians get drowsy before they have to climb up to the fourth level of faith. They're so comfortable in levels two and three that they don't want to move higher. They stagnate instead of holding fast and growing. And the door stays shut.

"But he answered, 'Truly I say to you, I do not know you'" (Mat. 25:12). He didn't say he never knew them. He simply said he didn't know them.

To know Jesus intimately, we have to let Him in. We must obey Him. We must turn everything over to Him and meet Him regularly in His Sabbath. The word "know," as used in the Bible, means more than our English version of the word. It signifies an intimate involvement and communication that goes beyond the comprehension of most. All the uttermost secrets are shared; nothing is held back. We turn everything over to Him.

When Jesus said, "I don't know you," it meant your heart wasn't willing to share with Him on His Sabbath, feasts, and new moons, and you didn't release to Him all that He paid for on the cross as your Savior and Redeemer. Your pride and carelessness caused you to shut the door to the wedding with Jesus.

"Be on the alert then, for you do not know the day nor the hour" (Mat. 25:13). This means that we must be ready for the test, be ready to give and turn things over to Jesus. Jesus is saying, "I am the Bridegroom, and I can delay My coming until I'm certain that the foolish have committed their course."

Are you being prepared for intimacy with Jesus for His return? The warning is out. The call comes quickly. Buy your oil now while you can still do so. If you don't, soon the door will be shut to you.

Don't be caught up in Satan's blankets of boredom, drowsiness, distraction, and nonchalance, and thus end up falling asleep permanently. I pray that we will all meet together at the wedding feast with the Bridegroom—and rejoice together.

Chapter Ten:

Will You Escape the Great Tribulation?

While the church sleeps, events in prophecy are speeding up at a rate never seen before. That's because we're extremely close to the last events of this age and to the imminent return of Jesus Christ.

I explained earlier how I have always been impressed with God's power, but in recent years I have begun to stand in awe of his amazing foreknowledge. In the book of Isaiah, He says, "I am God, and there is no one like Me, declaring the end from the beginning…" (Isa. 46:9–10).

God knows exactly what's going to happen before it happens. Whether it's knowledge of what will happen to us personally or a foreknowledge of all the events of mankind's history, He knows it all. Yet He always respects our free will. He gives us every opportunity to do the right thing, and when we fail, He redeems us and all our sins and mistakes by the blood of the Son He offered us, Jesus.

God is love (1 John 4:8). And since that's who He is, not simply what He does, it should be spelled with a capital L. Our Father is Love. Because He is Love, He warns us of what is about to happen so we can prepare.

He also prophesies events long before they happen in His Word, the Bible, so we can stand in awe of His foreknowledge and eternal perspective. Throughout the Bible He encourages us to think about things with His perspective, the Eternal One.

He tells us to be still and quiet, meditating on the truth that He is the Eternal God (Ps. 46:10). He has even set aside a specific day of the week that most Christians have ignored, a day in which we rest and meditate upon His eternal plan for mankind. That day is the Sabbath, which is Friday sunset to Saturday sunset.

It's the day that prophesies the time of the culmination of God's plan of love, expressed in more detail in His feast days during the year. It is the day when we look forward to eternity, when time will no longer exist. God inhabits eternity, the eternal dimension.

Even those who keep Sunday never seem to get off the not-so-merry-go-round of weekly cares and troubles to pause, be still, and know that God is God, the God of eternity.

Those who do stop and rest God's way, and on God's day, have a better concept of this God of eternity. Actually, most Sabbath-keepers have a better grasp of prophecy because they understand the eternal perspective of God. It is also His day of revelation. Meeting Jesus the Revelator allows us to receive understanding directly from Him about what He's doing and what is going to do in the world.

Because the Sabbath is the day that celebrates Satan's defeat, those who obey understand many concepts (Ps. 111:10). They can see what Jesus is preparing prophetically to counteract and overcome what Satan has planned to do.

Hebrews 3 and 4 speak of that eternal rest and tell us we are to rest as God did, meaning we cannot fully understand eternal rest unless we keep the weekly Sabbath rest. It's the day we picture infinity. We will inhabit eternity as God does. Actually, we already are eternal, but we haven't yet tapped all the indescribable joys of eternal life with our Father, Brother, and Comforter of Love.

Our God is good. He wouldn't have given us the Sabbath unless it was good for us. It is good for what it does for us spiritually, emotionally, mentally, and physically. It is also good for what it represents—God's eternal love. It is the day that foresees the time when all mankind will love and worship the true God in the Millennium.

What's more, it prophesies the eternal rest the whole earth and all the inhabitants it has ever had will experience. They will know Jesus and have the opportunity to bask in His love forever. What a blessing God has given us—a day to celebrate His love and show Him how much we love Him!

Heartwarming Story of a Timeless God

A friend recently sent me an email that our church received years ago. It brought home God's timelessness. He knows the end from the beginning (Isa. 46:10). He knows long before we pray what we will ask (Isa. 65:24), and He knows if we will ask in faith or in fear.

The email came from a doctor working with children in Africa, relating a striking example of God existing outside of time. This doctor lost a mother in delivery, leaving him with a premature baby that would die without a hot water bottle since he had no incubator. The bottle would have to come in a parcel, which had never happened, but that would take months. The situation looked impossible, but not for ten-year-old Ruth.

"Please, God," Ruth prayed, "Send us a hot water bottle today. It'll be no good tomorrow, God, as the baby will be dead, so please send it this afternoon. And while You're about it, would You please send a dolly for the little girl so she'll know You really love her?"

A parcel arrived that afternoon! The doctor opened it in front of all the children. After opening the top part, which held clothing, he reached down into the box and brought out—you guessed it!—a hot water bottle.

Little Ruth exclaimed, "If God has sent the bottle, He must have sent the dolly, too!" Rummaging down to the bottom of the box, she pulled out the small, beautifully dressed dolly.

That parcel had been on the way for five whole months, packed up by the doctor's former Sunday school class, whose leader had heard and obeyed God's prompting to send a hot water bottle, even to the equator. And one of the girls had put in a dolly for an African child—five months before—in answer to the believing prayer of a ten-year-old to bring it "that afternoon."

We serve the awesome God of eternity! He is not limited by time.

Dwelling in Heavenly Places

Shall we lay down our time limitations and enter Jesus' day of joy, representing eternity? Satan is a prisoner of time. We aren't. We rejoice together as a family that inhabits eternity, a family that's not limited by time. We rest in faith with Jesus on His Sabbath because we aren't concerned about "losing" a workday. We are no longer in the rat race. We have gained eternal life. We celebrate being more and more outside the limits of time.

God does tell us, however, to redeem the time, to make good use of the time God has given us on this earth. Satan knows He has shortened his time to rule the world, and that Jesus is coming back soon (Rev. 12:12). Those who are engrossed in worldly ways will be in a woeful state, whereas this verse says that those who dwell in heavenly places will rejoice.

Those who dwell with Jesus (Eph. 2:6) and put their spirits, empowered by the Holy Spirit, ahead of the flesh and earthly ways, will be able to rejoice because they're dwelling in the eternal perspective.

They look to Jesus in the heavens and inside them to redeem their time and to use it for the glory of God.

They don't wait until the last minute like the foolish virgins of Matthew 25. They take extra oil in their flasks that represent, among many things, their time of intimacy with God. They aren't too rushed to take time out to be still and be with God in close fellowship. Seeking Jesus is their main goal in life. They constantly seek to have more of Jesus. He is all they need. He is their Source.

If you've been squandering your time in fleshly pursuits that you've put ahead of Jesus, or if you have sought to do things in your strength rather than to "cease striving" (as some translate "be still" in Psalm 46), it's time you consider one of the purposes of prophecy.

Standing in Awe of the God of Eternity

Prophecy should make us stand in awe of the God who declares the end before the beginning. It should make us so full of awe and reverence that we seek Jesus so we can change to be more like our Father in heaven (Mat. 5:48).

Peter says it well, even though the end of this age hadn't yet come at that time: "The end of all things is near; therefore, be of sound judgment and sober spirit for the purpose of prayer. Above all, keep fervent in your love for one another, because love covers a multitude of sins" (1 Pet. 4:7).

The end of this age is nearer than most think. And Peter tells us it's time to give spiritual matters top priority. It's time to go all out and seek Jesus. He is Love. He will cast out the fears that plague even many Christians in these last days. Love never fails. And God's love in us is the only way we'll be able to face these end-time trials.

In fact, walking in that love and growing closer to Jesus will even keep us protected in the worst of the trials. The "hour of testing" (Rev.

3:10) doesn't have to come upon those who truly seek and obey Jesus and walk in His love.

Escaping the Worst of Times

While I don't believe in fear tactics, it might be helpful for those who are lulled into a false security by the conveniences and entertainment of our modern life style, especially in the "have" nations, to see what God does prophesy as "all these things" (Luke 21:36).

Jesus is talking, in both testaments, about a time of

> great tribulation, such as has not occurred since the beginning of the world until now, nor ever will. Unless those days had been cut short, no life would have been saved; but for the sake of the elect those days will be cut short. (Mat. 24:21–22)

Historians record that parents ate their children in the fall of Jerusalem in 70 A.D. But Jesus says the coming time will be the worst ever.

Understand that while God allows free will and foreknows perfectly what men will do and what will occur, He is in control. He is sovereign.

Nevertheless, NASA has predicted that sun variations in late 2012 or early 2013 could cause electromagnetic pulses that have the ability to destroy our electrically and electronically sustained society, stopping computers from working and bringing life to a standstill, catapulting us back into the nineteenth century. If you lived in that century, you might be able to fend for yourself. But most don't have self-sustaining farms and wouldn't know how to survive on them if they did.

What would happen if such an event occurred soon or in some future winter? Many, if not most, would die, and what would occur when spring arrived and millions of corpses lay on the ground? Pestilence would spread quickly.

While we don't know all the details of what will happen, God does give some indications, especially to our Anglo-Saxon nations. And our society, especially Christians, don't seem to want to read the prophecies that describe the macabre scenario.

Yet what Jesus describes in the curses against Israel are exactly what will happen to a modern Israel who doesn't know their identity. The downfall of the Anglo-Saxon nations described by the curses in those "boring Old Testament passages," as men see them, is outlined in some detail.

The many Christians who aren't "doers of the word" are one day going to see themselves in the mirror of God's Word in these neglected verses (James 1:22–26).

Those who survive will finally be still and "know that I am [Jesus]," says God when He brings them back into the original Promised Land. "There you will remember your ways and all your deeds with which you have defiled yourselves; and you will loathe yourselves in your own sight for all the evil things that you have done" (Ezek. 20:42–43). He's talking here to the "house of Israel" (Ezek. 20:44), the lost northern tribes, not the house of Judah, whose descendants inhabit the tiny nation of Israel today.

Speaking the Unspeakable

We won't go through all the gory details here, but Jesus does record some of the worst regarding mothers and fathers eating their children because there's nothing else to eat (Deut. 28:53–58). These are the consequences of the disobedience to God displayed so openly by our Western nations. God allows the law of cause and effect to run its course in the form of curses, words that warn of failure if we don't take God's laws of love seriously.

The peoples of our nations, especially our leaders, have gone down a path of rebellion that leads to a destruction that cannot be averted. We are seeing a concentrated effort to expunge the name of Jesus from America.

America has thrown Jesus out of the picture. Many may be surprised to see how God looks at Manasseh, whose name means "forget." Manasseh (the United States) has long ago forgotten God's Sabbath, and most today would consider that a minor issue, even a disputable one. Yet when you read what Jesus says about it in Ezekiel, you may be surprised to see one of the major reasons why destruction is coming upon this nation.

Ezekiel 20:11–24, speaking to the house of Israel, not Judah or modern Israel but the Anglo-Saxons, says that one of the main reasons these believing nations were cast out of the original Promised Land, and will be cast out of their newfound promised land of America, is the breaking of the Sabbath.

Notice Ezekiel 22:26:

> Her priests [the pastors of modern Israel] have done violence to My law and have profaned My holy things; they have made no distinction between the holy and the profane [losing all principles of right and wrong that were still somewhat evident in the 1950s, accepting any sexual aberration that God condemns as normal], and they have not taught the difference between the unclean and the clean [whether it be unclean meats forbidden by God or unclean moral practices]; and *they hide their eyes from My sabbaths*, and I am profaned among them.

They pretend the Sabbath is not in the Bible, when they know in their hearts the only Sabbath mentioned in the Bible is the one starting Friday evening and ending at Saturday sunset. They know Sunday is not in the Bible, but they hide their eyes from the truth, inventing all kinds of ridiculous excuses to twist the clear Word of God.

Can Everybody Be Wrong?

After all, anybody who is anybody keeps Sunday. The vast majority of the churches keep Sunday. Surely the majority must be right. How could they be wrong? And why would God expect us to buck the majority and risk being persecuted? The arguments sound so convincing that most Christians have swallowed them.

Many of the pastors are actually warlocks, as some in the know have shared on the Freedom Blog. One pastor was surprised to hear this, but when he asked around, he found out that other pastors in his city were known warlocks, and witches[24] had infiltrated even the church he pastors.

Here is his blog comment:

> At first when I heard that warlocks have moved into being pastors, I said no way, so I asked around and I got back that more than half of the pastors in my city are known to be warlocks. Every church seems to have witches running important areas in them, including my own. How did the churches get so infiltrated?

24 *Witches are practitioners of evil and supernatural powers. They invoke the demonic world to control and cause harm to others, even though they often claim otherwise, especially in the lower levels of witchcraft. They can be either male or female, but the males are usually referred to as warlocks, the higher levels exercising great power for evil.*

The answer came from one of a number of strong believers who have had much experience on the dark side, and who speak with authority:

> The masons and others have been placing warlocks into churches for years. Plans for compromising the churches have been going on for years in order to bring about the rising beast power in Europe. The program is nearly complete.

She later added this comment:

> ...the program started shortly after the reformation from the [universal] church. The warlocks stopped the daughters from keeping the Sabbath. All [daughter] churches belong to [the universal church] because of the Sunday worship and the warlocks trained to infiltrate the daughter churches.

The strong believers on our blog have great credibility. Thousands have asked them questions about witchcraft and dreams and have been astounded by their accurate answers. We know them by their fruits.

Satan has done his dirty work of deception so well that if you believe in a seventh-day Sabbath, you're considered part of a fringe element, if not a cultist. Yet God condemns in Isaiah 5:20–21 "those who call evil good, and good evil."

Yet the name of Jesus and meeting Him in His Sabbath will be the two main gut checks of the last days for those who claim to be believers. These items will be the litmus test. Only those who obey will be spared the Great Tribulation. Will you follow the crowd to destruction, going along with what is popular? Or will you follow the narrow road?

Who Will Escape?

Some prophecies give us general revelation, and we need the Holy Spirit to fill in the gaps and give us additional understanding. This is true when it comes to those who are at the throne of God in the last days (Rev. 7:9), raptured to heaven before the Great Tribulation, or martyred during this time of trouble and thus rising with their souls and spirits.

Do you remember that Jesus wondered whether He would find faith on the earth in the last days? Will He find faith in us? He always gives us free will. We have a choice.

Will we allow ourselves to be engulfed and overwhelmed by the many fears that have been spoken out in these last days? Will we speak *about* the mountain of time and other pressures with which Satan attacks us, as we all have done at times, or will we speak *to* the mountains of problems in our lives in faith and thanksgiving?

Cults have given strange interpretations of the famous 144,000 to be sealed and protected in the end time. They are those whose faith emulates that of their father, Abraham. They come from the twelve tribes of Israel, only twelve thousand from the nation of Israel (or those of Jewish heritage dispersed in the world). Because Dan bowed to the "women" (or false churches) and tried to be a judge, as his name implies (his Hebrew name signifying a judge), in his own strength, he is the only tribe not included.

However, twelve thousand from each of the tribes, including the Anglo-Saxon nations, will be included. These are indeed a special group of the elect, but they do not compose all the elect in the last days. Indeed, an innumerable multitude from all nations (including America and the Commonwealth nations) will either escape the Great Tribulation or delay obedience but repent and be martyred during that tribulation time and rise to heaven. This last group will miss part of the marriage feast, but they'll be in the first resurrection and reign as Jesus' bride with Him over the earth.

The elite group of 144,000 is referred to as "the bond-servants of our God" (Rev. 7:3). They are both physical Israel and the "Israel of God"

(Gal. 6:16), a special part indeed of Israel, the believers. Their number indicates that they'll be the gatekeepers of the twelve gates of the holy city. We see them standing with Jesus in the heavenly Mount Zion (Rev. 14:1), and later they'll stand with Jesus as priests in the temple at the physical Mount Zion in Jerusalem.

These believers have a special anointing from God. They "have not been defiled with women [or men]" (Rev. 14:4), having never married but been set apart for God's service in a special way. They have never committed adultery physically or spiritually.

We must also understand that women in the Bible represent churches, in this case false churches: "These are the ones who have not been defiled with women..." (Rev. 14:4). They are unpolluted.

Will You Have the Courage to Obey Jesus?

This group of 144,000 has renounced any allegiance to false churches that teach lies. Most Christians today have not yet come to that point. But we can, and thus be part of the great multitude from every nation, including the tribes of Israel, who come out of Babylon and the woman who rides the beast, the great universal church. The lies of doctrines of demons are so accepted by the majority that you really stand out if you say no to these false doctrines.

You can understand why God said the way of error was broad but the path of truth narrow. Take, for example, the almost universal observance of feast days that aren't mentioned in the Bible except in derision (Jer. 10:1–4; Deut. 12:29–32). The holidays most people observe today have clear roots in pagan worship, but somehow they must be okay, many think, because everybody is keeping them.

Yet God says not to follow the crowd to do evil (Ex. 23:2; Mat. 7:13). When you disregard the First Testament, it's easy to miss the clear evidence that the apostles and others in the New Testament kept the days ordained by Jesus Himself in Leviticus 23.

When I researched *Bible Code Broken!*, I found even scholars that keep Sunday such as Willy Wordorf making startling admissions. He openly admits, as do others, that the first-century church in Judea, which had a minority but definite Gentile composition, kept the same days Jesus kept.

While a few departed from that faith once delivered by Jesus in the second century, beginning in Rome, it was not until a pagan emperor came along in the fourth century who wanted to combine paganism and Christianity that the heresy became accepted as church doctrine.

The universal church took over. The Sabbath and the holy days Jesus and the apostles kept were maligned. Sunday, Christmas, and Easter reared their ugly but accepted heads and the pristine spring of the church Jesus founded became a polluted river.

Be On Guard Against Deceivers

Jesus' main admonition to His end-time disciples was that they were not to be deceived (Mat. 24:4). Have you been misled? Is it possible that you're not yet one of those elect who would stand firm and heed Jesus' warning of the last days? He said, "Come out of her, my people, so that you will not participate in her sins and receive of her plagues" (Rev. 18:4).

Who is she? She is a false church with daughters who have followed her false ways. Those daughters protested certain doctrines, but they didn't reject her pagan days, which were falsely baptized Christian. Satan made sure that a change from Sunday-keeping to the Sabbath wasn't part of any reformation.

The daughters didn't protest Sunday, Christmas, or Easter. The devil infiltrated the churches with warlock pastors who steadfastly resist the truth and pollute the church with lies, all the while persecuting true believers who would step out in faith to keep God's days.

The deception is so complete today that many will say, "You're never going to take Christmas away from me!" They justify their stance with human and demonic reasoning, and it sounds so appealing, in the same way that Satan's spiel to Eve sounded so right.

While the context is the final signs and wonders of the false Christs that will arise at the very end, Satan's goal has always been "to mislead, if possible, even the elect" (Mat. 24:24). Although the King James' translation of this verse ("the very elect") may not be totally correct, we can see that God speaks of levels of faith, and that the very elect refers to those in the higher levels.

Those modern Israelites who show themselves to also be strong spiritual Israelites reflect the faith of the father of the faith, Abraham. Isaiah speaks of these faithful ones: "Listen to me, you who pursue righteousness, who seek [Jesus]..." (Isa. 51:1). Notice that this is an end-time prophecy, part of the several chapters in this section that God has inspired us to speak out every Sabbath during the current tribulation so we may be prepared to escape the Great Tribulation.

Isaiah speaks here of the faith of Abraham. He says, "Look to Abraham your father..." (Isa. 51:2). Those friends of God like Abraham, who follow his example of great faith, will also be few in the last days. More of the elect and very elect will come in the "great multitude" (Rev. 7:9) from every nation. They are also special and will be protected as part of the Bride of Jesus.

How Will You Respond to These Truths You Won't Hear Elsewhere?

We believe God has blessed us with special knowledge of end-time events, knowledge that has been hidden from those who follow the false traditions of today's Christianity, those who do not yet understand the importance of keeping God's days and grasping the real identity of Israel in prophecy.

We believe what you read in this book are truths you will not hear in the same way in any other book, and many prophecy books have been published, all saying their scenario is the correct one. It will be your task to prove according to God's Word the fruit of what we relate here.

While we hope you see the importance of understanding even the small details of biblical prophecy revealed here, our greater hope is that you take seriously one of the most important purposes of prophecy. Prophecy is a warning for end-time believers to wake up, to begin to obey by coming out of the world. And that world includes the religious world, a world of falseness, a churchianity that has lost its foundations (Ps. 11:3).

Will you come out and be blessed? Or will you clinch your teeth of religiosity and defend with belligerence the falseness you have accepted without every stopping to prove it from the Bible? (1 Thes. 5:21)

If you want to see 1 Thessalonians 5:23 fulfilled in your life—your spirit, soul, and body, in that order!—being preserved complete and without blame as you stand before Jesus in a rapture and come back with Him to rule, then you need to practice the verse most don't: 1 Thessalonians 5:21. We quote it from the King James Version: "Prove all things [according to the Word, the whole Word, not simply the last fourth of it]; hold fast that which is good [true]."

It's not too late to change now. But soon the door to the marriage feast may be shut. Those who delay can still be a part of the latter part of the marriage feast, but why miss any of it? And at what price? You will lose your physical life for Jesus. Why go through such a trial when you can avoid it? Why be obliged to prove your loyalty in times of great distress when you can prove it right now by simply obeying?

The Great Worldwide Harvest of the Last Days

The fate of the church and the world still depends on the free will of believers, even of those who read these lines. However, I'm confident that Jesus has delayed His coming so that the church can get ready. Merciful and gracious, He is the Grace that will empower us to do our job and turn the hearts of the children to Father Love so the earth doesn't have to be smitten with a curse.

A great harvest of souls around the world is prophesied for these last days. It isn't necessarily fulfilled in the millions of Africans and Asians packing stadiums or open fields who accept Jesus without follow-up discipling—or even worse, who accept "the Lord" without truly getting to know who Jesus is or calling upon His name.

This prophecy will be fulfilled, subject to the free will of believers, by the formation of a "great multitude which no one could count, from every nation and all tribes and peoples and tongues, standing before the throne and before the Lamb, clothed in white robes, and palm branches were in their hands" (Rev. 7:9).

God's prophecies have a number of fulfillments, because His mind and the languages He uses are conceptual in nature, broad in scope. So "the ones who come out of the Great Tribulation" (Rev. 7:14) and who have been cleansed by Jesus' blood in the very last days can be those who come out of this tribulation by escaping from it, being raptured to heaven before it occurs.

That's not all. This verse can also apply to those who delayed and yet repented and gave their life as martyrs. They won't be in the first and best rapture, but they'll still gain a place of honor in the Kingdom and won't miss out of the entirety of the marriage feast in heaven.

They serve in the temple of God in heaven, and they will serve as priests in the temple of God on earth during their reign with Jesus on this planet. Despite wonderful promises of tears being wiped away and hunger and thirst forever satisfied (Rev. 7:15–17), the Bible never says that these or other saints will live forever in heaven, as the popular lie contends.

Who will these elect be? Will you be among them?

We know some who won't unless repentance comes. Malachi prophesies that some will be tired Christians who see life as a burden and ask God continually why they don't see results and have walked "in mourning" as Christians (Mal. 3:14). Unless they repent, they won't be among the bride who is ready to meet the Bridegroom Jesus.

God will replace those tired Christians in the marriage feast with those to whom God extends mercy at the very last. God will go "into the streets and lanes of the city" to call "the poor and crippled and blind and lame" (Luke 14:21). If those who are invited to the marriage feast are too busy, distracted by worldly cares, or too preoccupied to answer the invitation, God has already chosen others who will glorify Him by allowing Him to work mighty changes in their lives.

Those diligent ones who answer the call, and those last-minute invited guests who respond, will either be in the twelve thousand of each tribe of Israel (Anglo-Saxons and some countries in Northwestern Europe) or in the great multitude from all nations, including the Anglo-Saxon ones.

Where will you be?

Chapter Eleven:

Job's Story of 2012—The Flip Side of Hell

Joy in the morning has been a theme for songs and movies, and it's one of the major themes in the Word of God. Job prophesied it. He spoke words in Hebrew with manifold meaning, words that both foretold what would begin to come in the darkest night of the year 2012 and revealed the darkest end-time despot as barren, having to surrender to the coming Light of Jesus as He returns to the earth.

Could it be that Job's words transcended time? I believe his words, spoken by a man Jesus declared righteous, authorized God to say in Genesis 1:5, "And there was evening and there was morning, one day."

A complete reading of the Bible reveals God as the God of day and Satan as the God of night and darkness, a darkness that will cover the world beginning in the winter of 2012. In many ways, late 2012 opens doors to hell, but Job reveals the other side of the story as well—the heavenly side.

In spite of all the negative prophecies that depict havoc beginning in 2012, Job's words have great positive power, encapsulated in the words of David in Psalm 30:5: "Weeping may last for the night, but a shout of joy comes in the morning."

Isaiah expresses the good news this way: "The whole earth is at rest [millennial Sabbath rest, the seventh day of a thousand years] and is quiet; they break forth into shouts of joy" (Isa. 14:7).

The night often brings terrors, but the day brings the relief of light. Tests and trials come, but as we weather them, blessings follow. Dishonor, as in a prophet who is dishonored in his hometown as Jesus was, is followed by honor. A lie comes before the truth corrects it. The light of Jesus shining for the seventh millennium and beyond follows Satan's night of six thousand years of oppression.

Satan's subtle request of Jesus in Job 2:4 ("Skin for skin!") to have a physical body so he could have dominion on the earth in a greater way will be granted. The Dark Knight of personified evil will be rendered totally barren. He will be given a body and then mocked and thrown into a lake of fire, finally realizing how insane he was to think he could outthink God and defeat Him (Isa. 14:15–17; Rev. 20:10).

The good news of the Kingdom of God is that Jesus wins! He outsmarts the prince of darkness, as He did in the book of Job, and Satan's night becomes eternally barren. Jesus and His saints are victorious! God's government returns to earth. How and how soon depends on those believers who read these warnings and how they prepare.

Here are Job's words in Job 3:7 as they should be translated from the multifaceted, conceptual Hebrew: "Lo, behold and focus on this. That night is barren, sterile, desolate, and is wrapped up in itself so tightly that it's life is lost" (my paraphrase).

Gay Beast

Satan's request for a body included being able to possess an end-time son of perdition, whose nature is intimated by the conceptual word *galmud*, translated as "barren." It can have the meaning of fruitless or meaningless, meaning unable to reproduce.

The end-time son of Satan, often confused with the Antichrist, is actually the coming political and military leader of the United States of Europe (or whatever it may be called), also called the beast in prophecy.

This despot will fulfill the Hebrew meanings of this word, which include being wrapped up in himself, fruitless, and sterile because he will lust for other males. He will be an unhappy gay beast, to use a modern oxymoron. Daniel 11:37 says that he "will show no regard... for the desire of women..."

This evil man will be a child of the night. God works in the day, Satan in the night. And the day representing the time when God will begin to defeat Satan's dark works is the Sabbath day. Furthermore, all indications point to the day on which Job spoke out most of his prophecies—the Day of Trumpets, Job's birthday, and the day of the birth and return of King Jesus to bring His light to the world.

We have explained how Jesus took six days to "recreate" the earth His way, while Satan took six days of a thousand years to reform the earth in *his* image. So, Job was declaring all of Satan's work for six thousand years barren and fruitless. The more pressure Satan put on mankind at the end, the more sterile his kingdom would become.

In calling the night barren, Job also limited the time of darkness' final gasp for life to the length of the night. Since the maximum length of the night in the Jerusalem area, the center stage of Bible prophecy, is fourteen hours, Job was also prophesying an hour for a year as the limited length of Satan's end-time night.

Fourteen years is the length of the seven years of sorrow followed by the tribulation and Great Tribulation that would last, subject to the prayers and actions of believers, for seven years. In other words, God will honor Job's words and minimize Satan's dark times at the end.

Another meaning of Job's prophecy is that the darkest time at the end of the age would begin on a moonless night, a new moon. And indeed, that darkness began at the exact end of the six thousand years allotted to man, two thousand years after Jesus' birth in 4 B.C., or 1996, on the Day of Trumpets in the fall.

Job's statement also prophesies the opening of the third seal and the riding of the prophetic third horseman, the black horse of famine that would begin to reign (Rev. 6:5–6). All the seals would eventually be opened.

Winter Solstice 2012 in Prophecy

A striking aspect of Job's prophecy is that Satan's darkest night will begin in earnest at the most barren time of the year in the northern hemisphere,[25] the winter solstice. The many cultures that have foreseen 2012 as a great time of darkness are confirmed as we understand the forty years from 1972 and the abortion ruling, completing forty years in late 2012.

Jesus implied in Matthew 24:20 that the Great Tribulation would begin in the dead of winter. That dark winter could have occurred as early as the 2012 winter solstice, but an unprepared church has pushed that date years later.

"No joyful shout" (Job 3:7) refers principally to the cry of a baby being born. Any child born during the time of Great Tribulation would be a burden to a mother going through this horrible time of trouble (Mat. 24:19–21). Wherever famine or false gods abound, no joyful shout will be heard.

---

25 *Jerusalem, the center of Bible prophecy, is in the northern hemisphere.*

Those who curse the night will also curse the day (Job 3:8). The world of darkness, including the Christian world that worships tradition, will be aroused against those who are of the day, including those who keep the Sabbath day.

One of Freedom Blog's young bloggers shared an aspect of the Sabbath truth he learned while with a young Bible study group. They beat him up and sent him to the hospital for nine days! Thanks to prayers and forgiveness, God turned the situation around to His great glory, yet the incident shows how much Christians hate those who keep the Sabbath.

Another church youth group threw urine-filled balloons at a group of youths emerging from a Sabbath Bible study. The pastor of the attackers was chief of police in the town, illustrating that the attacks will come from both churches and governments.

When taken in context and in the conceptual Hebrew, the latter part of Job 3:8 should read as follows: "All those who curse, use spells, speak incantations, issue hexes, and practice divination, come! Curse the Sabbath day, the feast days, and the Day of Trumpets for the King. You who are skillful in the treasures of the ancient knowledge of curses, spells, hexes, and incantations, prepare, rouse, and incite for action the great serpent Satan, the fallen morning star, the king of the ways of Babylon, the confusion; come and twist the Sabbath day and the Feast of Trumpets" (my paraphrase).

1996 and Beyond

God has given us the grace to understand certain possible timelines of these last days. God did say that He reveals His plans and what is to come before it happens to His servants (Amos 3:7). All treasures of knowledge and wisdom are embodied in Jesus (Col. 2:3) and He pours Himself only into one day to meet and teach His people in a special way—the Sabbath. Revelation comes then. Prophecy is opened up to understanding. While it is not yet revealed when Jesus is coming back, prophetic timelines that depend on free will are available to those who search them out. In this book, I'll mention only one of a number of indications for a nineteen-year minimum span of time after the end of the six thousand years in 1996. Many others exist.[26]

Explorers have found the true Mount Sinai in Saudi Arabia, including the rock that was split, pouring out water for Israel in the desert. That rock was six feet across, with four feet on one side, a nineteen-inch gap in the middle, and two feet on the other side. This is an indication of the four thousand years before Jesus (who is the Rock) came, two thousand years after Jesus before His return, and the nineteen-year span which is an extension of the time of man.

The year 2015 would have been the transition year between the kingdom of Satan and the Kingdom of God. Jesus would have exerted His wrath for a full, extended year of 390 days beginning on the Day Trumpets 2015, returning at the end of this extended year, which would end on the Day of Trumpets 2016, 390 days after Trumpets 2015.

We know He will return in the future on a Day of Trumpets. However, we don't know what year it will be. Nevertheless, as the time gets closer, we'll be able to know more. The day of the first rapture, when the saints who have prepared will be caught up to be with Jesus for the marriage feast, is not the day of Jesus' coming back to rule. He receives His bride in heaven at the time of that rapture (the believers being "caught up" rather than Jesus coming down), but He doesn't return to earth before the end of that extended, last year of His wrath.

26 *1 Samuel 17 reveals that Goliath's height was six cubits and a span, representing six thousand years of man's rule and a span. Some have speculated that to hold the shaft of his spear, a nineteen-inch hand span is required. This would support the nineteen-inch gap in the rock found by archeologists at Sinai.*

We don't yet know when that will be, since it depends on the church's preparations.

The Bridegroom's delay in the parable of the ten virgins (Mat. 25:5) indicates that God foreknew the church wouldn't be ready to be Jesus' bride, and thus He would not return at the ideal date of the coming of the King, the Day of Trumpets in the year 2016. The time could come when God's servants will know the day of Jesus' return, yet probably not the hour, but it wasn't known when Jesus spoke to His disciples, and we do not know it today. We only know a general timeframe, which most Christians ignore or deny that it is even possible to know.

God has revealed to others, and to us, that the tribulation began on the Day of Trumpets 2008, the very day that the bottom dropped out of our financial system and an economic crisis hit the stock markets. But to get the full picture, we must go back to that fateful day of September 11, 2001.

Unless you keep God's holy days, you might not be aware of the fact that the correct day of Trumpets in 2001 was September 18, exactly seven days after 9/11. On that day of attack, we became painfully aware that God had removed His hand of protection from the leading nation of the peoples that were once called Israelites. Americans lost their identity as the tribe of Manasseh (which means to forget) because they abandoned the Sabbath, the very reason for their scattering among the nations, as Ezekiel 20 and 22 explain.

Whoever may have been the principal cause of this terrorist attack, God foreknew it all, even the shadow governments bent on a new world order and the destruction of America. God saw America's rejection of His Son Jesus, a principle on which the nation had been originally founded as a new promised land for His people. He didn't cause it, but He allowed it, as did the U.S. government that stood idly by and broke all protocol by allowing the planes to stay in the air.

The story from the mass media and the politicians was nothing but lies upon lies, cover-ups upon cover-ups, and God foreknew all that as well. The powerful propagandists will slur those who tell the truth as "conspiracy theorists," but they ignore the truth that Satan is the original conspirator. He is using his puppets, the secret societies and "misleaders" we are cursed with in our Western nations, to systematically destroy the U.S. constitution and the nation itself, as prophesied in the Bible.

It would be impossible to understand the history of the last half-century without knowing about the contacts our governments have had with aliens, knowledge that has resulted in the murder of those in the know who have dared to proclaim the facts.

While we air some of those facts on www.freedomtruthseekers.com, our main interest is not the titillating information hidden from the public, but revealing the truth of God's Word and His prophecies about the darkness to come and the subsequent bright light of Jesus that will soon illumine the whole world and the universe.

As these words are being written, we are several years into the time of tribulation. While it has certain parameters it cannot exceed, its length is variable according to how and how soon the potential virgin Bride of Jesus, the church, wakes up from its sleep and does the job God has called it to do (Mat. 24:14; 28:19–20; Mal. 4:6).

Times of Dullness, Darkness, Yet of Revealing and Restoration

Job prophesied a number of periods of darkness in history. One of them was the time Jesus asked His disciples to pray for Him (Mat. 26:38–41). They failed. They went to sleep, as have His disciples today. Jesus experienced the barren night Job prophesied; we have now entered another era of darkness and barrenness those same words of Job foretold. When we fail to pray for one another, we make the night barren for

Jesus and others. We allow a cloud of dullness to descend and a dome of darkness to be established over an area.

Those domes (demonic powers over certain regions invoked by witchcraft) began to form in a large way beginning in 1996. The ranks of witches and Satanists began to explode at that time, and a seed was established for this darkness when Germany and later the European Union made the casting out of demons illegal. Such important prophetic events often disappear from the records, but an article in the Edmonton Journal reported the event when it occurred. A new surge of persecution began against those who do not follow the doctrines of the universal church and who do not worship their leader.

Instead of standing up against the forces of evil and risking persecution, pastors and churches bowed before the evil (Jer. 10:21).

Not only was Satan authorized to begin in earnest his plan to bring a dark dome over the whole world and bring about a night in which no man could do God's work, but these events opened the door for the reign of fear, terrorism, scarcity, loss, and murder. We saw the first signs of their reign on September 11, 2001.

On that day, God opened a small door for repentance for all of Israel (the United States and the Commonwealth) and Jacob (the unbelieving nations and all unbelievers). America was given seven days to repent, but the nation chose to mourn, not to change.

As Jonathan Cahn explains in *The Harbinger*, America's leaders even reacted in pride, reflecting the words of Israel's leaders in Isaiah 9:10. They said, "We will rebuild!" The implication is that we are strong in our strength and we don't have to rely on God, humble ourselves before Him, or change our ways.

This first harvest of fear through terrorism started on the Day of Trumpets 2001, the seven years of sorrow, foreshadowed by accounts in Job.

The clouds of dullness began to manifest in 1996 with Christians being encouraged and seduced into rejecting the truth of the Word. Even Sabbath-keeping churches began to turn away from God's days.

While witnessing the light, the love of the Father, the sacrifice of Jesus, and the coming Kingdom of God will crack open any dome of darkness, Satan is gaining ground in forming a dome over the whole world. The day of darkness is here, and it will last for a minimum of nineteen years (1996 to 2015).

The darkness will begin to intensify beginning at the winter solstice of 2012, but it began in 1996. At the same time, God opened in that year a new era of revelation and restoration for those who would seize it. To those who obeyed the Word, God released an anointing to use the words of love against the domes of darkness. Those who would love Jesus enough to obey Him (John 14:15) were given great power over the demonic world.

The barren night can thus be counteracted by powerful gifts God has made available to every believer. They include the power to forgive sins, to speak in a heavenly language to our Father in heaven, and to do great miracles, even more than Jesus did (John 14:12). But how many Christians are ready to receive these gifts? Precious few.

Few believers, if any, are walking in all the gifts God has made available to us. But they are available for the asking, according to our level of faith. God is patient with His people, yet He wants to give them all He has. Some are asking in fasts for the release of the Benjamin Blessing (explained in my e-book, *New Moons—New Lives*).

While perfection in these and all areas of spiritual growth isn't a requirement to be raptured and escape the Great Tribulation (Luke 21:36), God wants to see His people submitting to Him and growing. Those who choose not to obey and grow will need a boost in their faith level.

An Anointing to Die?

A new anointing will be released to those who are late in their decision to keep the Sabbaths of God and keep the testimony of Jesus. They will be given a rare anointing—the anointing of the martyr. This group will not prepare itself fully for the day at hand and heed the warning to seek Jesus while He may be found. They choose to fight darkness without a full deck. They have allowed the cloud of darkness to blind them to what God is revealing and doing now and to the power and authority God has made available.

Darkness kills, steals, and destroys. It makes the night barren. But we don't have to stay in the dark. We can seek the light of our Father through His Word and obedience.

Are you walking into the cloud of dullness by neglect, thus allowing the dome of darkness to kill you? If you recognize your need for Jesus as Satan's barren night suffocates the world in these last days, you won't be deprived of the "joyful shout." You will be keeping the days that celebrate Jesus' return to the earth to bring joy where sorrow and hopelessness have abounded. You will be keeping the Sabbath day and God's holy days, including the Day of Trumpets. You will "know the joyful sound" (Ps. 89:15) of the *shofar*, signaling Jesus' triumphant return. You will meet Jesus in His days, and it will be said of you, as it was of those who celebrated the Feast of Trumpets millennia ago in Nehemiah 8:10, "Do not be grieved, for the joy of [Jesus] is your strength."

Late 2012 doesn't need to be for you an open door to hell. It can be the gateway to all the gifts of heaven. Receive them and grow in grace and knowledge (2 Pet. 3:18), even knowledge about Satan's end-time schemes, which include giants and aliens.

Chapter Twelve: What You Haven't Heard about Giants and Aliens

Some readers may get a bit jumpy when they see this chapter heading. Wait a minute. Give me an opportunity to explain. It's a long story, but I don't think you'll skip anything. These stories are true, but they're stranger than fiction.

People love to put other people in categories. Such a pigeonholing procedure is neither just nor loving, but people keep doing it. The prevailing view is this: anyone who talks about aliens must be some kind of kook.

You can easily debunk this misrepresentation by doing a Google search for "Chuck Missler Nephilim." His video, "Return of the Nephilim, UFOs, Aliens, and the Bible—Part 1 of 2" (search for Part 2 as well) is one of the best-documented proofs of UFOs from respected members of our society. Missler spent thirty years in the strategic community of the Department of Defense.

Missler quotes Edmund Spencer, who warns against "condemnation before investigation." The Bible says it is foolish to answer a matter before hearing it and tells us to prove all things (1 Thes. 5:21).

Astronauts aren't kooks. Consider a transcript of an interview on Larry King Live, where Larry spoke with Dr. Edgar Mitchell, a distinguished former astronaut. You can do a web search for Larry King's interview with Edgar Mitchell and find it easily. The transcript is quite revealing. Mitchell, of Apollo 14, is quoted in an April 1996 broadcast of Dateline, saying, "NASA is covering up what really happened at Roswell, New Mexico."

Major Gordon Cooper reported seeing UFOs in space.[27] Cooper saw a green UFO on May 15, 1963, a UFO that was at the same time tracked by Australian radar. He testified before the U.N. that UFOs are visiting this planet. In May 1996, he said, "We are being visited by aliens."

Gemini 7 astronauts saw a UFO in December 1965. In total, thirteen astronauts have gone on record as seeing UFO's in space.

Stripping aside all the hoaxes, the evidence of the existence of UFOs is overwhelming. Multiple, competent witnesses have seen them. They have been plotted on radar, leave tangible traces on the ground, and are photographed. They have been clocked at speeds in excess of six thousand miles per hour, making right angles turns, and they can dematerialize without a trace. They are physical, but having been produced by Satan, they have advanced technological abilities.

Common sense would tell us that the cover-up of the Roswell crash in 1947 is so weak as to be laughable. Modern technology has shown that the paper the government spokesman held in his hand as he lied about the crash in Fort Worth, five hundred miles away from the event and days after it, revealed that a crash did occur and alien victims had been secured.

Alien abductions are, on the one hand, too bizarre to accept, but on the other hand, too frequent and consistent to ignore. At least three percent (some say ten percent) of the population has reported them. These abductions often involve the implanting and harvesting of human

---

27 See http://www.syti.net/UFOSightings.html.

fetuses. Genetic manipulation has been a tactic of Satan for thousands of years.

Many crop circles are hoaxes, but some have been examined by scientists and are unexplainable in normal terms, including samples from a barley field near my home in Edmonton, Alberta.

I believe in proving all things and finding the truth. Do you?

Naysayers, Beware!

Am I a conspiracy theorist? I do believe Satan is the great conspirator and that he has a plan to counter God's plan. It does indeed involve a plan for a one-world government, or a new world order. Actually, no one-world order will rule, but the world will be separated into three ruling orders, the European beast power, the Islamic empire ruled by the Arab Antichrist (or biblical King of the South), and the Asian bloc.

The thirteen astronauts who came forward about UFOS all had naysayers, but their integrity won out.

I also have my naysayers. Some call my organization a cult simply because we keep the Sabbath day. Do cults exist that keep the Sabbath? Yes. However, they're not cults because they obey God by keeping the fourth of the Ten Commandments; they're cults because they aren't willing to be corrected by the Word of God, and because they worship men more than Jesus.

We do not fulfill the criteria for a cult. We love Jesus and put Him above every man. We have shown ourselves to be willing to be corrected when anyone shows us where we are wrong according to the Word of God. We realize we aren't the only ones who know Jesus and that those who don't know about the Sabbath are just as much believers as we are.

The sensitive and sometimes graphic material I include in Appendix II regarding aliens and giants is considered by some to be speculation.

I cite others and their websites that speak of these giants and aliens. I don't necessarily agree with all they say, but I wanted to provide some source material for those who think I'm dreaming all this up.

I believe our presentation of these subjects is unique. Some of my conclusions come from divine revelation, combined with a study of ancient writings and sources, some of which may have been deliberately deleted by authorities for reasons I leave you to imagine.

I also realize that my understanding of the Hebrew may not coincide with what you find in concordances and scholarly works. The problem is that the vast majority of scholars do not go back to the *ancient* Hebrew.[28] The definitions they provide for Hebrew words are limited since much of Aramaic and less ancient Hebrew[29] is also limited in scope and doesn't include the vastness of conceptual meanings as confirmed in other ancient Hebrew writings. Rabbinical scholars that specialize in the ancient, conceptual Hebrew have confirmed many of my definitions.

Furthermore, my church is comprised of fervent lovers of Jesus who meet Him on His Sabbath day to receive revelation from Him. We keep His holy days. During the Days of Unleavened Bread, we have lain down to Jesus the leaven or sin of falseness, especially that of keeping the holidays of the Christian world.

I realize that few Christians today believe what I do about the term "Lord." God revealed to me several years ago the importance of using the mighty name of Jesus instead of this weak title. I realize, however,

---

28 *As is often the case with foreign invasion, Judah lost its ancient Hebrew language when the nation was taken captive by the Babylonians in 604 B.C. When they returned after seventy years, the pure original language was polluted by Chaldee and Aramaic. It lost its rich, conceptual nature. Furthermore, when Jerusalem fell in 70 A.D., Hebrew became a dead language, reverting almost completely to Chaldee and Aramaic. Modern Hebrew is more akin to Yiddish than the ancient Hebrew.*

29 *For further information, visit http://www.israelect.com/divinepageant/Kabbalah.htm.*

that many use "Lord" mixed with "Jesus" and do get results. Our church has seen dramatic changes when we apply God's instruction to use by invoking Jesus only by His name.

In Appendix II, I explain the meaning of the word "Lord" (or "the Lord") used by itself without the name of Jesus following it, and its connection with the popular Christian holidays.

Our church has seen by revelation and experience the power of the name of Jesus. We often use the Hebrew name *Yashua*, Jesus' original name, because of its powerful, conceptual meaning in Hebrew. However, I believe the notion that we must speak His name in Hebrew is one of many false doctrines espoused in churches today.

Consider this: the name of Jesus, as translated by the Holy-Spirit-inspired authors, is [Iēsous]. God didn't inspire the original Hebrew name *Yashua* to be included in the New Testament scrolls. This means that the One who died for "every tribe and tongue and people and nation" (Rev. 5:9) doesn't require us to say His name in Hebrew to be saved, healed, or delivered.

Satan introduced false gods long before Jesus came. The fact that His name in Greek resembles the name of the false god Zeus is no reason to avoid it. Zeus meant "healer," but Jesus is more than that; He's the Healing Savior. If God wrote Jesus' name in the Greek language in the inspired and infallible original biblical texts, that means we can say His name in any language and receive powerful results.

Naysayers Versus Truth Sayers

In the following section, I'll refer you to some who speak similar truths. Even though I don't agree with everything they say, I do salute their courage to speak out.

William Cooper was a government insider who spoke openly, at the risk of his life, of the aliens and the corresponding government cover-up. He was murdered for his courage. So he has some well-deserved credibility.

Cooper said that the movie *Close Encounters of the Third Kind*, for instance, was based on a *true* story. You read that right. Hollywood fare isn't always the work of someone's imagination. He also said that basically all we hear from the government and media are lies. He stated that unless we understand the alien connection and their interplay with the governments of this world, nothing in the last half-century of history makes any sense.

We live in a world of lies, and people love to have it so. That may sound surprising, but it's true. Most people, even Christians, prefer to hear comfortable lies than the truth.

I don't want people to tune me out from hearing the truth, so I've included much of my more sensitive and astounding research in Appendices II and III. Not everyone is ready for those truths. Furthermore, some may not understand how I can make these claims. All I can say is that they don't have the background I have.

As I mentioned, our church keeps God's days. We obey Jesus, albeit imperfectly. We are attuned to the voice of the Holy Spirit, whom Jesus promised would lead us into all truth (John 16:13), even the inconvenient truths.

Here, you will receive the truth. I may not give chapter and verse for every scenario I advance, but these writings are a product of a perspective of the Bible that is broader than most, aided not only by reading between the biblical lines, connecting the dots of "a little here, a little there" (Isa. 28:10), but also benefitting from an apostolic understanding of the vast, conceptual meanings of Hebrew words that explain the character and actions of the giants and aliens.

My friend and apostle prayed to God years ago for an understanding of the conceptual Hebrew. While pastors mocked his prayer, he has since worked closely with a prominent rabbinical scholar who has been amazed at his insight and has even learned from my friend. I see this as confirmation that his prayer was answered. I see further confirmation in the understanding it has given me of the Word of God and how it all fits together.

Daniel said that "knowledge will increase" in "the end of time" (Dan. 12:4) and "those who have insight will understand" (Dan. 12:10). Paul also spoke of apostles and other five-fold ministry members who would bring us "knowledge of the Son of God" (Eph. 4:11–16).

Because of God's mercy and grace, and because we have obeyed (Ps. 111:10; Acts 5:32), we can see the whole prophetic picture and how it all fits together. Some points are only proved when we see how that perfect fit comes. I pray you will be able to receive the revelation I have received. It may surprise you.

Government Coverups of UFOs

The existence of aliens was not a surprise to God. He foreknew everything Satan would try to do to counteract His plan of salvation.

The truth is, I was once an unbeliever—not only in Jesus, but also in UFOs. I grew up during the flying saucer era, first accepting the intimidation by the government that the only place for ufologists is the loony bin. Then I accepted Jesus and initially believed these aliens must be demons, not fleshly beings. Accepting the truth opened my eyes to new understanding. What a surprise!

You will be surprised, too. The truth is a fascinating story that dispels so many falsehoods and actually prepares us for the future, when aliens will be a part of the fulfillment of prophetic end-time events. I believe we can handle the truth better than the blatant lies from governments.

While UFO sightings by important government officials have gone virtually unnoticed and unreported, a journalist was recently fired for her interviews with respected citizens of Stephenville, Texas. Seems the truth was too hot to handle. It's always easier to make it disappear.

But neither the truth nor the UFOs have disappeared. In fact, UFO sightings—a fact throughout the world's history, evidenced in art throughout the ages—have markedly increased in the last few years, especially since 1996, which happened to be the end of the six thousand years allotted to man.

In 1997, thousands of residents of Phoenix, Arizona saw what was without any doubt an unidentified, unexplainable, extremely large flying object over the city. Residents woke up to weathercasters mocking anyone who pretended to have seen this craft, and the lying word for two months or so was… mum. That is, until ABC finally reported it, definitely not with the speed at which some UFOs have been clocked.

Now pilots and government personnel are reporting UFO sightings, and some are demanding that the government stop the cover-up.

But don't hold your breath if you think the government will begin to tell us the truth and nothing but the truth. We do hope you can breathe easier when you hear what we have to say from the Word of God. God's Book covers everything—and it never lies. From beginning to end, the Bible is a book of truth—truth that even most Christians have never heard. And most Christians don't start reading the Bible where we will begin, at the beginning.

The Big Bang?

It's quite simple. Compare Genesis 1:1–2 and Isaiah 45:18 and you'll see the Hebrew words *tohu* and *bohu* (void, waste, in a state of confusion) mentioned in both passages. He is the God of order (1 Cor. 14:33, 40). God is not the author of confusion (*tohu* and *bohu*). Satan is.

Something evil from an evil one had to happen to cause the confusion. The spacing between the Hebrew letters in these verses indicates, as science agrees, that God created the earth about four and a half billion years ago.

No, Bible thumpers. Not six thousand years ago. That was the time of the "*re*-creation" and Adam's creation. A number of verses, while they have several fulfillments in time, refer to Satan's first and subsequent rebellions and attempts to overthrow God on His throne (Isa. 14:12–14; Ezek. 28:14–14; Rev. 12:7–9).

God placed archangel Lucifer on earth to prepare this planet for man (Ezek. 28:13). But sin began to enter Lucifer, making him into the adversary and rebel called Satan. He ascended with one-third of God's angels, which were under his charge on earth, to God's throne in the northern sky, called in the Bible "the recesses of the north" (Isa. 14:13).

The consensus of scientists is that many of the dinosaurs were destroyed about sixty-four million years ago. My colleagues and I believe we have received divine confirmation that it was more likely 66.6 million years ago, since Satan's soon-coming rebellion will involve those same numbers: 666. This first rebellion of Satan caused God to cast him down to earth—a dark, devastated world—and the resulting cataclysmic battle caused the earth to shift in its rotation.

It's little wonder that when we gaze into the heavens we see few stars in the northern sky. God had to unleash his power through physical means to pulverize Satan as he fell from God's throne. Jesus was part of the battle, of course, and witnessed this colossal event (Luke 10:18), remembering that He was long before "watching Satan fall from heaven like lightning."

Big bang? No, the only big bang was when God banged Satan out of heaven.

Scientists have found evidence of another kind of big bang. They believe the giant crater we call the Gulf of Mexico was created at that very time by a giant asteroid, one of the weapons of destruction used in the titanic battle Satan waged against God. The change in the earth's rotation and the dust created by the great asteroid resulted in the ice age that froze the dinosaurs in their tracks. Everything fits.

Lucifer, who had become Satan by this rebellion, fought God because of pride and jealousy. He was jealous of the future race called mankind because he knew they would be made in God's image (Gen. 1:26–27), unlike the angels, and would wield godlike power, which he coveted.

"Evilution" *Did* Occur

After Satan saw his first defeat at the hands of God, his efforts were stymied. But this serpentine critter is a poor loser and doesn't like to throw in the towel. Satan's dinosaur creation didn't work, because a catastrophic ice age suddenly destroyed most of them. Satan was left with a chaotic earth, his power to create by fiat withdrawn by God. Now he had to resort to genetic manipulation. It was indeed "evilution"—a real evolution invented by the evil one himself.

Some may cite John 1:3, which states that Jesus created all things. He did. When Jesus gave Lucifer the power to create life on earth to prepare it for man, it was in actuality Jesus doing the work. When we lay hands on people for healing, we don't do it in our power, but in the power of Jesus. Jesus is doing it through us.

In the same way, Jesus created through Lucifer. When Lucifer became Satan, he misused that power to create ugly dinosaurs to threaten the life of man that was to be created rather than truly prepare the earth for man.

And Satan had another plan. What better way to mock God than to gradually evolve a man-like creature who would gain power and threaten the existence of the real thing to come—mankind made in God's image.

Much evidence exists to show that long before Adam, Satan indeed mocked God by using the genetic manipulation now referred to as evolution to bring about humanoids who had a certain intelligence and civilization. Archaeologists have found many artifacts and skeletons that predate the creation of Adam six thousand years ago.

A difference, however, exists. These man-like creatures did not have the Spirit that God breathed into Adam, making Adam and his progeny sons of God. Shocking though it may be for misled fundamentalists, evolution did occur. The Creator God allowed it because He gave free will to Lucifer who became Satan.

Some fundamentalists use evidence of human footprints in conjunction with dinosaur footprints in Texas to try to prove that man and dinosaurs coexisted. What they don't realize is that humanoids coexisted with dinosaurs, but mankind didn't. Satan produced humanoid aliens long before Adam, but once God created man, no dinosaurs roamed the earth. No dinosaurs are mentioned entering the ark before the Flood.

Satan thus began to cause physical life to evolve into an advanced, man-resembling creature. He was planting future seeds of doubt that God was the Creator. God *is* indeed the Creator. Satan is a false creator.

About 12,600 years ago,[30] Satan made another attempt to take over God's throne, using the humanoid aliens he had produced and

30 *This date is evidenced by certain verses in Isaiah and East Indian traditions, as well as research explained on the History Channel's series on Ancient Aliens (Episode 4). This episode explains unusual "ley lines," or ancient structures lined up in Ireland and Scandinavia, that were most likely markers for*

their advanced spacecraft to leave earth suddenly on a space mission in the form of another *coup d'etat* to overthrow God's government. The sudden departure and the fumes of these craft were the apparent cause that produced another ice age on earth and made the planet even more devastated.

Crystal Technology, Amazing Structures, and Robot Wars

The advanced technology of these aliens who left the earth at that time was far ahead of what we know today. Sumerian manuscripts also give ample evidence of an amazing, crystal technology that existed from Adam's time to the Flood. Even certain Hindu texts speak of amazingly fast planes powered with this advanced technology. Evidence shows that antigravity devices also existed. Crystal energy allowed large objects to be moved effortlessly.

What other explanation could exist to explain the amazing structures around the world such as the Ajanta Caves in western India, Baalbek, Lebanon, Heliopolis in Egypt, and Labella in Ethiopia—not to mention the temples in South America, Mexico, and the underwater temples near Japan?

Don't believe the lie that all previous humankind consisted of only ignorant, grunting cavemen. We may like to believe the Fred Flintstone fantasy, but we need to come out of Stone Age thinking to recognize the advanced technologies of the past.

The Sumerians record that "the father of man" (Adam) walked with God on all twelve (sic) planets. Those feats certainly caused Satan to

---

UFO travel. The placement of these structures was based on the stars of the constellation Cygmus. The "Northern Cross" is actually a cross placed by God in the sky to show that Jesus would have to come to die on a cross.

become even more jealous as he planned his ruse to tempt Eve in the garden.

Some earth formations can only be explained by accepting the fact that these aliens lived on earth but traveled among the stars. No earthbound knowledge could explain the astounding accuracy of measurement exemplified by so many of our planet's ancient monolithic structures, as exposed on the well-researched TV series *Ancient Aliens* (whose speculations are not always true, but whose facts don't lie). Similar structures have been found on Mars.

The humanoid watchers waged robot battles (on our radio site we have published the photos of robot heads found on the moon). The aliens had the giants build large statues to glorify these humanoids, whose statues we see on Mars.

One word the Bible uses for aliens is *guwr*. They were humanoids called "watchers," to be distinguished from the "hosts of heaven" created by God in Genesis 2:1. God made beings that, according to the Hebrew word for "hosts," implied, among many meanings, "learning vessels with souls and bodies." They were either neutral or good, since God doesn't create evil beings.

Both Satan's humanoid watchers, created on earth and traveling in the heavens, and God's hosts, who also had the intelligence to make spaceships, are referred to in Isaiah 1:2, when God commands, "Listen, O heavens…" Jesus Himself calls these watchers and all the eyes that exist in the universe to focus on what He is about to do on the earth.

The *guhr* were humanoids, abominations, or developments of genetic engineering from Satan. They existed before the last ice age (and were probably the cause of it) about 12,600 years ago when they reached their peak.

Glossary of Alien Terms

Humanoid, Humanoid Watcher, Enemy Alien: Manlike product of "evilution" (Satan's genetic manipulation) originating on earth and having been sent to other areas of the galaxy and/or universe. Satan genetically engineered these aliens to mock God, who he knew would create man to be higher than him. They are the avowed enemies of God, and Satan wants to use them to attack God's throne in the last days. They kidnap humans to take advantage of their gene pool and use their energy. They left the earth around 12,600 years ago at Satan's second rebellion, and they are those who return in UFOs. They are part of a race of eight or nine varieties that have warred between each other and are used by Satan to instill fear.

Hosts of heaven: A general term that can refer to inanimate stars or to angels. It can also refer in the Hebrew to beings created by God in Genesis 2:1 who are "learning vessels," called upon by God to learn from what mankind is doing on earth (Isa. 1:2).

Alien (in general sense): Foreigner; any being not part of man or humankind that is alien or foreign to this earth; believer in Jesus (even we believers are sometimes called aliens, since we are of a different, heavenly kingdom, not an earthly one.)

Transmuted humans: Those humans who have had their genetic structure combined with humanoids, who wanted to see if they could reproduce that way and have a soul like man.

Unwrapping Satan's Cover-up

Much goes on behind the scenes as Satan prepares to fulfill the ominous prophecies God foreknew and wrote throughout the Bible, not only in the Book of Revelation, but also in the books of Job and Isaiah. The powers that be are not always the powers that are, and the real power of evil working behind the scenes is that of the god of this world—Satan (2 Cor. 4:4; Rev. 12:9; Eph. 6:12). While he is the greatest conspirator, he works through human instruments.

The stars and planets tell a story. NASA photos reveal the large face of a humanoid[31] carved in the mountainous surface of Mars and pyramids that are almost identical to the Great Pyramid found on earth.[32] Who made them? And why is the fact that no spacecraft has been able to land on one part of Mars hushed up?

The only valid answer is that these feats of engineering are products of giants at the behest of the alien humanoids fabricated by Satan's evolutionary process. They left the earth, but they have returned many times. And prophecy shows they will return—with greater visibility.

Jesus prophesied that the last days would be like the days of Noah (Mat. 24:37). Since aliens and giants were powerful at this time, we know these aliens and giants will indeed return in force.

The English government recently opened many of their heretofore-secret files on aliens. Larry King interviewed a high military official who had seen a UFO. King asked if the U.S. would also open its files as the British have done. His response was, "Only if they [aliens] land on the White House lawn."

---

31 *NASA likes to downplay these astounding images, but at this link you can see the original photo of the face in 1976 (http://www.msss.com/mars_images/moc/extended_may2001/face/1976pio.html).*

32 *You can see the pyramids here: http://www.greatdreams.com/cydonia.htm.*

You would be surprised to know how many U.S. presidents have either had contacts with aliens or have been informed of their existence. Ronald Reagan called on the nations of the U.N. to realize that our greatest enemy was from outer space.

While documentation is hard to obtain, strong evidence exists to suggest that the cover-up is a deal between the government and the aliens allowing the U.S. to use alien technology. It is evident from the disappearance of important files that a presidential edict was issued long ago to keep the existence of aliens a secret and to mock anyone who would spot aliens or UFOs. As more and more reputable sources verify their existence, it will become increasingly difficult for the government to lie to the public.

Ancient Hindu and Sumerian writings speak of phenomena that are unexplainable without an admission of the existence of humanoid aliens.[33] You can find more at UFO.whipnet.org. More sites are available in Appendix II. While wild speculations may abound on some of these sites, I believe they provide evidence from the original Hebrew understanding of aliens in the Bible.

Is the government really trying to protect us so we don't get scared? Or are they also trying to cover up their secret dealings with these creatures who they're trying to tell us don't exist? The giant cover-up must stop.

---

33 *"According to Dr. V. Raghavan, retired head of the Sanskrit department of India's prestigious University of Madras, centuries-old documents in Sanskrit (the classical language of India and Hinduism) prove that aliens from outer space visited India. There is… a mass of fascinating information about flying machines, even fantastic science fiction weapons, that can be found in translations of the Vedas (scriptures), Indian epics, and other ancient Sanskrit text…" (Nikhil Shantala, http://nishantala.com/2011/02/05/were-hindu-gods-none-but-ancient-aliens/).*

Giants (*Nephilim*) Mentioned in Your Bible

Numerous civilizations predict in their writings the imminent return of the giants. What are these giants, described in the Bible as *nephilim*, and what do they have to do with you?

I realize that anyone who speaks about giants and aliens is considered a conspiracy theorist, and that a strong bias exists against what you are about to read. The truth, however, is that giants are mentioned in multiple places in the Bible. Genesis 6:4 mentions these giants, and Numbers 13:33 talks about them. Jesus warned that the last days would be just like the days of Noah (Mat. 24:37), and we know that in Noah's days giants roamed the earth.

In the original, conceptual Hebrew, aliens are also mentioned and described as being not from this world. We aren't speaking of people from another country, which is one of the meanings of the word in Hebrew. What people don't understand is that the Hebrew language has words with vast, multifaceted meanings, some which present a description of the humanoid creatures created by the false creator Satan by genetic manipulation.

One of my friends has two friends who were deployed in Afghanistan, two friends who don't know each other but who told him the same story. They both encountered giants in the mountains there, but the government didn't want these facts to be known.

Have you ever wondered why we have so many stories in our culture, and every other culture on earth, about giants, UFOs, castles in the sky that floated around with all sorts of beings in them, and even strange creatures like gargoyles ("gourish," from the Hebrew *guhr*?), monsters, and such? Were these stories fact or fiction? Did you know that every religion on earth acknowledges giants?

The Bible says these stories are fact. It tells us their root purpose, their designer, and their destiny. The Bible even prophesies the return of the giants.

Have you noticed that science books don't say anything about giants? Anthropology books also don't talk about giants, even though four thousand skeletons have been found, ranging in height from about ten feet all the way up to thirty-six feet. Some are identified as having six fingers and six toes (2 Sam. 21:20).

We can see in the Greek language that giants are mentioned in Revelation 9:14–16, during the wrath of God. It should be noted that the horsemen are the first four seals that appear when the seal is broken. A horse is a beast of the field. The four messengers (the meaning of the word "angels") are the four horsemen, or four generals who are genetically altered.

The Greek word translated "horsemen" doesn't properly translate into English. It implies the shape of a man but with the strength and height of a standing horse on two legs. It can also mean a genetically-engineered giant. These giants are currently bound or in prison, and they will soon be released to destroy a third of the earth.

Some of the mentions of giants and aliens in the Bible aren't as obvious as others, yet the word "foreigner" can have various meanings. Foreign gods are mentioned.

In fact, we see the end-time beast in Europe having the help of a foreign god (Dan. 11:39). That foreign god can include, in the original language, an alien in the sense of a humanoid watcher. After all, Satan produced these beings genetically to fight God. Why would he not use them again, bringing them back to be part of his forces to defeat God in the last days?

Most people have no idea to what degree aliens could be involved in end-time prophecy. Nor do they realize what effect the DNA of these Satan-produced creatures has had on them.

The truth is that you have been polluted spiritually and even physically by Satan's deception and by the giant DNA he has produced in you. You need to be cleansed. And God has the cleansing solution you need.

Virgins, Wake Up and Rest in God's Sabbath

As we have seen, virtually the whole church has been lulled to sleep, in part by being inebriated with the wine of the false doctrines of the universal church. The midnight cry will soon come, and is indeed already sounding, and it will soon be time for the virgins to wake up. In His delay, Jesus is mercifully giving us all time to repent.

He is even calling, after virtually two millennia of deception, for His bride to come back to Him by meeting Him on His day, one of His methods for sanctifying His end-time bride. The letters of the Hebrew word *Shabbat* signify a return to the covenant and the cross of Jesus. He wants His bride to be pure in every way, including being free from the pollution of the giant DNA and the corresponding perversion and compromise that has infiltrated the church.

How can we be fully cleansed unless we meet with the Sanctifier, the Holy One (*Yahovah Makkadesh*, as He calls Himself when referring to the sign of His end-time people) on the Sabbath day? (Ex. 31:13) Those who want the full cleansing will meet for their weekly wash in holiness on God's holy day. They will take the Passover and take regular communion so that the blood of Jesus can cleanse them from the unholy DNA they received from Satan's world.

The giants weren't allowed on the ark, since they were evil and had no mates. In the same way, God doesn't want unholy DNA in the ones

He will rapture to be with their Bridegroom Jesus in the last days. They will be holy in spirit, soul, and *body* (1 Thes. 5:23), or at least in the process of purification.

We can only achieve that purity by God's grace. Jesus will empower us to put things in the right order, allowing our souls and bodies to be led by the Holy Spirit, the Sanctifier, in our spirits.

Those whom aliens have abducted are numerous, and they are the ones even our website's most Spirit-filled bloggers have had challenges trying to help. I pray that as you hear their pleas for help, you will not treat them as crazy but have compassion on them and pray for them.

UFOs and Alien Abductions

Facebook was abuzz when a number of our bloggers spread the word that we were creating a post on UFOs and the trauma of alien abductions. Many who have kept these frightful experiences to themselves all these years have opened up and shared the stories that brought them ridicule rather than help.

Ellias wrote: "My wife and I were driving through the mountains when we got buzzed by a UFO. On their second pass over us, my wife suddenly developed heart pains. The third pass over us resulted in a massive heart attack of which she did not survive. My wife never had any heart troubles in her life. She wasn't even frightened by their presence. Why would they do such a thing?"

Henry wrote: "At the end of World War II, I saw a UFO just before leaving Germany. It was about ten meters by thirty meters. It hung over a research center for about twenty minutes, then it just disappeared. The research center was said to be doing time travel research. Do you think that it was a time ship sent to pick up evidence of its work with the Nazis? And will it return before Jesus gets back?"

David shared this: "I have seen nine UFOs so far in my life. All of them were close enough that I knew they weren't balloons or earth-made planes. The first one and the last two were seen just east of Vegreville. I think they may have been following some grid, looking for something. I do not trust the authorities so I have never reported these sightings officially. I do not understand why the authorities are working against the truth."

Oscar wrote: "Until 2006, I always thought that people with UFO sightings were smoking something illegal. Then on my way to Camrose I was buzzed twice by what can only be described as a flying saucer. The paint was burnt off the hood and cab of the truck."

Meeshka shared this comment: "In Russia, I was able to see spacecraft three times. Each time they appeared, I felt a tormenting fear and a desire to destroy coming from them. I do not like UFOs."

Boyd related this: "I have seen UFOs twice now. Once in Phoenix and the other time was just south of Winnipeg. Both times I was amazed at how many people were there to see it up close and were denying what they saw. There were hundreds of excuses to justify what they saw. How can so many people be so afraid of the truth?"

Donald shared some of the consequences of seeing UFOs: "In 1999, I reported a UFO that I saw land behind the governor's mansion. The governor invited the aliens into the mansion and talked with them for over an hour. I was then institutionalized for ten years, where I got electric shock treatment, two broken legs for attempting to escape, and endured days of torture at a time. God bless America, the land of the free."

Ken continued in the same vein: "I reported several UFO sightings that I reported to the government. They called them weather balloons, yet they confiscated my digital recorder and cancelled my credit cards until I agreed on tape that the sighting was a lie. How can they get away with such horrible abuse, with theft and with constant lying?"

Dean shared a series of amazing comments: "On July 24, 2011, at about 10:55 p.m., on a farm north of Alberta Beach, we saw a strange craft hovering over the barn. We were too afraid to go out there to see what was going on. About ten minutes later, the UFO flies away at great speeds and no sound. Six of my cousin's cows were gone. They had been locked in the barn because of the bugs. Why would they steal all his cows?"

A half-hour later, he followed with this: "Do you want to hear something weird? My cousin just phoned and told me that a man in a U.S. military uniform drove onto his farm and offered him six replacement cows if he wouldn't publish any information on what happened. He signed the form. But what does the U.S. military have to do with UFOs?"

Dean got this answer: "More than likely these cows were taken for food for the prisoners in the craft, but they have also been known to be taken to experiment on as well."

A pastor reported on his congregation of two hundred: "A quick check through church records has shown that four people reported seeing UFOs within the last seven months..."

Ronald's grandmother had the best answer to aliens: "All of my family have seen UFOs. We even saw a woman abducted at Sylvan Lake, Alberta. Our grandmother told us from the time we were small to say, 'Evil ones, be gone in the name of Jesus, for the blood of Jesus is against you.' It has always caused them to leave us alone and fly away immediately. We have learned not to fear them, even though our grandmother warned us that they are very cruel and very evil."

That grandma knew what she was talking about!

All Abductees Can't Be Lying

Even more comments came in about abductions, like this one from Yolanda: "Myself and four friends were all abducted in 1994. All of us have cancer in the third rib down from the collarbone on the right side. Both the police and doctors call this a coincidence, and say that it proves nothing. Do you think the police are paid to act stupid on such things?"

Alex wrote: "My life has been ruined because of these UFO abductions. I lost the hearing in my right ear and the sight in my right eye because of something they did. The doctors do not know what caused it or how to heal it. I really hate these aliens."

Doctors were also involved in Teressa's experience: "My mom has been abducted twice and I have been abducted once. We were both left with scars and lumps under the skin that the doctors are afraid to take out. We both agree that we were left with the impression that these aliens are very evil."

Scott's experience made him consider suicide: "I was abducted twice that I know of for sure. When I was thirteen and again when I turned nineteen. Both times I was sexually abused and had needles withdraw fluids from different areas of my body. They didn't seem to care about the pain they were putting me through. The last abduction was the worst because they put something in the back of my skull. I have had blurry vision ever since it was installed. I have considered killing myself to stop the pain."

Raj commented: "Six people from the next town were abducted by a UFO. About one hundred people saw this event, yet no news is coming out about this abduction. All pictures that have been attempted to be posted have been removed within the hour. What does this hiding the truth mean?"

Raj added this: “I have seen three UFOs in the last four years. At first I thought I was seeing things, until I got within fifty feet of the ship. At that time I realized that the other ships were real. My skin got burned when the ship took off.”

Lola related some of the trauma of abductions: “Yes, alien abduction is possible and does happen. I have seen my friend grabbed right out of the car in front of me. She has had trouble remembering things ever since it happened. X-rays show several metal chips in her brain and in the spinal cord at the back of her neck.”

Norra shared her pain: “In 1992, I was abducted while on vacation in Mexico. I was twenty-three at the time. They stole my ovaries. It has been a living hell ever since then. Severe crippling pain that nothing seems to relieve [and] the loss of my husband because he did not want a sterile wife. And even the rejection of my family…”

John related his loss and disbelief: “My cousin was abducted about two years ago. When we found her, she had been left beside a road bleeding from left breast to her belly button. When the doctors examined her, they found that a lung and kidney had been removed. The police reported it as self-mutilation. She died about three months later. Why do officials lie so much when it comes to UFOs?”

Darryl vividly describes what he witnessed: “A horrible fear takes hold of a person who has been abducted. For me the pushing of metal objects into my skull and private parts was bad enough. But I had to watch the other person in their examination room being systematically taken apart while they were still alive and conscious. They were pumping something into his veins that seemed to be keeping him conscious and alive as they removed his insides. It reminded me of German war experiments on the Jews. Have we been already taken over?”

One of our inspired bloggers answered: “Darryl, we would like to suggest that you use the blood of Jesus in the communion service to deactivate these metal objects and dissolve them harmlessly. It is very necessary for you to turn your helplessness over to Jesus and your futile attempts to save yourself and the disemboweled man. This new moon would be a most wonderful time to do this. Then it would be very prudent to have a trauma communion for the healing of your brain and mind. UFOs were heavily involved in *all the activities during Hitler's time.* Your victimization is also a turnover item for the new moon. As long as the saints continue to pray and use God's Word against the beast and its government, they have not yet taken over."

Brent unveils the cruelty of the cover-up: "They say that confession is good for the soul. They lie, especially when you talk to the government. They do not represent the will of the people. They do not act for the benefit of the people. So who are they representing? I saw a UFO land south of the Clear Lake Military Base. I was assaulted when I reported it to the base gate. I was told that I never saw anything and if I kept talking I would never see anything again. Who is in control of this country anyway? Are the aliens from the UFOs in control of everything?"

Cover-ups and Biblical Revelations

These are only a few of the comments we've received. While it is reported that about ten percent of North Americans have seen UFOs, the government and the media would like us to believe that these people are mentally unsound. But too many military officials and astronauts have given testimonies for all these eyewitness accounts to be made up.

It has become increasingly easy to see that the lies are in the government camp rather than in the mouths of these eyewitnesses. What may surprise you more is that God spoke of these aliens in His Word. His plan to call only a few in this age was aided by the cryptic way in which He wrote the Bible (Isa. 28:11–13), using ancient, foreign languages that He knew in advance would be mistranslated.

Those who believed and obeyed all of God's commandments would understand and put the pieces of the Bible puzzle together (Ps. 111:10). God would anoint His servants to understand the Word through the original languages to teach the saints (Eph. 4:11–13; John 16:13).

Few understand that the Hebrew has multiple meanings, far beyond what James Strong understood, such as in the word "host" or "hosts of heaven" (Gen. 2:1; Deut. 4:19), *tsaba.* One of its meanings is "those who live on solar systems that are not that of earth." The truth comes out of the Hebrew! It may not have been translated, but it is still the Word of God.

Deuteronomy 4:19 refers to more than astrology. God warned against the worship of His hosts, the hosts that are humanoid watchers, and their impressive UFOs, the stars, or the angels.

In verse 20, He explains the need of His people to be genetically pure. He had brought them out of the iron (*barzel*, in Hebrew) furnace, crucible, or melting pot of Egypt. [34] We are called to be of golden character and pedigree, not of the lowly iron used for war.

Many witnesses have testified that they've received alien DNA when abducted, and alien and giant DNA are products of mankind's perversion into humankind. This perversion can only be broken by Jesus' blood as we take repeated communions. God wouldn't have put these warnings in His Word if it weren't to be a problem, and it's no coincidence that this concept followed the verse about the hosts of heaven.

Several passages dealing with aliens are found in the book of Lamentations, a prophecy about the end-time believing nations ("daughter of Zion," Lam. 2:1), especially in the time of tribulation.

God foretells (Lam. 4:2) that believers at the end would be "regarded as earthen [human] jars, the work of a [not *the*] potter's hands!" In clearer

34 *Bar means "seed" or "seed of his father," and zel refers to a false creator god. The Hebrew word kuwr, for furnace, also means "to have mixed genes not of mankind, a people not created pure by God."*

terms, they would become polluted in their DNA because of rampant sexual sin (Lam. 4 6; 2 Tim. 3:1–9), and some would unite sexually with the humanoid watchers in UFOs. Not all believers know their identity in Jesus enough to know how to resist these attacks.

Aliens in the Bible!

The original Hebrew of the following verses reveals an alien connection:

> They hunted our steps so that we could not walk in our streets; our end drew near, our days were finished for our end had come. Our pursuers were swifter than the eagles of the sky; they chased us on the mountains, they waited in ambush [UFOs can make themselves invisible] for us in the wilderness. (Lam. 4:18–19)

Jeremiah continues his prophecy for the last days: "Our inheritance has been turned over to strangers, our houses to *aliens*" (Lam. 5:2).[35]

Not all aliens mentioned in the Bible are from outer space, but these verses definitely include the UFOs. Their occupants track people they want to abduct for the purpose of extracting their DNA to improve their own, tracking down their victims like the roaring lion that produced them. They think that by stealing mankind's DNA they can obtain the spirit God gave him and thus attain eternal life, or at least harness his energy.

As the above verses state, these craft are swifter than eagles. They have been clocked on radar at three thousand kilometers per hour, and they make ninety-degree turns without stopping.

---

35 *Both Hebrew words for strangers and aliens find their root in nekar, akin to nephilim. Ne signifies those with plant DNA or seeded with plant scent, whereas kar is similar to kuwr, a crucible or mixing pot, humanoids with mixed genes.*

As we have seen, alien spaceships aren't always evil ones. The hosts of heaven God created are beings that are intelligent and have a purpose (Gen. 2:1; Isa. 1:2). In Job 38:32, the chapter that reveals God's end-time secret weapon against the giants, Jesus challenges Job: "Can you lead forth a constellation [*Mazzaroth*, in Hebrew] in its season…?" One of the many meanings of that Hebrew word is "an armada of ships that travels between stars." UFOs are in the Bible, often hidden in the Hebrew.

On our blog, Joseph related his sad experience with UFOs: "My wife has been abducted twice now and both times she came back cut up and in a lot of pain. How do they track a person? Because we have moved eight times and still they found us. She thinks that she will not live through a third attack and abduction. Is it three strikes and you're out when it comes to abductions?"

One of our regular and inspired contributors wrote this in response: "Joseph, a ufologist told me that they track with some sort of chip in the jaw, or it gets attached to the spinal cord. He also said there very, very few people who have ever talked about a fourth encounter… We pray that the blood of Jesus shield you and yours from any further attacks. Seek to use the Word of God against your enemy in accordance to the will of God. It is more powerful than they are."

It is indeed the blood of Jesus that defeats these enemies, and we need the power of the blood more than ever in these last days. Here is a declaration you could use in times of severe attack: "No demon can withstand the power of the blood of Jesus. Satan has no authority or power to form a weapon against His blood. We overcome by the blood of the Lamb and the word of our testimony. We abide in Jesus, our High Tower of Defense. Jesus is our Rearguard. We walk with and in Jesus, and no weapon of Satan can separate Jesus and us. Nothing can break through the blood of Jesus."

What brings forth the need for the blood of Jesus in this end time is the fact that a last days falling away has already begun, even though the major apostasy will occur when the man of sin is revealed (2 Thes. 2:3). Witchcraft and Satanism are growing faster than Christianity by far, and some Christians, due to their disenchantment with the emptiness and falseness of present-day Christianity, have joined their forces.

One of our excellent bloggers, who has much experience in the dark arts, explains why this is: "The first thing that pushes women out of churches and into witchcraft is the number of spells of seduction. Second, the lack of leadership. Third, the amount of lies and lying that they have to put up with, especially in the church. Fourth is the amount of hypocrisy that pastors will speak out to justify disobeying God in order to keep wrong traditions. Fifth is the provable doctrine of demons that has been incorporated into church belief. If you have to worship Satan in the churches, you'll feel comfortable worshipping him directly through witchcraft."

Hunting and Tracking Abductees

While the number may be small, an important phenomenon is also occurring. Some witches who are also prostitutes seek out the humanoid watchers from the UFOs in order to have sex with them, binding their lonely and empty souls to the watchers and/or giants for power and sexual pleasure. The phrase used for their activity in Ezekiel 13:18 can also apply to the humanoids in UFOs:

> Woe to the women who sew magic bands on all wrists and make veils for the heads of persons of every stature to *hunt down lives*! Will you hunt down the lives of My people, but preserve the lives of others for yourselves?

Both the witches and the humanoids hunt down lives. The watchers in UFOs will track down their victims of enslavement, usually with chips placed in the spinal area. As we have seen, one woman moved eight times, unable to elude her captors. Witches and humanoids both seek the light and life energy of mankind. They also claim parts of the bodies they capture as a trophy for their DNA value.

To "preserve the lives [or souls] of others for yourselves" means to use spell attachments to disturb their souls, depriving them of peace and rest, even tormenting them by keeping them enslaved to the spell caster or their demon guardians.

As with the giants who will return before the wrath of God, they sometimes try to attack and abduct believers who don't have their identity in Jesus firmly established. The song fifty years ago about a giant purple people eater reveals Satan's subtlety in influencing our society and preparing them for the *nephilim* and watchers. These giants weren't just part of a song. They existed long ago at the time of the Flood, and they targeted the purple or royal people—the believers. The song says they wanted to be part of a rock band.

Rock music is loud and dulls the senses. The "veils" (Ezek. 13:18) are similar in their purpose. They are principally veils of disorientation that keep people from seeing and hearing what they need to hear and see. Their brains are dulled. This usually starts with spells of seduction that are becoming more and more common. Young people who watch the popular witchcraft movies become victims of these veils, which can quickly become chainmail bonnets and/or spiritual crockpots over their heads if they are Christians who refuse to allow Jesus to change them and bring freedom.

The witches especially work against believers. When they see a zealous person who loves Jesus enter a certain church, they pronounce spells that invoke the demons of panic, such as *Hermes* (also known as

Mercury, the hurry-up, messenger demon), and intimidation to bring on many forms of overload, especially for young, junior pastors, with the goal of causing mental breakdowns.[36]

"For handfuls of barley" (Ezek. 13:19) refers to cheap thrills from a prostitute or a lying priestess who sells lies. The phrase "fragments of bread" indicates being addicted to mind-altering drugs, such as the sexually stimulating speed and crack. Priestesses who lie would sell themselves and be slaves to these addictions. Sexual activity would give them a legal right to bind their partners' souls to themselves or their masters (warlocks or humanoids), and they would be food for those masters. Both witches and humanoids in UFOs can be included in these passages.

In Ezekiel 20 and 21, Jesus declares that He is against these magic bands, bindings, bonds, and false vows and He will tear them off. Anything that ties us to giant DNA can be removed through the body and blood of Jesus, who knew He was coming to die to set us free. No other bondage breaker exists.

Being hunted like birds or flying ones (Ezekiel 13:20) means being picked up for the flesh to be roasted and/or being focused on the skies, curious about and longing for UFOs and the giants as if they were a part of one's destiny—to be saved by them as a substitute for our Savior.

Satan has put a craving for such encounters in our nature, engendered by the power of sin, an entity and an instinct that is activated at conception and which can only be overcome by the power of Jesus. This "sin… crouching at the door" of our hearts (Gen. 4:7) brings seduction, deception, and delusions of salvation other than those realized through Jesus. Our bloggers have even reported pastors who teach rapture by UFOs. The animal DNA that is part of our unbelieving past is responsible for these instincts, which must be turned over to Jesus.

---

36 See "Witchcraft Spell Break-off" in A-Z section at www.freedomchurchofgod.com.

Turning the Pain Over to Jesus

Lucille had much to turn over to Jesus: "Can a person who has been abducted be set free from the nightmares of that abduction? I have been in psychiatric care for five years now and they are a waste of time. I think that I'm worse off now than I could have been if I was never under their care."

She received this excellent answer from another blogger: "Lucille, after much prayer, we were shown that it is your unforgiveness that has created the nightmares. You have not forgiven yourself, nor have you forgiven God for allowing this to happen. Write everything down and then turn each point over to Jesus to deal with on this upcoming new moon. I would also suggest that you ask for the grace of forgiveness to start the process. We bless you with peace to your soul."

Leslie related this: "Ever since I was very small, my mother has said that I am the child of a space creature. She said that she was taken into a spacecraft when she was sixteen years old and a creature made her pregnant. If my father was an alien, what does that make me? Could that explain my extra-long finger and super night vision? And do you know why no one in my mom's family will accept me or acknowledge me?"

An experienced blogger wrote this: "Leslie, you have a lot of things to deal with. The first is the label of being a space child and a bastard. You can reject these and turn them over to Jesus. If you know Jesus, you can turn over the wrong identity and declare that you are a child of God the Father. Second, your mother's abduction and rape, this needs to be turned over, as it tells you that you are worthless and a product of sin. Third, your mom's family, they have cursed you with being the bastard, being unacceptable, and being a disgrace. Turn this over to Jesus and reject their curses in a communion service. And fourth, night vision is not normal for humans. However, long fingers are common in every society. You must turn your rejection of yourself over to Jesus. When you reject your body or any part of it, your body will reject you. Start thanking your Father in Heaven for your life, your purpose, and for the uniqueness that He has given you. Also thank Him for the favor you have with your family. Be blessed with freedom and peace in your heart."

Beverly wrote: "How does a person with this condition [father-hating] deal with an abduction? My dad is very certain that my brother was abducted by aliens. He has never been the same since he went missing for eight hours when he was on a camping trip when he was fourteen years old. Our dad saw a UFO take off from the woods, and he went there and found my brother naked and having numerous cuts upon him."

She received this wise answer from a prayer warrior: "Beverly, from what I understand, your brother would first go into denial and shock. Because when he called for help, no one answered, he would be in unforgiveness and betrayal. If he was camping with your dad, he would associate all his pain towards his dad. Then he would think that everyone betrayed him to the point where everyone was against him and out to get him. He would be as stable as a cat on a hot tin roof. Anger-rage would flare uncontrollably at even the mention of the abduction, because it could not have taken place if he was in charge and control. And finally, he will mock everyone who attempts to help him see past his pain."

If you are reading this and have had an abduction experience, know that in spite of the severity of the trauma, Jesus isn't limited in his ability to help and heal you.

The aliens and giants are a part of Satan's end-time plan to destroy the church and the entire earth. While they aren't the crux of the gospel of the Kingdom of God, they cannot be ignored if we're serious about returning to our Father Love and being the pure Bride of Jesus.

God has given us time to wake up and change. What will we do?

We pray that you'll be able to understand our hard-hitting Appendix II, an account of world history you haven't heard. We believe it can change your past and your future.

Chapter Thirteen:

You've Heard It All Wrong—Learn from Daniel!

If your prophecy diet is the standard fare most Christians gobble up, you've heard it all wrong! And one man who can cut the confusion for you is Daniel, that prophet whose messages were for our time—the last days. Let's learn from Daniel. He didn't understand all God gave him to write, but we can!

Daniel is full of prophecies for this end time. We will treat in the space we have some of the most important.

One of the prophecies of Daniel that came at the expense of diligent fasting and prayer applies to the church today. The archangel Gabriel delivered an astounding prophecy that has many meanings, and several aspects and layers of fulfillment. He called Daniel "highly esteemed," meaning in Hebrew "considered as righteous, holy, beloved, and worthy."

That's how our Father also sees us because of Jesus. The reason some of these conditional prophecies have not yet come true is that God's people have had a hard time seeing themselves as God sees them, as God saw Daniel.

Gabriel revealed that seventy weeks had been "decreed for your people and your holy city [Jerusalem]" (Dan. 9:24). So, the first fulfillment applies to the people of Israel, which includes all believers, since that is what "Israel" means. Most have overlooked this part of the prophecy, and understandably so, since this is the prophecy of the coming of the Messiah, exactly on time at His first coming.

The city of Jerusalem and what happens there is another line of fulfillment. The same verse speaks of a time when sin will end and the atonement of Jesus will begin the process that will eventually bring in "everlasting righteousness" for all.

The translators, however, added the word *place* in italics after the phrase "and to anoint the most holy." It should not be there. God is speaking of a time when the latter rain in the last days will bring reformation and revival to the church—*if* the church does its part. God prophesies that we are to be anointed in the fullness of the Holy Spirit.

A foreign leader ordered the rebuilding of Jerusalem twice in history. The first was in 457 B.C. Seventy weeks is equal to 490 days, and using the day-for-a-year principle (Ezek. 4:6; Numb. 14:34), that means 490 years. But the prophecy said that after seven weeks (forty-nine years) and sixty-two weeks (434 years), a total of 483 years, the Messiah would come. And in 27 A.D. Jesus did come into His ministry, exactly 483 years later. In the Bible code, the name *Yashua* appears every twenty-six letters, so it is confirmed that the prophecy involves Jesus.

Shortly after that period of 483 years, or the last period of sixty-two weeks of years (or 434 years), "the Messiah will be cut off and have nothing…" (Dan. 9:25). He was crucified, losing all His worldly possessions on His last day on earth before dying for us.

The same thing began to happen for God's chosen people, physically and spiritually speaking, sixty-two weeks of years, or 434 years after the second order to rebuild Jerusalem, in 1542. Since 1976, the church has been increasingly affected by poverty and loss of zeal.

After seven years of construction, a Turkish leader gave the order to finish the temple's rebuilding in 1542. God's people, principally the lead nation, America, began in 1976, under the leadership of a weak president, to lose the prestige they had previously enjoyed. Foreign nations no longer feared to speak evil of the United States. Even Hitler had hesitated to rail against America, but now she began to lose the pride of her power. Iran defied the U.S. by taking large numbers of hostages. The blessings of Abraham began to be lost.

Christians (spiritual Israel) were also cut off from God's blessings beginning at that time. The Messiah and those who belong to Him would be cut off just as He was. Christians began to fall into a lackadaisical slump, lacking in zeal and overall prosperity. Physical and spiritual poverty have affected the church as a whole since that time.

Gentiles to Regain Power in the End Time

"Seven periods of times [or seven times]" were to pass over the Gentile king who ruled Babylon (Dan. 7:16). The Book of Revelation, when compared with Daniel 12:7, shows that a time, times, and a half a time are equivalent to three and a half years, so a "time" is equal to a year in prophecy. Seven years would be seven times the biblical year of 360 days, or 2,520 days.

Applying the day-for-a-year principle, that brings us to 2,520 years. As Nebuchadnezzar lost his power for seven times (seven years), so the Gentile nations would only come into full power over Israel (the U.S. and the Commonwealth more than Judah, modern-day nation of Israel) 2,520 years after the fall of Babylon in 539 B.C. That would bring us to 1982.

Because of what Satan did in inspiring pride in King Nebuchadnezzar, Satan lost the power he could have had in using the Gentile nations to dominate Israel. He lost the right to sit on his earthly throne until the end of these 2,520 years. Then he would be able to wield power over the believing nations through the pagan nations. Those nations would trample down Jerusalem until Jesus' return ends the "times of the Gentiles" (Luke 21:24).

In 1976, Israel (notably America) began to lose the blessings of Abraham and thus looked to the Gentile nations for protection. So, God had to allow the Gentiles to be the protectors of the U.S. and the Commonwealth. Behind the scenes, major steps in European unity and power came in 1982, opening the door for Gentile protection rather than God's protection of His physical people.

Apart from those hidden events, in a general way the U.S. began to lose God's protection after 1982 and rely more and more on the Gentile nations for protection, even in economic terms, since the national debt began to soar. The "times of the Gentiles" is essentially the time at which the non-believing nations take over the land of the believers—the U.S., the Commonwealth, and the small nation of Israel. More and more, America is betraying its ally Israel in favor of the Palestinians.

Luke 21:24 says, "Jerusalem will be trampled underfoot by the Gentiles until the times of the Gentiles are fulfilled." Those times will be fulfilled or ended with the return of Jesus.

God gave the modern Israelite nations the blessings of Abraham, and they have ruled since the early 1800s, dominating the world. But from 1976 to 1982, we saw the beginning of their demise. The times of the Gentiles came in, which will culminate in their treading down Jerusalem and the return of Jesus to stop the Gentile domination. He is the Stone that was cut out that destroyed the statue of Daniel 2.

The "people of the prince who is to come will destroy the city and the sanctuary" (Dan. 9:26). Satan is that prince who used other princes or rulers, in this case the Romans, to destroy Jerusalem and its temple in 70 A.D.

Titus and other Roman leaders were types of the coming beast power in Europe, along with a great church that will come against Jerusalem in the end time. The armies of the Gentiles will tread down Jerusalem.

Before we look at the connection with Daniel 8, we shall look at the last part of Daniel 9:26: "Its [his] end will come with a flood [of armies]; even to the end there will be war; desolations are determined [that phrase, in Hebrew, indicates terrorism]."

The Challenge for End-time Believers

Daniel 9:27 applies several ways. Probably the most important way is that Jesus made

> a firm covenant [the New Covenant in His blood—the ninth biblical covenant] with the many [all mankind who would be given the opportunity to know Jesus, either in this life or in a future resurrection, and who would choose to follow Him] for one week [a period of seven years], but in the middle of the week[37] he will put a stop to sacrifice and grain offering…

Jesus was crucified or "cut off" (Dan. 9:26) after half of that seven-year period, or three and a half years. Since the prophecy has already referred not only to Jesus but also to those who have Jesus dwelling in them (the "most holy" of Dan. 9:24), and since Jesus rose and ascended

37 *While the week is seven years in fulfillment, Jesus was actually cut off in the midst of a literal week, Wednesday, the Passover day that year, to rise three and a half days later at the waning moments of the weekly Sabbath (Luke 23:54; Mat. 12:40).*

to heaven, only to live inside believers through the Holy Spirit, it is those holy ones who are called to fulfill the rest of the prophecy.

What a challenge for us believers today! God has thus prophesied that, subject to our free will, He will cause a powerful reformation and revival in those of the church who truly desire to be the spotless Bride of Jesus. He wants to "anoint the most holy," to cause the light and glory of Jesus to rise on believers in the last days (Isa. 60:1–3; Acts 2:17).

God's perfect will was for that revival to occur in the last three and a half years of the days of sorrow that preceded the Tribulation, which we are now in at the time of this writing. But since the church wasn't ready to prepare itself, God had to honor our free will. The nonchalant and fearful Laodicean attitude has hindered the church.

We need to call on the spirit of repentance so that we can move forward to accomplish this prophecy. For the prophecies of Acts 2 and Joel 2 to become reality, for the fullness of the prophesied end-time outpouring of the Holy Spirit to occur, the church must begin to heed God's prophetic warnings and wake up.

Jesus does not want to have to do the work Himself (Isa. 59:16). The prophecies are conditional, so they allow for that sad possibility. The question is, will we allow it?

The time is short. The time of sleeping and coasting is over. Evil is overtaking the world, and God is saying to each of us, "Who will stand up for me against evildoers? Who will take his stand for me against those who do wickedness?" (Ps. 94:16) It is certainly not by wallowing in sin that we resist wickedness. God warns us to be rid of uncleanness (Isa. 52:11), to rouse ourselves and rise spiritually (Isa. 51:17).

For those who are waking up, open your spiritual eyes to understand the amazing prophecy of Daniel 8.

The Antichrist—Only One of Four End-time Despots

Daniel 8 presents the historical type of another man from the last branches of the Greco-Macedonian Empire that precedes the Roman Empire, a man named Antiochus IV, or Epiphanes. He prefigures one of the rulers who will cause the famous "abomination of desolation," the end-time Syrian *mahdi* (Arab Antichrist), the "one who makes desolate" (Dan. 9:27; 11:31). Whereas Antiochus sacrificed swine flesh on the altar of the temple, the mere presence of the "son of perdition" (or beast) in the temple will also be an abomination and a blasphemy. The Antichrist will simply add to the degree of abomination.

The Antichrist, prefigured by Antiochus (who was indeed ruler over Syria), will almost certainly come once again out of Syria, or its modern equivalent, as the Arab messiah. This Arab leader will probably do the same as Antiochus by sacrificing pig's blood on the temple altar to mock the Jews.

The Antichrist will make the sanctuary unclean and give legal right to the beast, the man of sin or perdition, to establish his headquarters in Jerusalem and specifically in the temple, claiming he is God. He can then claim God's city and put his throne on the holy mountain of God.

Daniel 11:44–45 describes that time. The many that the beast will "destroy and annihilate" will include the Antichrist, which is why we only see the beast and the false prophet thrown later into the lake of fire (Rev. 19:20). Both the Antichrist and the false Jesus will already be dead when that event occurs.

While we hear talk of a new world order, several groups of nations will rival each other in seeking to control that world order. The beast, or European power, will rule one-third of the world, flexing its military and economic muscles. The Germans and other Europeans have a power base in South America, with many of the Nazis who went underground after World War II having gone to that area. Other British colonies around the world could also join with the beast power as they stand in awe of his signs and wonders.

It appears more and more that technology, "a god whom his fathers did not know" (Dan. 11:38), will help the beast to succeed. Chips inserted into the hand and forehead will likely mirror the main mark of the beast, Sunday and false holiday worship (Rev. 13:16; Ex. 13:9).

We do read of a time after the beast's wound has been healed. As he comes back to life with a new personality, the whole world will stand in awe of him (Rev. 13:7–8, 14–16). Resistance will also come, however, from the other world power blocs. We see the "king of the South" resisting this northern beast power in Daniel 11. The Bible also speaks of resistance from the northeast (Dan. 11:44), a power bloc called "the kings from the east" (Rev. 16:12), which will exert its strength much later during the wrath of God in that last prolonged year of 390 days.

The "king of the South" (Dan. 11:40), or Arab Antichrist, will oppose this beast, or King of the North. This southern king will oppose the beast militarily and economically, and is already beginning to formulate such an opposition. This Arab bloc will constitute the second third of the world area that the Antichrist will rule, while the Asian bloc of nations will rule the other third.

America and the Commonwealth nations will be neutralized by the European beast power. America (Manasseh) is no longer the military powerhouse it once was, and plans to cut defense spending would make it only a regional power, a power soon to be destroyed by a German-led (descendants of ancient Assyria, Isaiah 10:5) Europe.

Solar flares and/or cyber-attacks and electromagnetic pulse attacks will possibly be the factors that make North America a sitting duck for Europe to plunder. A return to nineteenth-century technology, by bringing an end to electric power, would render helpless a people who rely on our modern system. They would be easy prey for foreign enemies, notably the powerful beast allied with the false prophet and false Christ.

The rise of these evil powers has been fueled by the rise of witchcraft and Satanism. Moreover, the shedding of innocent blood since 1972 through legalized abortion has been a blood sacrifice preparing the way for their evil deeds.

Jesus said, "For many will come in My name, saying, 'I am the Christ,' and will mislead many" (Mat. 24:5). This can be understood two ways: many will say Jesus is the Christ, and many others will say, "I am Jesus the Messiah." The four end-time leaders will all claim they are Jesus to some degree, or in the case of the Antichrist, superior to Jesus.

Four Men—Not One

Four men, not one, will come on the scene to deceive in this end time. They are the *false prophet*, *the false Christ* (false Jesus), *the beast*, and *the Arab Antichrist.*

The *false prophet* claims to be the "vicar of Christ," meaning Jesus' replacement on the earth. The way is being prepared by kingmakers behind the scenes who have no qualms with poisoning those leaders they don't want for this end-time evil.

The *false Christ* and the false prophet give allegiance to *the beast* and cause his mark to be taken by people. But the beast will ultimately destroy the "harlot" (the false church led by the false prophet) (Rev. 17:16). Satan always uses competition among those he chooses as his instruments.

The Antichrist, or Arab Messiah, claims to be greater than Jesus and is opposed to Him, while the others essentially claim to *be* Jesus.

Confusion reigns in the world of prophecy teaching. Prophecy proponents can only see one Antichrist coming on the scene. Some are now declaring that the Antichrist is Arab rather than a European leader. They're right that the Antichrist will be Arab, but they're wrong to believe this man will be *the* Antichrist or *the* only end-time despot. The beast is not the Antichrist, and the Antichrist is not the beast. One is the King of the North and the other the King of the South.

Daniel 8 describes this Syrian leader and his abomination. History records that Antiochus sacked the temple, erecting an altar to Zeus, and on December 25, 168 B.C., he offered a pig to Zeus on the altar of God, causing the Maccabean Revolt.[38]

The prophecy of the 2,300 days in Daniel 8 begins with the clash between the goat and the ram—that is, Alexander the Great and the Persian king Darius. The battle that opened all Asia to the Greeks occurred in 334 B.C., at the river Granicus.

As in Genesis, even though Daniel refers to the daily morning and evening sacrifices, a morning and an evening equal one day, or 2,300 days. This had a literal day fulfillment of six years and 110 days in actual accomplishment.[39]

---

38 *Al Maxey. The Silent Centuries. Accessed: May 31, 2012 (http://www.zianet.com/maxey/InterLst.htm).*
See section entitled "Greek Rule" as it relates to the Ptolemies and Seleucids (332–168 B.C.).

39 *This was the period of apostasy (rebellion) that began in 171 B.C. and ended in 165 B.C. with the cleansing and restoration of the*

The day-for-a-year principle, however, also applies (Ezek. 4:6; Num. 14:34). The same length of time *may* also apply in the end time, but we must consider another exciting *possibility.*

The angel Gabriel explains to Daniel the basic meaning of this vision of 2,300 days in Daniel 8:20–22. The ram represented the Medo-Persian Empire, the goat the kingdom of Greece, and the large horn its first king (Alexander the Great), out of which four kingdoms would arise. This prophecy was fulfilled. Alexander's forces—composed of thirty thousand soldiers—moved so rapidly that Daniel 8:5 says they traveled "without touching the ground."

After the death of Alexander by fever in Babylon, the kingdom was divided between Alexander's four top generals, with Seleucus obtaining Syria and Babylon in the east, Cassander ruling Greece and Macedonia in the west, Ptolemy ruling in Egypt to the south, and Lysimachus ruling over Thrace, Cappadocia, and northern Asia Minor in the north.

A Decisive Battle

In the Greco-Persian battles, Adam Clarke, in his commentary, confirms the violent and unusual victory of the Greeks over the Persian army at the river Granicus. This victory occurred in 334 B.C., so that's the beginning mark of the prophecy, which you can read in Daniel 8:9–14.

It is commonly known that the "little horn" was Antiochus Epiphanes, the king of Syria. Although the Romans subdued all four Greek dominions, the little horn came out of the Seleucid horn because it's seen as expanding to the east and to the south, meaning that it had already conquered the northern and western horns. This occurred in 65 B.C. when Rome conquered Syria.

Temple in Jerusalem by the revolt led by Judas Maccabeus.

This means that the little horn could apply both to the Syrian leader (Antichrist) and to the Roman leader (the beast) in alliance with the false church, since in history Rome swallowed up the little horn that was Syria. In any case, they both defile the temple in Jerusalem, one leading the way for the other.

> Antiochus' empire spread across the whole Middle East, and he hated the Jewish religion. Says the *Critical, Experimental Commentary* by Jamieson, Fausett and Brown:
>
> ...Greece, with all its refinement, produces the first—ie., the Old Testament *Antichrist*... He wished to substitute Zeus Olympius for Jehovah at Jerusalem... Identifying himself with Jupiter, his aim was to make his own worship universal (cf. v.25 with ch.11:36): so mad was he in this that he was called Epimanes (maniac) instead of Epiphanes (illustrious). None of the previous world rulers... had systematically opposed the Jews' religious worship.... He is the forerunner of the final Antichrist, standing in the same relation to the first advent of Christ that Antichrist does to His second coming.[40]
>
> This commentary continues the story of Antiochus:
>
> ...He not only opposes God's ancient people, but God Himself. The daily sacrifice—one lamb was offered in the morning and another in the evening (Ex. 29:38,39)—was taken away—by Antiochus.[41]
>
> The first book of Maccabees tells us the details:

---

40 *Robert Jamieson, Andrew Robert Faussett, and David Brown. (Grand Rapids, MI: Eerdmans, 1999). Volume 1, p. 427.*

41 *Ibid.*

> The King forbad burnt offerings and sacrifice and drink offerings in the temple, and [ordered] that they should sacrifice swine's flesh... Now in the fifteenth day of the month Kislev [December 25], they set up the abomination of desolation upon the altar... and they did sacrifice upon the idol-altar, which was upon the altar of God. (1 Macc. 1:20,24,54,59, KJV)

The first book of Maccabees relates that Israel made a covenant with the heathen, forsaking God's covenant and circumcision (1 Macc. 1:11–16). Isaiah 28 speaks of a future "covenant of death" the tiny nation of Israel will make with the Gentile nations, a covenant that will backfire on them.

The Abomination of Desolation

In 168 B.C., Antiochus plundered and desecrated the Temple in Jerusalem. Werner Keller describes the setting up the worship of Olympian Zeus in God's temple and the death penalty for keeping the Sabbath and circumcision as "the first thoroughgoing religious persecution in history"[42]

The cutting off of the sacrifices lasted three and a half years (see also Dan. 9:27 and 12:7). Josephus declares in *The Jewish War* that Antiochus "put a stop to the constant practice of offering a daily sacrifice of expiation for *three years and six months...*"[43]

The period of the abomination of desolation itself—when the Temple itself was defiled—lasted exactly three years, from 168 to 165 B.C.

---

42 Werner Keller. The Bible as History (London, UK: Hodder & Stoughton, 1980), p. 315.

43 Josephus. Wars of the Jews. Book I, Chapter 1, 1.

Josephus confirmed this and recognized that "this desolation came to pass according to the prophecy of Daniel, which was given four hundred and eight years before..."[44]

But the vision was principally for the time of the end (Dan. 8:17). A day is often a year in prophetic terms, so this brings us forward 2,300 years to the time of the end. So, 2,300 years from 334 B.C. is 1967 A.D.

Gene Faulstich, in his book *History, Harmony and Daniel,* writes that the he-goat running into the ram was fulfilled when "Alexander routed the Persian armies after crossing the Helespont in 334 B.C."[45]

He continues:

> The timespan given for the fulfillment of the Temple is 2,300 evening-mornings or days. In the interpretation of prophecy, it is normal for a day to become a year. Since the prophecy concerns itself with a Greek defilement of the Temple, it is interesting that from Alexander's defeat of the Persians, who gave to the Jews permission to rebuild their Temple, to the Jewish capture of the Temple site is precisely 2,300 years. Alexander met Darius III the Medo-Persian monarch at Hellespont in 334 B.C. on the seventh of June. The Persian army was destroyed and Darius fled, leaving some of his family behind. According to Plutarch, Alexander was about to engage Darius at the end of the month of Artemisius. The next month (Daesius) was a month that was avoided by the Greeks for it was thought to be a bad omen. Alexander caused it to become a second Artemisius, thereby avoiding the possible engagement at the wrong time. In 334 B.C., the month of Artemisius extended from May 9 through

44 *Josephus. Antiquities of the Jews. Book XII, Chapter 7, 6.*

45 *E.W. Faulstich. History, Harmony & Daniel: A New Computerized Evaluation (Chronology Books, 1988), p. 93.*

> June 7. Spring was late that year, so Alexander chose not to make it a leap year by adding one month as should have been. It seems more than coincidence that the Syrians should open fire on the Jews on April 7, 1967, which was 120,000 weeks after Darius met Alexander. The Temple mount was taken exactly 2300 years (solar) to the day, after the confrontation at Hellespont, on June 7, A.D. 1967. The prophesied battle between the he-goat (Alexander) and the ram (Darius III) took place on June 7, 334 B.C. Exactly 2300 years later on June 7, A.D. 1967 the Jews took control of their Temple site again.... Artemisius 28, 334 B.C. (Alexander vs. Darius) + 2300 years = Sivan 28, A.D. 1967 (Six Day War). At the same time, the king of Greece was overthrown, and Greece was no longer a monarchy. In April of A.D. 1967, military units seized the royal palace, government offices and leaders, and radio stations. Three army officers then took the power of a military dictatorship, thus ending the kings of Greece.[46]

Faulstich explains that the Greek Kingdom spanned 2,300 years—from Alexander, the first king, to the last king, Constantine II, who went into exile to Italy in April 1967.

Israeli 1967 Blitzkrieg—Dramatic Fulfillment of Prophecy

There's more. In 1967, the state of Israel defeated the combined armies and air forces of the surrounding Arab nations in only six days. In less than three hours, the Israeli air force destroyed three hundred Egyptian aircraft on the ground, losing only a few planes. Israel seized the West Bank from Jordanian forces, as well as the Old City of Jerusalem. In

46 *Ibid., pp. 96–97.*

135 A.D., Emperor Hadrian had expelled the Jews from the old city. In 1967, Israel cried out in victory, *"Har ha'bayit b'yadenu!"*—"The Temple Mount is in our hands!"

The Jews thus seized the Old City of Jerusalem and the holy Temple Mount, where two temples had been constructed. In 70 A.D., Roman armies under Titus and Vespasian had conquered the Jews and destroyed the Temple. The 1967, victory prepared the way for the rebuilding of the temple.

Moshe Dayan cried out, "We have returned to our holiest of holy places, never to be parted from it again." A small nation of a mere two million people had conquered armies from Arab nations with a population of over 140 million.

Some believe we are not in the time of the end. But this prophecy was given to Daniel for the time of the end, proof that we are in that time now.

The days of Antiochus were only a foreshadowing of the Great Tribulation. In *Antiquities of the Jews,* Josephus adds this:

> ...but the best men, and those of the noblest souls, did not regard him... on which account they every day underwent *great miseries* [forerunner of the Great Tribulation] and bitter torments: for they were whipped with rods, and their bodies were torn to pieces, and were crucified, while they were still alive and breathed: they also strangled those women and their sons whom they had circumcised, as the king had appointed, hanging their sons about their necks as they were upon the crosses. And if there were any sacred book of the law found, it was destroyed...[47]

47 Josephus. Antiquities of the Jews. Book XII, Chapter 5, 4.

These were beastly occurrences, and soon a group of prophetic beasts will appear, beasts that have been misunderstood. It's time we understood the differences between these beasts.

A Beastly Bunch

Since the Bible is full of symbolic beasts, we need to understand their interrelation. The fourth beast of Daniel 7, the Roman Empire, is quite close to the first *beast of Revelation 13*, which comes *from the sea*, meaning a group of people sharing the same ideology rather than one individual. In fact, this beast is a combination of the revived Roman Empire in Europe and the great false church allied with it. Satan will allow this beast to sit on *his* throne, giving this beast power over hell and the demons.

This beast of Daniel 7 is allied with the false church and is used by Satan to perpetuate and make stronger his Sunday deception. Satan established the first day of the week to celebrate his government and mark of submission. Can we see why following the popular religious tradition can trap us into following the beast later?

If we accept any gift of Satan, we open a door to leaven "the whole lump" and begin to worship Satan. When the Sunday lie is revealed to us as a lie, and we submit to it, we are submitting both to Sunday and to Satan. We are worshipping his government, his money system, and his ways.

Don't be deceived. Submitting to Satan renders us cowards who follow the cowardly loser, Satan, rather than the Victor, Jesus. If we obey any part of evil, we will eventually obey all evil.

When you face Jesus, what will you say? "Jesus, I was only following the leaders who brought me to You. And all the famous ones kept Sunday. The church I came into when I accepted You kept Sunday. How was I to know?"

Do you think He'll be satisfied with your answer? Will He say, "I gave you My Word. You have never read in My Word that you should keep Sunday. So why did you believe those who told you a lie? Why did you follow a multitude to do the evil that seemed right because nearly everybody was doing it?"

If you don't want to follow the end-time beasts, the time to examine yourself is now. God is merciful. However, the time is coming for a choice.

The Beast of Revelation 13:11—The False Christ

The *other beast comes out of the earth* (Rev. 13:11). He seems to be coming from the grave, possibly resurrected by demonic power by actually having a demon take possession of his body to control and speak through it. He could also be a humanoid alien formed by genetic engineering.

This is the beast which we know as the false anointed one, the *false Christ* (or Jesus). He will surely be charismatic and appealing. He'll be acknowledged by the previous beast to be the savior of man. His tongue is corrupt and tantalizing. He will mesmerize people by his charming ways.

The job of this false Jesus is to make people worship the first beast and bring followers into blind submission so that they are unable to repent or receive correction. They won't even be able to acknowledge the gospel preached at a certain time only by angels. They'll believe they are on God's side, the winning side.

The *false Christ* will have the power to produce great signs, such as calling fire down from heaven. He may use a method like anointing people with tongues of fire to obey every word of the beast. What a way to counterfeit the Pentecost miracle!

Satan will empower him to walk on air, walk through walls, and cause the bodies of the dead to rise. He will be unable to put souls in those bodies, but he can have demons control them. He will be a master manipulator, specializing in betrayal and control. He will claim, as the spirit of control does, to be Jesus. That will be the claim of this end-time false Christ.

His name will be a household word. He will be worshipped as a false savior. He is the epitome of the white horse of false religion depicted in Revelation 6:2. Jesus comes on a white horse, but with a sword, not a bow. The false Christ will try to conquer the world by proclaiming world peace.

If we love miracles more than truth, we will be deceived. If we follow the "way of Cain" (Jude 11), we could easily fall into Satan's trap.

Walking in the Way of Cain

Like Cain, the first false messiah, the false Christ will hate the truth and truth seekers, proclaiming the real Jesus and His followers to be heretics. And as Cain killed Abel, he will martyr the believers who are still on the earth, those who have not been raptured. Those whose insignia is the eight-pointed star of Cain will follow the false Christ as he follows the way of Cain.

Cain was cursed as a restless wanderer, barred from Sabbath rest. The false Christ will encourage people to take the mark of Cain and the corresponding "mark of the beast," the keeping of Sunday. There will be no rest for the wicked in the last days. They will work continually as they worship the financial system of the beast.

Daniel 11 gives detailed prophecies, many of which have already been fulfilled and can be historically documented. Daniel 11:40 begins to speak of the end time, referring to Mussolini's revived Holy Roman

Empire's invasion of Ethiopia. This was a forerunner of the King of the North fighting the King of the South.

Remember that the Syrian forerunner of the Antichrist, Antiochus, was swallowed up by the Roman Empire, who thus at that time replaced Syria as the King of the North. Assyria had been the original King of the North, and Nimrod, under a different name, was the original King of the South.

The European revival of the Roman Empire will be the end-time King of the North. Most prophecy teachers believe wrongly that Russia will invade the Middle East in the last days. They fail to see the simple truth that Ezekiel 38 refers to a millennial Israel "of unwalled villages… those who are at rest, that live securely… into the land that [has been] restored from the sword" by Jesus' return to the earth (Ezek. 38:11, 8).

Their whole prophetic end-time scheme is thus flawed, especially because they don't understand that the U.S. and the Commonwealth represent Israel. Germany and the United States of Europe will invade the U.S. and take many of them captive. That same revived Roman Empire will then invade the Middle East.

Russia comes into the picture only much later, in Daniel 11:44. Russia is to the northeast of Jerusalem. The revived European Roman Empire will fight the Russian's Far East alliance, and Jesus will defeat both as He returns.

Who will comprise the alliance of the King of the South is not yet crystal clear, although we see in Psalm 83 that Assyria (Germany and the United States of Europe) will be joined by a number of Arab nations, including possibly the Philistines (who may in part be the Palestinians), against the tiny nation of Israel. Northern Africa has historically been the area of the King of the South.

Psalm 83 agrees with Daniel 11:41, showing that these Arab nations are allied with Europe and are thus spared when Europe, the King of the North, invades the Middle East after the King of the South "collides" with him (provokes him). It remains to be seen whether this provocation is simply military or if it involves a deprivation of oil from the oil-rich nations of the King of the South. Daniel 11:43 says that Europe will gain control of "gold and silver and over *all the precious things* of Egypt" (Dan. 11:43). "All the precious things" could definitely imply oil.

Jesus Will Protect The Faithful and Their Children!

The good news for faithful believers is that we have a Defender in Jesus, and Jesus has appointed a strong archangel to stand guard over "the sons of your people" (Dan. 12:1). The "time of distress such as never occurred since there was a nation until that time" in this verse refers to the Great Tribulation. Jesus will assure (through Michael, the angelic defender of Israel) the true believers that those "found written in the book [of life], will be rescued."

When we live in fear, however, we worry about things we shouldn't be concerned about. We ask questions that do need answers, but we don't always find the specifics spelled out in the Bible. That's where faith comes in, and faith means we know that God's name is Love for a reason. He always acts in love.

One of our bloggers asked this question: "If Jesus comes back too soon, what will happen to our children? Will He just kill them off because they didn't qualify?"

Our answer didn't provide the details he wanted, nor has God revealed all the specifics now: "Your children are sanctified when you're in Jesus. His plan wouldn't be to kill off children. Love is not a murderer. When our children are sanctified, God assigns them guardian and ministering angels. These angels are responsible for caring for and teaching the children of the saints."

God isn't limited by anything, even a believing woman who's pregnant. He has a plan for every possibility. It's a matter of trust and faith, a matter of knowing that, as the expression goes, God is good all the time.

God is indeed good, and He knew that the church wouldn't be ready to be raptured at the outset of the Tribulation, even though He warned us to get prepared—in our case, showing us the timing that was His perfect will.

Our church received a cryptic revelation from Matthew 26:2 just before the Feast of Tabernacles in 2006. Following the day-for-a-year principle, and understanding that the Passover symbolized the rapture, we came to understand that God wanted us to be ready for the first rapture in two years' time from 2006. While God wanted His church to be spared even from the Tribulation, being raptured to heaven for a seven-year period before the ideal time of Jesus' return, He foreknew that we would allow Satan's attacks and delays to affect us.

Where Are You?

Jesus is still asking us, as He asked Adam, "Where are you? Where are you in relation to Me? Are you ready to repent? Do you really want My ways of love, or do you want to allow Satan to delay your growth and your wholehearted commitment to My ways?"

We have had many warnings in Freedom Church of God, and we relay them to our listening audience at www.freedomtruthseekers.com. Many years ago, we heard a sermon telling us that the time to "diddle" was over. How often God sent prophets to His people Israel with the same message: "Return to Me!"

Who will be faithful to the end? Daniel 12:10–11 says that many will be purged and refined and understand the truth, even the true meaning of prophecy. Now we see through a glass darkly, and not all details of prophecy are crystal clear. Such is the case with Daniel 12:11–12.

Daniel 12:11 tells us that from the time the sacrifices are stopped in Jerusalem, there will ideally be a period of 1,260 days (three and a half years), followed by an extra thirty days. The prophecy seems to go backwards to an event that will precipitate other dramatic end-time occurrences, perhaps the fatal wound incurred by the beast, who is then miraculously resurrected and assumes great power and prestige forty-five days before the abomination (1,335 days in total before the very end). Those who wait in patient perseverance in obedience will be blessed and protected (Dan. 12:12). Will we?

Jeremiah holds out a promise to those who will be faithful in the end time in 29:11–13:

> "For I know the plans that I have for you," declares the [Eternal], "plans for welfare and not for calamity to give you a future and a hope. Then you will call upon Me and come and pray to Me, and I will listen to you. You will seek Me and find Me when you search for Me with all your heart."

The choice is ours. Prophecy moves on. Will we?

Time Will Tell: A Prophetic Timetable

Billions of years ago (probably nineteen)—Creation of the angels and then the universe.

66.6 million years ago—Satan's first rebellion.

4004 B.C.—"Re-creation" of devastated earth after Satan's second rebellion (12,600 years ago; Satan loses the rule of his first estate, the earth).

718 B.C.—Captivity of northern tribes of Israel + 2,520 Years (seven prophetic times) = 1803 A.D., the date of the Louisiana Purchase, opening the door to Abraham's blessings upon modern Israel (U.S. and Commonwealth).

457 B.C.—Decree of Artaxerxes + 483 Years (seven weeks of years, forty-nine years and sixty-two weeks, 434 years) = 27 A.D. Messiah would come into His ministry 27 A.D. (Daniel 9:25–26).

June 7, 434 B.C.—Battle at Hellespont, where the goat of Daniel 8 (Alexander, Greece) defeats the ram (Darius III, Medo-Persia).

4 B.C.—Birth of Jesus on the Day of Trumpets.

June 7, 1967 A.D.—Jews take control of Temple area (the way is prepared for rebuilding of temple and making sacrifices) exactly 2,300 years after the Battle at Hellespont (in the day-for-a-year principle, 2,300 days).

1996—End of six thousand years allotted to man and Satan on the Day of Trumpets.

2015—End of nineteen-year span of time. Ideally a transitional year and originally planned for wrath of Jesus and His return on the Day of Trumpets 390 days later in 2016. The Bridegroom delayed His return, since the bride [church] wasn't ready.

September 11, 2001—God gives the U.S. seven days to repent after 9/11 attacks before the Day of Trumpets on September 18, 2001, beginning seven years of sorrow if no repentance (Matthew 24:8).

September 29, 2008—Financial crisis begins on the Day of Trumpets, beginning the tribulation, ideally projected to last for three and a half years, until spring 2012.

Spring 2012—Originally planned time for beginning of the Great Tribulation. The Bridegroom delayed events because His bride, the church, wasn't ready to be raptured at the ideal time (Day of Trumpets 2008), and the unpreparedness of the church therefore delayed the beginning of the Great Tribulation, at which time a prepared church would be raptured (Rev. 3:10).

???—Great Tribulation begins and lasts for three and a half years.
???—The Day of Trumpets begins an extended year of 390 days of the wrath of God against His rebellious enemies.
???—The Day of Trumpets and the return of Jesus to rule the earth.

Chapter Fourteen:

You're Done, Devil!

While God has an overall plan of prophecy, so does Satan. The problem for Satan is that God knows everything he'll try in advance and has beat him to the punch at every turn. God knows the end from the beginning, so he knows all the twists and turns and has a plan for every scheme of Satan, every weapon in his arsenal, every aspect of his M.O. (*modus operandi*).

God's holy days, days that the Christian world has overlooked, detail God's plan and ensure Satan's defeat. If Christians had kept them, prophecy would be much easier to understand. Each feast has an important meaning, and even a prophetic significance.

The Feast of Unleavened Bread brings out one of the most important anointings of God's people. Do you know what it is? We all, of course, have individual anointings, or empowerments, given by God to perform what He has called us to do. We will consider a few biblical examples.

Abel was a prophet and a witness of righteousness, Enoch a martyr for righteousness, Noah a preserver and a teacher. Job was designed as a light to men and as a walker in righteousness.

Abraham was anointed for faith, faithfulness, and fatherhood. Isaac was anointed into the joy and prosperity of faithfulness. Jacob, who became Israel, was anointed into increase and nationhood. David was anointed for praise, victory, and kingship, while his son Solomon was called by God to bring peace, to establish the roots of wisdom, and to establish elaborate building projects.

Isaiah was anointed into judgment and to the calling forth of the King, which is why we can call his book the gospel according to Isaiah. Jeremiah was anointed to be the director of change. When he moved, nations fell and were reestablished elsewhere. Daniel was anointed for the sealing of Babylon's destiny.

Jesus was anointed to be a martyr, a sacrifice for all mankind. The Holy Spirit fashioned Jesus' body according to the Father's design. Unlike the first Adam and those of us who have followed him, Jesus wasn't made of the dust of the earth. And while Satan put enormous pressure on Jesus, and He was especially vulnerable before His baptism at age thirty, He did not have to defeat the power of sin or hardwiring of the brain that come with sons of Adam who are of the dust. That's why we need His grace (empowerment) to defeat Satan and sin in our lives. That's also why God gave us this feast, so we could lay down sin and falseness to Jesus.

Like Jesus, however, we are all designed perfectly for our anointing. Adam was also designed for his anointing, to subdue and multiply. Jesus was designed to resist Satan, to preach, and to die for mankind.

We are anointed as kings and priests, not for our glory but for the glory of the King of kings and the High Priest of priests. Few are called now as martyrs, but we are called to refrain from loving our lives unto death—to be willing to sacrifice our lives if necessary and surrender the desires of our flesh to Jesus. We are anointed with the abundant life, to live and not to die (Ps. 118:17).

Dying to Self Opens Door to Life and Victory

We only die to ourselves and to our fleshy ways, which is one of the main reasons we keep the Feast of Unleavened Bread. As we deny our right to eat leavened bread, we also learn to deny ourselves, bringing death to self so that we can truly live.

None of us are anointed to be destroyers. We are anointed to be victors over the destroyer Satan and his *modus operandi*—his schemes and lies and the falseness he has brought into the world, even the Christian world.

We have a great calling. We are called to bless rather than curse and to bring forth freedom, calling back the Kingdom of God on this earth. We are called to be preservers of mankind for the Kingdom of God. We are anointed for being the balancers of truth over deception and delusion. When falseness and deception speak, it is our job to balance and neutralize them with the Word of God. That's one of the main aspects of our anointing.

John says that Jesus came "for this purpose, to destroy the works of the devil" (1 John 3:8). Jesus lives in us, so we have His anointing in addition to our individual anointing. In fact, Jesus has already defeated Satan and destroyed his works. We are called to use the authority Jesus gave us to enforce the victory He won.

John warned us the same way Jesus did in Matthew 24. In 1 John 3:7, John said, "make sure no one deceives you." He follows in the next verse to show the very reason Jesus came into the world, and the reason He comes to live in us. That purpose is to destroy the works of deception that Satan devised.

Jesus said on the cross that His purpose was accomplished when He said, "It is finished." But it is not finished in our lives until we enforce it. We are the enforcers. And the purpose of the Feast of Unleavened

Bread is the purpose of our lives, to resist evil by speaking against it and acting against it, overcoming evil with good.

How can we do this, and how can we be ready to escape "all these things" of which Jesus spoke in Luke 21:36, events that begin to explode in late 2012, if we are in love with Satan's falseness? We can't. That's why God gave us the Feast of Unleavened Bread. All week we can lay down to Jesus the falseness and lies of Satan with which he has deceived us.

This feast is the feast of purification of the Bride of Jesus. The time is short, and yet most Christians have been deceived into avoiding this important festival. The wake-up call God issues before late 2012 is a call to keep His Sabbath, feasts, and new moons. They help us understand God's plan of love and equip us to understand and destroy Satan's methods of deception and destruction.

The Importance of History

One of the great lessons of history is that men have not learned their lessons. And one of the main reasons Christians have such little faith and power today is that they lack knowledge about the history of Satan's first estate.

God first created the angels about nineteen billion years ago. They had a time of learning before Jesus spoke the words that caused the universe to be created, probably a billion or so years after the angels' creation. Jesus created the earth later, about four and a half billion years ago.

God gave Lucifer the government of the earth so he could prepare it for man. So, the earth was Lucifer's first estate, his area of rule. He rebelled, however, with a third of the angels 66.6 million years ago, and God thrust him back to earth. At the same time, God sent a great asteroid hurtling towards earth, creating the area that is now the Gulf of Mexico and causing the cataclysms which divided the land into continents.

It was only 12,600 years ago that Satan lost his first estate of earthly rule. At that time, his second rebellion failed in an attempt to invade the throne of God with his humanoid-driven spaceships. His loss was confirmed when the Holy Spirit's hovering over the planet in Genesis 1 pushed him and his demons down into hell.

Satan's second estate (or period of earthly rule) began when Adam sinned, establishing Satan as god of this world.

When we fail to understand, or desire to understand, the pre-Adamic world and Satan's first estate, we plan to fail in our battle against Satan. We become ignorant of Satan's schemes because we don't see how they started. Buffeted by Satan, our faith fails. We must understand pre-history if we are to learn Satan's tactics.

God foreknew all that Satan, man, and He would do and even wrote the history of man in the stars. The Cygnus (or Swan) Constellation, also known as the Northern Cross, is a striking example. Ancients worshipped the humanoids produced by Satan in the pre-Adamic period and some humanoid watchers that came from the stars.

Plato discovered 2,500 years ago that fifteen "ley lines" encircled the earth as if they were equators circling the planet at different spots. He knew that the earth was divided into 120 triangles produced by these fifteen lines or "equators" drawn around the globe. They followed geometric and magnetic power grids.

In turn, at fifteen points these ley lines intersected at especially important magnetic power centers. Those who worshipped the sky gods and the places where they came from (the stars) built, with extraterrestrial help, intricately and mathematically designed structures along these intersecting points, referred to as navels of the earth. These structures mirrored exactly the formation of certain star groups such as

Orion, especially the belt, at the exact time of Satan's second rebellion 12,600 years ago.

When you see a bird's-eye view of the three Egyptian pyramids, for instance, you can see two of the pyramids in a straight line, but the third only a bit offset in alignment with the other two, as if they were a perfect, earthly model of Orion's belt. A structure in Boyne Valley, Ireland is a copy of the star group Cygnus (or Northern Cross).

In its fourth series, *Ancient Aliens* has an interesting program involving ley lines. The structures built along the intersecting points of these lines, the navels of the earth, also served as points that UFOs used to guide their flights.

The ancients believed the area of the Northern Cross, which points to the dark center of our galaxy, was where creation began, and it was, since it was the God who inhabits the northern sky who spoke the creation. They called it the beginning and the end, meaning that the end would come about when the earth entered in the last days into that dark center. It does exactly that in December 2012![48]

---

48 *Much controversy has surrounded the Mayan predictions for the winter solstice of 2012. John Major Jenkins is the most credible scholar who has written about it, and you can do a web search of his findings. He states that a rare alignment in the precessional cycle will occur on the December solstice in 2012, when the sun conjuncts the center of our Milky Way galaxy. Precession is the wobble of the earth that is completed every 26,000 years. Some say this entry into the dark part (or rift) of our galaxy actually began in 1998 and would continue until 2016, but they explain that our solar system enters visually into that dark zone precisely on December 21, 2012. These dates are interesting, since the timespan of an additional nineteen years added to the allotted six thousand years given to mankind to rule the earth began in the fall of 1996. It would be a time of spiritual darkness, culminating in God's ideal timing—a time of intense darkness called the Great Tribulation that God purposed to begin in the spring of 2012, growing much darker by the winter solstice, since witches and Satanists would call for the man of sin to manifest at that time. The darkness was prophesied to end with the return of Jesus in 2016. At least, that was the plan had the church been ready. December 21, 2012 would thus be a time of intense darkness, especially in a spiritual sense. The importance we place on this date is only supported (rather than proven) by the Mayan prediction of the dawning of a new age. The important matter for God is the forty years since the legalization of the spilling of innocent blood through abortion and the end of a generation of forty years, the end-time generation of unusually rampant sin that would bring sure judgment.*

December 2012 won't be the absolute end of this age, but it signals the beginning of the change into a new age. How could the Mayans and many other cultures have known this if they hadn't learned it from Satan's alien star travelers that visited earth?

The swan formation was also pictured as a dagger or sword, showing that Satan would attempt to ascend to the throne of God to try to dethrone the Creator. The ugly duckling will attempt to take God's throne, but he'll take a losing "swan dive," as the star group is also dubbed.

The Cross Prophesied in the Sky!

Yet this star group is also shaped like a cross, showing that Jesus would have to die to save man from this rebellion, which would influence men especially at the end time.

Who would have known that our great God would fulfill Psalm 19:1 in this way? David writes,

> The heavens are telling of the glory of God [and His glorious plan for man]; and their expanse is declaring the work of His hands [including His defeat of Satan on the cross, which redeemed men, the work of His hands, to be a part of His Family]."

In Psalm 8, David also mused on that awesome plan for man as he beheld the stars. God has also pointed Abraham to the stars (Gen. 15:5).

While some may dispute the astronomical importance of the winter solstice of 2012, the biblical basis of our prediction of spiritual darkness has an unshakeable foundation. God will not be mocked. Sin has a penalty, and that important date is a point of no return. Sin's price will be paid; darkness will greatly increase, signifying that the shining light of Jesus' return is imminent.
If the church continues to be unwilling to be prepared and fulfill its mission, total annihilation will result by the fall of 2028. The final twelve years after 2016 represent a period of total judgment without mercy.

Satan took the star picture God made and perverted it into astrological signs, even encouraging people to worship the stars. Nevertheless, our awesome God foreknew all of Satan's schemes and had already provided the sacrifice of His Son on the cross, the central moment of history, between the beginning and the end, to foil Satan's plans.

As the earth enters the dark area of the galaxy in December 2012, our world's ancient monolithic structures will once again line up with their corresponding star formations. This important event will signal the beginning of the end of this age and the imminent third major rebellion (thirteenth in all) of Satan. This will be his last rebellion before Jesus returns with His light of glory to rule as He casts out the darkness.

It's essential that we understand the plans of the enemy and his history if we are to see his defeat in our lives today and walk in the power of faith in the last days.

Satan will only become history in our lives when we understand his history, his two major rebellions and a third to come, as well as his complete history of his minor rebellions. You are about to discover the plans of the enemy so you can see his defeat in your life and be part of seeing his defeat in the world in these last days.

Rebellions Sponsored by Satan

To understand what Satan is about to do in late 2012, we need to understand the rebellions he has inspired in history, which reveal much of his methods. They are listed below:

1. He led a third of the angels to try to take over God's throne, probably 66.6 million years ago. God had sent him to earth to prepare it for mankind, but inspired by pride and jealousy, Lucifer became Satan. The result was that

God, in the heavenly battle that ensued, had to bring cataclysms on earth. Scientists believe that the Gulf of Mexico was formed at that time by a gigantic asteroid.

2. When God withdrew Satan's creative powers, the devil resorted to mockery by making humanoids that resembled the future mankind he knew God would create, as well as *nephilim* or giants, both of which he created by genetic manipulation. The alien spaceships that left the earth to attack God's throne caused the great ice age on this planet that left it in a state of confusion when God set about in Genesis to "re-create" the earth.

3. Satan's deception and destruction of the Garden of Eden was his effort to stop God's plan of love.

4. In Genesis 6, we see demons and modified sons of the false creator Satan (demons and humanoids—good angels don't lust or mate with women) manifesting to mate with women, producing men of renown and giants on the earth. Because of genetic pollution, all men have been born with the corrupt DNA of those giants, allowed after the Flood because of the corrupt genetics of the wives

of Noah's sons. That's why communion, and especially the Passover, is necessary for believers to be free from this genetic pollution.

5. Next came the rebellion of Nimrod and the Tower of Babel.

6. Satan then inspired the Pharaoh of Egypt to destroy the people of God.

7. Assyria and Babylon took Israel captive in Satan's effort to cause God's physical people to lose their identity.

8. Antiochus Epiphanes, a century before Jesus, profaned God's temple and city, prefiguring the future Antichrist who the Bible indicates will rise as Antiochus out of Syria to be the Arab messiah and King of the South. The Arab world is already preparing a coin made partly of gold that will put the U.S. dollar to shame and rival the euro. The current confusion and rise of Islam in the Arab countries of Africa and the Middle East is a preparation for the rise to power of this soon-to-emerge Antichrist.

9. When Constantine, led by Satan, couldn't defeat Christianity from without, he feigned becoming a Christian to destroy God's people from within the church. He succeeded in introducing over five thousand doctrines of demons into the organized church, the vast majority of which were never rejected by the protesting daughters of the universal church God is calling people out of today (Rev. 18:4). The four friends of Job represented the world's four major religions, the last of which, Elihu, represented the protesting daughters of the great church, patterned after Nimrod's deception. The laws Constantine established to persecute Sabbath-keepers are still on the books and will be used to martyr true believers who aren't prepared to escape the Great Tribulation.

10. Frederick the Great led a crusade for public ignorance and deception.

11. Napoleon tried to smash those who were rising up to proclaim the good news of the Kingdom, and he invaded those areas where Sabbath-keepers (such as some of the Waldensians) had fled.

12. The short-lived Hitler-Mussolini axis, prophesied in Daniel, set the stage for the tenth and last resurrection of the Roman Empire in Europe, which will be the seventh revival of the Holy Roman Empire.

13. The United States of Europe, in whatever form it may take, is about to burst on an unsuspecting world, even on a Christian world that is confused about prophecy and is either asleep or about to fall asleep. As I write this, the "Berlin Club" of *ten* nations (as prophesied) has met for the first time to revive the project of European unity.

14. Satan will be released for his final and futile attempt to defeat God and His people near the end of the thousand years of peace Jesus will establish on earth.

As we approach the thirteenth powerful but futile effort of Satan to defeat God, we must be sure that we're not defeated and destroyed by Satan. God has called us to defeat and destroy him and his method of operation. We must know his schemes.

Deception, Intimidation, Compromise, and Fear

Satan's methods haven't changed. In his effort to steal, kill, and destroy, he lies. He deceives. He has deceived Christians since the subtle creeping in of the Sunday heresy in the second century and the patently pagan Constantine was used by Satan to water down truth and attack those who would defend it.

He has seduced and deceived Christians in these last days not to take God's Word seriously and to play roles, taking Jesus' name in vain and treating the Word with contempt.

Today he is waging a war of intimidation against believers, attacking them in the courts and media, causing the lukewarm, Laodicean church to cower in fear. The pressure to compromise has never been greater. "A little compromise won't hurt anybody," some say, "and that way we can get along well with everyone." That's the prevailing attitude, an outlook that Jesus says will cause Him to vomit those who adopt it out of His mouth (Rev. 3:16).

It's not too late for lackadaisical Christians to turn the spirit of compromise over to Jesus, but it's almost too late. The love of Jesus' followers is growing colder by the minute, because lawlessness is abounding. When Christians compromise with God's law, they break the boundaries of protection that the laws of love give. Fear enters.

Those anointed to speak out against and destroy Satan's methods of deception are allowing themselves to be destroyed, not only for a lack of knowledge but also for a lack of obedience.

Jesus gave us His blood to pay for our sins; His cross to turn our compromises over to Him; and His Sabbaths, new moons, and especially His Feast of Unleavened Bread to turn over all the lies and falseness of Satan. But we have until now refused to accept what He offers. Jesus is saying to us believers, "Prepare to meet your God" (Amos 4:12). We either meet Him at the altar, turning over our sins, or we meet Him at the woodshed, where it won't be pretty. He's giving His church time to repent (Rev. 3:19; 2:21), but the time is growing shorter by the day.

The Lion of Judah is roaring through His servants (Amos 3:6–8), but who has believed and responded to their report? (Isa. 53:1) Will we? Will we listen to the swan song of the world's religions' "worthless physicians," represented by the friends of Job who smear believers with lies? (Job 13:3) Or will we hear and obey the truth that will set us free? (John 8:32)

The world is groaning for the manifestation of the mature sons and daughters of God to rise in these last days (Rom. 8:19–21). Why? The answer is that it's not only our fate we decide, but that of the whole world. We are anointed to be the salt that preserves the world from total destruction. Have we lost our savor? Have we hidden our light?

We don't know for sure how bad December 21, 2012 will be. But we know that at some point in time solar flares could erupt that take parts of our planet back a century, bringing our electric and computer-based society to a standstill. How we react to God's warnings will determine the severity of the events to come.

The details of what could or will happen in 2012 aren't as important as the need for nonchalant believers to wake up and prepare for a rapture. The words and actions of believers are paramount at this crucial time. It's critical that we understand the power of Job's prophecies for evil and good in these last days.

Jobs Powerful Words and Us

Job struggled to understand why so much suffering came upon him, a man who even Jesus called righteous. When he began to allow Satan to vent through him, Jesus still considered him righteous because he never cursed God; he only questioned Him and misjudged Him. While he began trying in Job 9:27 to forget his complaints in his own strength, he let all the negative thoughts spew out of his mouth in Job 10.

Satan used those words. But so did Jesus.

His words prophesied the hopelessness of latter-day Christians who would also allow their mouths to speak the words of Satan rather than the words of God. But his words at the same time opened a door of hope for those who would lay down their misery and negativity to Jesus and learn to obey Him by speaking His words into the evil circumstances of these last days.

The choice is ours, and time is running out for the making of those right choices.

This righteous man said in Job 9:28, "I am afraid of all my pains, I know that You will not acquit me." Space does not permit explaining in detail the multiple meanings of the Hebrew words used in the sentence. I have endeavored to state the meanings as simply as I dare:

> I am openly and constantly aware of all the pain I have endured, borne witness to, had bound to me, been wounded by, and sorrowed grievously about. I anticipate a never-ending increase in pain that advance relentlessly upon me. I am openly and constantly aware of all the pain I have endured and sorrowed grievously about. I anticipate a never-ending increase in pain that advances relentlessly upon me. I know by personal experience how fixed God is in allowing instruction by pain, so I now realize that God has decreed my lot in life. I am thus forced to respect His power in leaving me prisoner to my guilt.

That verse prophesied the mindset of many Christians today. Job's words here, and in a number of other statements, prophesied that Jesus would come to take our pain.

Job was saying that pain and persecution would come to those who seek Jesus, and since all pain comes because Jesus allows it, all our pain must be turned over to Him at the cross. Jesus had to pay for all causes and effects of pain in order to be our Redeemer, Restorer, and Deliverer.

Because of Job's words, Jesus would have to drink voluntarily of the dreadful cup His Father set before Him to provide a way of escape and defense for those who surrender to Him and walk in *His* righteousness. Whenever we fall short, His blood and priestly work as our Advocate guarantees our forgiveness and restoration.

In the expanded translation of Job 9:29, Job expresses the feelings of many believers today, feelings they need to lay down to Jesus:

> As I am deemed by You to be accounted judged and declared wicked, vexing, troubling, and one who departs from righteousness, goodness or holiness, and filled with iniquity, rebellion, and wicked dealings, why then should I grasp at righteousness, exhaust myself being upright, labor to do good, and exert myself by seeking God in a way that is blocked by Your curses?

Compare Malachi 3:14, which describes a modern church that feels it has wearied itself by serving God in vain.

Job 9:29 sums up why Jesus had to die and establishes the coming of forty prophecies proving that Jesus is the Messiah and the One who broke the power of the curse, sin, and death.

Job's declaration and prayer in Job 10:2 for God not to condemn him is an awesome prophecy that obliges God to find a way for all men who ever lived on earth to find the pathway to the Father through Jesus. Satan thought he had Jesus trapped here by Job's words, since such a feat seemed impossible. But the Father, Jesus, and the Holy Spirit already knew the end from the beginning and outsmarted Satan, using the words Job spoke, planning a way whereby almost all mankind would be eventually saved.

That's not the only good news in Job's words. Listen to what he says in Job 9:27: "Though I say, 'I will forget my complaint, I will leave off my sad countenance and be cheerful…'" The Hebrew word *paneh* (*panah*, or countenance) becomes the opposite of the word or concept that follows. Here the word that follows is *balag* (grief, or sadness). The simple meaning of *paneh* is "to turn," meaning to turn your face to someone, leading to the next meaning: "face," or countenance (Ps. 119:132,135, where "turn" and "face" are both *paneh* in Hebrew).

The definitions of *paneh* are: to comfort yourself with words of life; to place your troubles, pain, losses, and cares behind you (implying that you cast them off to Jesus); to break free from the negative; to remove fear from the forefront and speak out words of a conqueror; to change the old, stale bread for fresh showbread (we can apply that to the spring feast, when we cast out the old leaven to feast on the unleavened bread of sincerity and truth); to cast off a wrong outlook to be restored, refreshed, renewed, and reconnected to love. The concept of the word is to lift up your countenance in a bad situation to change your attitude.

Here is the expanded translation of Job 9:27:

> I will persist and be committed to change by forsaking what drags me down, what makes me sad and negative, and what leaves me powerless, feeling abandoned, and lacking purpose, energy, and life. I will vehemently reject negative thinking, speaking, and any use of my time that pulls me downward. I do this in order that I may face a change in attitude, being uplifted, restored, refreshed, redeemed, and reconnected to love and joy. I will be renewed from grief, sorrow, selfishness or selfish

concerns, destructive thoughts, and negative speaking so that I may be strengthened by the Word and promises of God.

What Job expressed is exactly what the Days of Unleavened Bread are designed to do, and that's why Satan has deceived most Christians into ignoring this feast. But a remnant is rising up who will take advantage of the purpose for which Jesus came and the purpose of this feast—to destroy the works of Satan and sin in our lives.

We who understand must follow God's admonition in Hebrew 12:1–2, laying aside on Jesus' cross the sin that so easily entangles us, "fixing our eyes on Jesus, the author and perfecter of faith."

Seven is the number of completion and perfection. God gives us seven days to learn to be free from sin and to learn to destroy all the works of Satan in our lives as we, by Jesus' grace, speak out against his method of operation, a method using seduction, deception, intimidation, compromise, and destruction.

All creation is waiting for the manifestation of the mature sons of God who will defeat Satan and his works by the blood and the power of Jesus. The victory is ours if we take it.

The Passover teaches us to accept the grace of forgiveness God offers us in the New Covenant. As we look into the face of the person whose feet we wash, we look into the face of everyone who has ever hurt or offended us, and we say or think, "I see you clean in God's sight and my sight, free from the evil one and in peace and unity with our Father Love."

We thus escape the rut in which unforgiveness and offense have placed us and we recognize that the grace of forgiveness is ours.[49] In keeping the Feast of Unleavened Bread, we have seven days to give to

---

49 Order my ground-breaking book, God's Fruit of Forgiveness, on our websites.

Jesus all that hinders us and walk in His righteousness, firmly planting our feet in the ways of love.

We recognize that we have access through the New Covenant to all the graces and wisdom of God in Jesus, who lives in us. We can walk in the joy of a bride being cleansed and prepared for the greatest Bridegroom of all time, Jesus, who we have accepted as our Savior, our Redeemer from all sin and falseness, and the Divine Master we have chosen to obey.

The lesson all believers need to learn—to be ready to meet their Bridegroom— is the lesson of Passover and the Days of Unleavened Bread as expressed in Psalm 130:3–4, which I shall paraphrase:

> If You, Father of love and forgiveness, should mark down our sins forever in Your book, who among us could stand? But there is forgiveness in the blood of our Passover Lamb Jesus, so that we may then stand in awe of You and go forward by the grace of Jesus to leave all the ways of sin in our lives so we can fully enter the joy of Your salvation.

God's days of celebration offer us the only way to compromise Satan's M.O., especially his end-time schemes. You and your family don't need to let fear invade your life if you allow in Jesus and His love. The years 2012 and beyond don't have to be times of disaster for you. If you submit to Jesus and His ways and days, you will emerge victorious.

Chapter Fifteen:
Don't Be Left Behind in Truth about the Rapture

Is the rapture for you, or are you caught up in the religious ruckus, confusion, and controversy? What's the real backbone of truth behind the rapture? Could the truth be that there is a pre-Tribulation rapture for some, a mid-Tribulation rapture for others, and a post-Tribulation rapture for the tardy? The Bible reveals three raptures. The first is imminent. Do you want the best escape route, or do you want the calamity?

Books and movies have catapulted the subject of the rapture into the minds of even unbelievers. In the Christian arena, opinions abound. Everyone seems to be sure they know what it is and yet, on the other hand, it seems no one is sure. No one agrees on the what and when of the rapture.

In all the religious wrangling, do you feel left behind by it all? Confused?

No wonder. Some say the rapture will be pre-Trib (Christianese for Tribulation), others post-Trib, and still others mid-Trib.

The key to open the door to understanding is to ask a simple question: could they all be right?

In most cases, the answer would be no. If you're saying something different about the same subject, someone must be wrong. And indeed, imperfect theology has affected all three camps.

But consider this: the only way the three camps could all be right, at least in part, is if the Bible spoke of three raptures. And it does. As surprising as that may sound, I aim to prove the truth of that statement.

The Bible says that the truth will make you free (John 8:32). While God wants His people free from error, the most important thing is for us to be spiritually ready for whatever comes. I hope also to provide help in spiritual preparation.

While enough verses properly translated in our language enable us to discover the basic truth, some of the details are filled in once you understand the conceptual nature of the original languages, especially the Hebrew.

The true story of the rapture—or rather, raptures— is stranger than any fictional accounts or movies. While few have discovered the simple truth, you can find it within the pages of that black book by your bedside—if you open the Bible and prove all things (1 Thes. 5:21).

Show Me the Money

Ridiculous scenarios in movies and novels have made the truth about the rapture hard to believe. Mockery and skepticism abound. Like some who want to see the hard cash before they'll believe the deal, others must see the word "rapture" in their language in the Bible before they will believe. This "show me the money" approach isn't an honest one. But interestingly, a Greek word connected with the rapture concept is pronounced almost like our English word money. So be patient, you *will* see the "money."

But if you're waiting to see the English word "rapture" in any of the major translations, you may be waiting until… well, the rapture.

A person once told me jokingly, and with pun intended, "I liked my high school, but it was just the principal of the thing." In God's school, we learn in principles. It's the principle of the thing, not the words themselves.

Most Christians believe in the Trinity, however they may envisage the triune Godhead of Father, Son Jesus, and the Holy Spirit. Most have been convinced by the Word, or by His presence and personality as manifested to them, that the Holy Spirit is a Person. Yet you can search the Bible from Genesis to Revelation and you will not find the word "Trinity." That doesn't change the truth that God reveals Himself in His Word as a Trinity. The concept is there. And so is the idea of rapture.

While God says He created mankind male and female, and you can read some rather racy passages in the Song of Solomon, the word "sex" is not in the Bible. Yet you only need to turn on your television to know that sex is a reality.

Many believers don't even believe in a rapture. And as we have seen, great diversity of opinion exists among those who do believe in this end-time phenomenon. Let's begin to unravel the mystery by getting an overview of the three raptures from the point of view of the greatest Threesome in the universe.

Rapture: A God's Eye Overview

We need to take a heavenly overview of this maligned and confusing subject. We have seen that the word "Trinity" is nowhere to be found in the Scriptures. But the Trinity teaching is indeed there. And curiously enough, that very concept gives us a hint at unraveling the rapture confusion.

God is a Threesome who does things in threes. It is one of His numbers of completeness. He made man with spirit, soul, and body. The Hebrew Scriptures ("Old Testament") are composed of three parts, while the twenty-seven Greek scrolls ("New Testament") represent the perfect cube of three (three times three times three).

Jesus began His ministry at the age of thirty and died at thirty-three. The sign Jesus gave of His Messiahship was that He would be resurrected after three days and three nights in the grave just as Jonah was in the great fish (Mat. 12:40).

Three heavens are mentioned in the Bible, with God dwelling in the third heaven. God convened His people for festivals at three seasons of the year. Peter denied Jesus three times, and afterwards Jesus asked Peter three times (with different Greek words) if Peter truly loved Him.

Furthermore, while most of Christendom ignores the nearly seven hundred verses that prove it, God has a master plan that includes three general resurrections (see Appendix I).

Dont Be Left Behind in Understanding

Will you be left behind? Rapture teachers sometimes scare. Their books and movies can make your hair reach toward heaven even if you don't believe you'll be caught up there. The sad truth is that liberating truth has been left behind. Since the rapture is at our doorstep, it's time for the light of truth to dispel the shroud of confusion.

When we become convicted that the whole Bible is inspired (Mat. 4:4)—not just what we call the "New Testament"—and grasp the meaning of the original words used, the rapture truth becomes clear.

When we understand that all Scripture is the infallible Word of God in its original form (John 10:35; Ps. 19:7; 2 Tim. 3:16), we know that God cannot contradict Himself. Rather than picking and choosing verses that suit our idea, we need to take all the verses that deal with the rapture together (many more than you may think). The truth we thus discover is potent.

Three Raptures

If we believe in only one rapture, we see verses that contradict us. Paul wrote both letters to the Thessalonians to answer questions about the rapture. He clearly states that Jesus "rescues us from the wrath to come" (1 Thes. 1:10) and "has not destined us for wrath" (1 Thes. 5:9). That includes Satan's wrath in the Tribulation (Rev. 12:12) and God's day of wrath that follows (Joel 1:15).

The "lawless one" cannot be fully revealed until the very elect are "taken out of the way" (2 Thes. 2:7). That means that those saints who love God's law are no longer on earth sending up prayers that restrain this man of sin. Many scholars believe the only way to translate "taken out of the way" is "raptured." One of the meanings of Jesus' name in Hebrew (*Yashua*) is "rapture."

Not all Christians have the same level of faith, and Jesus established the following principle: "It shall be done to you according to your faith" (Mat. 9:29). Has the Jesus who is always the same (Heb. 13:8) ever failed to rescue the faithful? Daniel didn't become food for lions. The three men in the fiery furnace came out unscathed. Even in modern times, a Christian was left untouched when a large vat of molten steel fell on him. Other believers have perished in tragic accidents for various reasons. While we don't know why in every case, we know that dying in an accident goes against God's perfect will; somehow Satan is sometimes able to cut lives short.

God promises protection for those who prepare for the wrath to come, but some will choose not to prepare and heed His warnings. The Bible shows that a world despot will soon arise. Some Christians will be his victims. He will wear them down and overcome them—even kill them (Dan. 7:21,25; Rev. 13:7; 12:17). Some will have to persevere and prove their faith by laying down their lives (Mat. 24:9,13; Rev. 14:13).

It is impossible for the same group to be both rescued from wrath and suffer wrath. We see at least two categories of Christians—those who believe in a rapture to heaven for a marriage feast with Jesus and are "rapture ready," and those who must give their lives to prove their faith because they weren't counted worthy to "escape all these things" (Luke 21:36).

We even see another category of Christians, those who prove their loyalty during the first part of the tribulation and trust God for a physical place of protection. They are raptured out of danger in a second general rapture before the horrors of the Great Tribulation, which will last for another three and a half years, or "times" (Rev. 12:13–17).

Rev 12:17 refers to "the rest of her children," those who weren't ready for either the first or second rapture, but who will persevere even unto death in keeping all the commandments of love.

The Gathering of the Saints

The new Christians called at the very end, during the very last of the Great Tribulation and the wrath of God, will be the ones caught up in the third rapture (or the first resurrection), changed in the "twinkling of an eye" (1 Cor. 15:52). This is the return of Jesus to earth and the gathering of the elect, which occurs *after* the Great Tribulation (Mat. 24:29–31).

As the original language makes clear, three groups are gathered: those in heaven with Jesus in the first rapture (or those who died before the first rapture and are in heaven), those in a place of safety in this physical universe, and those who accept Jesus at the very end who are changed to rule with Jesus on the earth. All these groups will in an instant be given an immortal and glorified physical body like Jesus when

He was resurrected (Luke 24:39; 1 Cor. 15:52), with flesh and bone only, physical earth suits to rule with Jesus on earth (Rev. 5:10).

God is faithful. He will indeed protect those who believe in His protection, those who keep His commandments (John 14:15) and who are ready, with oil in their lamps (Mat. 25:1–13). Whether or not they enjoy the full protection or safety during the Great Tribulation depends on their response to Jesus' words, "Come, my people, enter into your rooms and close your doors behind you; hide for a little while until indignation runs its course" (Isa. 26:20).

If you want God's rapture rest, you must discard confusing teachings and humbly search the Scriptures, all of them, "a little here, a little there," so you won't be "snared and taken captive" (Isa. 28:10,13). If you listen and obey, walking in love and thankfulness, you'll be in the first rapture, which is the best.

If you're already letting your inner spirit man rule over your flesh, seated firmly in the heavenlies with Jesus (Eph. 2:6), you'll be able to be in that best rapture. Love will show the way.

The Key of Love

What you read above isn't some doctrinal whim. It's the only way to put all the biblical pieces of the puzzle together without contradiction. Truth brings clarity.

How could it not be true? Do we believe our God is Love? It's impossible for Him not to love us.

Those of you who read my book on healing know that God heals because He loves. If you're a parent, you know you'd never afflict your children with a deadly disease. Neither would our Father Love. Many Christians get sick and die because they don't realize who they are as sons and daughters of their Father Love. He loves them like He loves

Jesus. That is not, however, the way they feel. They don't accept the truth, by faith, that their Father loves them.

This same refusal to accept God's love can block the rapture concept in believers' hearts and minds. As my book on rejection explains, they feel rejected by God.

In fact, all my books deal with this key component of love. *Bible Code Broken!* opens the door to receive God's love on His day of love, the seventh day. This day sets us apart so we know who we are as beloved ones of God, so we know who God is (Ex. 31:13). To those who love Him by keeping His Sabbaths, He offers "a name better than that of sons and daughters" (Isa. 56:5).

Do you believe you're worthy of God's love? You may not be of yourself, but Jesus, who died for you and lives in you, makes you worthy.

A Telling Letter

A woman from Calgary, Alberta wrote me regarding the rapture. I quote from her letter, leaving out the name of the TV evangelist she cited: "God never saved anyone from being martyred. Look at all those burned at the stake by the [universal] church. [The evangelist] says it is the height of arrogance to think that *today's* Christians would be spared. They will have to prove their faith like saints of the past. I also have a book whose author says the same thing and ministers have said they also agree but cannot or will not preach it because the people would come unglued…"

The truth is that many Christians, including leaders, do not fully understand how much God loves them. When Christians do understand their identity in Jesus and claim their covenant rights as sons and daughters of the Most High, others often assume they're arrogant. Confidence isn't arrogance (Heb. 10:35). "The wicked flee when no one is pursuing, but the righteous are bold as a lion" (Prov. 28:1). They know who they are.

The mature sons of God don't fall asleep over the words of the Bible. They read them. They know them. They speak them with confidence and lay hold on the promises of God.

We have seen that the wrath of Satan in the Great Tribulation and the wrath of God in the Day of the Eternal are soon to come. Those who know who they are will learn about the rapture and claim the promises regarding it. They will confidently call on Savior and Deliverer Jesus, who rescues and saves them.

You don't have to be "unglued" by the negative pronouncements of well-meaning preachers. Your Father loves you. He would never make you go through the wrath to come. He would only allow it so as not to force your will. He doesn't want to see you suffer.

Martyr Mistake?

The irony is in one of the statements in this woman's letter. A great church has adopted a pernicious lie from the religion of ancient Babylon: penance. Suffer for Jesus. Please Him by enduring pain.

No! He endured pain *for* us. He was called to be a martyr. While every Christian must die to self and be willing to die physically, not every Christian has the gift or calling of martyrdom.

Jesus laid down His life for us. Persecutors may have thought they took His life, but the truth is that He laid down His life in a voluntary sacrifice (John 10:15).

We have Bible promises that will keep us alive until we have lived a full life (Ps. 91:16). Interestingly, the word for salvation in Psalm 91 includes the idea of rapture.

What God promised to a physical people applies even more to His spiritual people: "He permitted no man to oppress them… Do not touch My anointed ones, and do My prophets no harm" (1 Chron. 16:21–22). All believers are anointed with the Holy Spirit.

"The right hand of [Jesus] is exalted; the right hand of [Jesus] does valiantly [as valiantly as you believe He will]. I will not die, but live; and tell of the works of [Jesus]" (Ps. 118:16–17).

Many of the martyrs who died didn't have to die. They could have seen Jesus work a miracle to protect them and then tell of His works in their lives. Others were called to give up their lives and did. They forgave their persecutors and their blood cried out from the ground to bring about a future blessing on that land (Gen. 4:10).

Ironically, the same great church that taught people to suffer in penance and be martyred, whether it was God's will or not, is the same church responsible for shedding the blood of Christians who didn't agree with that church's doctrine. More believers have died for keeping God's day of love, the Sabbath, than for any other reason. Because of a lack of knowledge, some died needlessly.

The only reason we would need to prove our faith is if our faith needed proving. When we think our Father Love is unfaithful in delivering us from the wrath to come, we do need to go through the crucible of tribulation to prove we love God more than anything.

"Because he has loved Me, therefore I will deliver him; I will set him securely on high, because he has known My name…" (Ps. 91:14). That's the key: love. He loves us. We internalize and personalize that love, and we then love God. He then delivers us and sets us "on high."

Set on High

God has always rescued the faithful—those full of faith and love. In earlier times, Jesus hadn't paved the way to heaven by His death, resurrection, and ascension. But He was always faithful.

He saved Lot; wrath didn't fall on him as it did on Sodom. He had Noah build a boat, saving him and his family. The rain of wrath didn't drown Noah. Since Jesus had not yet opened the doors to heaven, He took Noah out of a land on which the wrath was about to fall.

Of course, God doesn't force you to be set on high. You have free will. You can stay here on the earth and go through the horrors of the tribulation. But our God of love offers you a way of escape. He wants you alert and "praying that you may have strength to *escape* all these things" (Luke 21:36).

Did you catch that? If you didn't, perhaps you won't be caught up in a rapture to stand before the Son of Man, Jesus. Those who are dead-set against any rapture may end up either dead or protected in a physical place of safety in a second rapture. But it's not the best way. You will escape some of "these things" but not "all these things."

How much do want to escape? Do you want to endure a few more terrorist attacks much worse than 9/11? Or pestilence, or famine? How much do you think Jesus loves you? And how much do you love Jesus? Those are the questions of the hour as the rapture approaches.

On high, or below? In heaven, or on earth? It's your choice.

Chapter Sixteen:

Last Days' Sex Craze—For Mature Readers Only

We are bombarded. Sex is everywhere. It's hard to escape. Illicit sex is on television, in the movies, in media commercials, and on billboards. Why is our society so sex crazy? A number of reasons explain the phenomenon, and this sex craze was prophesied in the Bible for the last days.

Jesus spoke a few words in His Olivet prophecy that we allude to frequently in this book:

> For the coming of the Son of Man will be just like the days of Noah. For as in those days before the flood they were eating and drinking, marrying and giving in marriage, until the day that Noah entered the ark… (Mat. 24:37–38).

What Jesus spoke wasn't the whole story. It was a brief summary of what we read in Genesis 6:1–2:

> Now it came about, when men began to multiply on the face of the land, and daughters were born to them, that the sons of God saw that the daughters of men were beautiful [and genetically good]; and they took [*laqach*] wives for themselves, whomever they chose…

The Hebrew word used here adds a different twist, and it is indeed a twist, which is one of the definitions of perversion. Sexual perversion has become the norm today, as it was in the days of Noah. Even those who call themselves Christians have allowed themselves to be inundated by the avalanche of sexual perversion extant today.

The apostle Paul spoke out a prophecy for the last days that confirms the other prophecies of end-time sexual perversion. What is most surprising is that his prophecy mainly targets Christians, those who are "holding to a form of godliness, although they have denied its power…" (2 Tim. 3:5).

This prophecy of 2 Timothy 3 also reveals some of the roots of this sexual perversion. We invite you to read these verses (2 Tim. 3:1–8, 13) and see the emphasis on sexual sins.

What do we see in these verses? We see sexual perversion and the love of pleasure that has characterized our time, but we see something else. We see an opposition to truth—lies and deception. This coincides with Jesus' main warning to His disciples against deception at the end time (Mat. 24:14).

Great opposition to truth existed in the days of Noah, just as it does today. Only one man and his family believed and taught the truth. The whole world refused to believe what Noah preached. The truth was perverted.

Twisting (perverting) truth opens the door for sexual perversion as well. The sexual perversion in the society of Noah's day was one of the open doors that allowed the sex crazed giants to come on the earth.

Taking a Bigger View of Take

The Hebrew word for "take" has many conceptual meanings that need to be considered. Here are some: to bring in as a person for abuse or abusing; to buy as a slave or a tool; to carry away against one's will; to be seduced by scent, hypnosis, or potion; to fetch away; to get at another's expense of loss; to enfold or wrap one's arms around to prevent escape; to take excess numbers of; to have many more than required; to force conception upon.

Are we getting a picture of this word's concept? Does it sound like real lovemaking? Here are some more definitions: to place in a position of receiving, with a sexual connotation (confirmed by a Hebrew scholar); to receive a male against one's will; to hold in reserve or in a harem; to seize or be seized for selfish purposes; to send forth as a right of homage or right of the tithe; to take away to one's stronghold; to use as a wife without love; to use indignantly; to win by size, power, might, or program.

These giants were enflamed with an animalistic desire for pleasure, and they had no morals. Satan put this desire to kill in their DNA.

We must understand that the *nephilim* were carrying out a program that Satan had programmed into them through the humanoid watchers. Wives were to be given by God to the husband he had chosen for them, not taken. They were not to be raped, clearly an action taken outside of God's will.

The skeletal records of many women show that their pelvic bones were crushed or strategically broken to allow a child of enormous size to be born. Thousands of skeletons have been unearthed of women who had their pelvic bones crushed in order to give birth to large children. The giants broke their bones and made the women suffer. Many did not survive the birthing process or were badly scarred.

The giants took wives for themselves, but it wasn't as if they went hunting for them. The indications are that the men lined their wives up to give them as offerings for these giants to take and abuse.

Does that sound like what was happening at Sodom and Gomorrah? We haven't quite come to that point today, but when the giants return at the very end, at the time of the wrath of God, the seeds of perversion will have been sown so that a similar situation could easily occur.

Why Jesus Had to Bring the Flood

Jesus saw the extreme wickedness and perversion on the earth, and He was deeply grieved. He would have to blot out those He had created (Gen. 6:5–7).

At stake today amid the extreme sexual perversion that has permeated our society, depending on the church doing its job, is also the destruction of all humankind and mankind from the earth, a curse of destruction on this planet (Mal. 4:6).

Jesus had to destroy the people on earth. But why?

Men were in subjection to the pheromones of the *nephilim*. They were turning their wives over to these giants so that *nephilim* genetic material could corrupt all flesh. Men weren't allowed to impregnate their own wives; only the giants could seed. The men were passive and impotent because of these pheromones.

Jesus, however, put a time limit (announced a judgment time) for man and the world, as we see in Genesis 6:3: "Nevertheless, his days shall be one hundred and twenty years." This length of time not only stated the new maximum lifespan of man; it was also the length of time that would pass before judgment would come on all those who polluted themselves with the giants. The watchers knew that God meant business, but mankind, under the influence of these *nephilim*, did not. The watchers prepared to leave earth and take as many of their giants with them as they could.

Genesis 6:4 states why God would have to take action: "The Nephilim were on the earth in those days, and also afterward…" This tells us that these *nephilim* were the cause of God's displeasure, and the limitations He had just placed on mankind resulted from this interbreeding and mixing of kinds.

Notice that the giants were on the earth during the days preceding the Flood "and also afterward" (Gen. 6:4). The watchers (or beings of the pre-ice age) were responsible for saving the lives of these giants through the time of judgment by water or earth-wide baptism. They weren't put into the ark for various reasons, including the fact that they weren't male and female, as Noah described the pairs he brought into the ark.

In order for giants to exist after the Flood, the watchers who worked with Satan had to take them off the earth before the Flood came. The time limit God gave, which encouraged the disappearance of the giants, may explain why Noah was five hundred years old before any sons could be born to him. Noah had to become clear of the giant pheromones so he was no longer impotent and could plant seed for children in his wife. Satan's purpose for the giants was to pollute the gene pool so that no woman could bear a seed or male child that didn't have *nephilim* DNA hardwired in to do Satan's will. Satan thought he could prevent the woman's seed (Gen. 3:15), the Messiah, from coming as Savior.

Satan felt that if these children of the giants could gain the promise of God for redemption, then he and his demons could also have a right for redemption. God made no plans, however, for them. They wanted to be redeemed and given full authority without ever repenting.

Uncommon Scents

You can see how Satan is preparing the world for the return of these giants. He is putting the accent on sex, and especially sexual perversion. Snce the scent of the giants will draw women sexually, Satan has prepared our last-days generation with scents that attract the opposite or same sex. The ranks of Paris perfumes have now been joined by the sale of pheromones that guarantee sexual attraction. Satan has made these giants to have a seductive scent that is absolutely irresistible. It is a scent that causes people to lose all their senses except the erotic ones.

Since Satan plans to bring the giants back soon, he is stepping up his perfume program along with the heavy sex saturation of our society. From the outset of mankind's sin, Satan has caused a pollution of the genetic make-up of mankind to transform them into a lower "humankind."

Humankind is much more susceptible to the effects of drugs—such as crack-cocaine, speed, and ecstasy, all of which are sexually arousing. Sexual sin has always paved the way for Satan's destructive power to be unleashed, and no exception exists when it comes to the return of the humanoids and giants. *L'eau de toilette*, followed by *nephilim* pheromones, will end up leading us to a moral cesspool filthier than anything history has ever known. It's time we wake up to the tragic consequences of our society's sexual looseness.[50]

Sex Gone Wild

The *nephilim* were designed to be extremely productive in producing seed. The legend of the giants says that a single one could supply seed for up to five hundred women in a single day. Women were driven mad by the pheromones. They would do anything to get anointed by the emissions of these giants so they could become pregnant.

These words are intended for mature audiences. God is pure, yet He spoke openly of sexuality in the Bible, speaking of women spreading their legs "to every passer-by to multiply [their] harlotry" (Ezek. 16:25). The Hebrew name Chedorlaomer (Gen. 14:1,4) included the meaning of having large testicles, as verified by a rabbinical scholar. God talks openly about women's breasts, telling married men to be satisfied with their wives' breasts (Prov. 5:19), and the Song of Solomon reads like

50 *On our website, we quoted an article about the sale of pheromones by a doctor who claims they are "supercharging the love lives of thousands of men" (www.ARAlifestyle.com).*

a handbook on marital sex foreplay. God records the story of Onan spilling his seed or semen on the ground (Gen. 38:9).

The graphic material we share here, and especially in Appendix II, is meant to warn of what is prophesied so we can avoid it and stay pure. It is not meant to seduce readers into practicing perversion.

Why should those God has called to warn the world, even the Christian world, about their sexual immorality be shy about stating things as they are? God is not a prude. He is quite open in His Word about sexuality. Our hope is that, in seeing the sexual perversions in history, you can make the connection with some of our church traditions today and open your eyes to what is going to take place soon. Traditions of these days of the giants were later followed by Babylonian and Canaanite customs. In the time of the giants, a cup of "holy" ejaculate from the giants (later from male prostitutes who dedicated their semen to the gods) was provided to anoint worshippers in dedication to the *nephilim* when entering the idolatrous place of worship.

Priests used phallic-shaped rods to dip into these cups (or pails) in order to sprinkle the congregation. In ancient Babylon, this procedure was done at the start of a sexual orgy. It represented the joining procedure of the *nephilim* with the woman. The priests would go in and anoint everyone in the congregation before having a sexual orgy that was supposedly blessed and holy. You could have sex with anybody there as many times as you wanted, but only on the first day of the week. Afterward, men and women would gather in temples honoring the genitals of the giants. They would press their hands together as a symbol that they were sexually ready for the *nephilim*.

Later the priests would perform a marriage ceremony, not only sprinkling a couple but throwing rice or grain seed, sometimes in a confetti style with crushed up leaves, to represent the blessing of the *nephilim*. These symbols supposedly brought a blessing so that the couple would have many "kids." Although ejaculate isn't used in modern marriage ceremonies, many are still confirmed by the throwing of some type of confetti.

The word "kids," by the way, is an abbreviated form of "kinds independent of divine sanction." Goats have kids that will mate with anything. Satan is referred to as a goat in the Bible, and Jesus separates His sheep from Satan's goats. So why not call our progeny children instead?

Bells rang out from places of worship in antiquity. For whom did the bells toll? They celebrated the perversions of the giants. The *nephilim* would often be forced to wear a bell on their genitalia so people would hear them coming into their area. They were even placed in steeples at pagan shrines and rung in order to call people—and *nephilim*—to worship.

Baal Worship

Baal was the name given to the storm god, and to a number of other gods who were either mighty men or giants. Baal is the how the word "Lord" is translated back into Hebrew. "The Lord" has multiple meanings of which most sincere Christians are ignorant. Baal was the title for a leader who had the biggest sexual endowment. Mayday around the maypole was a time of size comparison. The decoration of the maypole was a confirmation of the man with the largest sexual organ. He became the leader of the land.

Such a leader was called "the lord" in the Babylonian traditions, especially among the Canaanites, who were devoted followers of phallic worship. Even in India today one finds temples in which a woman isn't allowed to marry or have children until she has gone in and spent many hours holding onto these large phallic symbols. These women believe they are receiving the blessing of the giants to be fruitful in childbearing.

Referring to Jesus as "the Lord" is calling Him, inadvertently in most cases, by an uncomplimentary sexual slur. People excuse this deceptive practice by saying it's biblical. Not true. The translators of the King James Bible were more familiar with the ways of Babylon than with Jesus and weren't true believers in Jesus. This was Satan's way of polluting the Bible with pagan terms.

People today are often called to come to the altar to receive the Lord, not to come to Jesus, the Savior and Redeemer. They also are called to come to Christ or the Anointer. But the term Christ must be identified with Jesus before it can signify any true anointing.

This lord worship is a clear reflection of the Babylonian and Canaanite influences on religion. God clearly forbids the mixture of pagan and godly modes of worship of the true God (Deut. 12:29–32; John 4:24; Mark 7:6–9).

Men of renown were also worshipped as gods in their own right (Gen. 6:4). These children who came from the giants grew taller and stronger than their mothers, yet smaller than the *nephilim*. These "men of renown" became the basis of the Greek and Roman pantheon of gods. They were the root gods (or master gods) of the Hindu religions. Many African cultures have traditions of *nephilim* worship.

The Hebrew words for idolatry and adultery are linked. While biblically women symbolized false churches with which Israel committed adultery, women also pursued satisfaction from false gods who symbolized sexual prowess. Sexual revelry was a common element of idolatrous pagan worship.

Satan has deceived Christians today into using terms referring to false gods for the true God. We insist on using terms and doing things that are not of God, leading to the judgment of our nations, especially the supposedly Christian Western nations. Few, however, follow the real Jesus who condemns the use of such sexual terms in His Word. His promise to His bride is that He will soon "remove the names of the Baals from her mouth" (Hos. 2:17).

We can pretend that these prophecies only applied to outright Baal worshippers at the time. However, we know that God wrote the Bible for us in the last days especially, for those "upon whom the end of the ages [has] come" (1 Cor. 10:11). God told Daniel to "seal up the book until the end of time" (Dan. 12:4). Bible prophecy was written for us in this twenty-first century.

God foreknew that we would use the term "Lord" to call on Jesus in the last days. That's why He revealed to us in the year 2000 that we needed to call on the mighty name of Jesus, not on a lowly lord whose title implies a sexual perversion.

Shouting Ra, Ra! for Evil

Man was only interested in worshipping *ra*, the conceptual and vast word for evil in Genesis 6:5. What has happened in our society? We worship evil and call it good (Isa. 5:20).

The whole of society has become so sexually oriented that you are unable to log onto the internet without being bombarded. There's hardly a song you can listen to, even on so-called Christian stations, that isn't polluted in some way. The Christian stations have songs that praise "the Lord." *Ra* was a lord. A derivative of this word, Rah or Ra, was the name of an Egyptian god-man or *nephilim.* He's the one people adore today as Santa Claus (Satan's Claws).

The ancient world was, and even our world today is, devoted to the worship of *ra* (evil) and of serving *ra*. Pre-Flood man was totally devoted to *ra*. He would die to serve evil. He would sacrifice his wife, his children, and his animals to serve wickedness. No act of cruelty or crudeness would be spared.

Genesis 6:5 means that mankind could not and would not think anything righteous because only the thoughts that pleased *ra* would enter his mind. Mankind, swayed by the altered genetic structure made possible by the humanoid watchers, was playing a satanic recording stuck in sin. They could only be made to sin. They weren't interested in anything righteous.

Genesis 6:6 shows Jesus' grief for having made man. The lust that Jesus saw in men's and women's sexual involvement with the *nephilim* greatly hurt His heart. He was repulsed by their desire to do evil, to love evil, and to bind themselves with sickness and infirmities.

God had offered man life, abundance, peace, and happiness. Man, however, wanted every perversion Satan could offer him, unwilling to stay pure, true, chaste, and faithful to the wife God had for him. Men took on the spirit of mockery. God's promises, His Word, and His covenants meant nothing.

Sexual slavery to evil meant everything. Anything men could do to get more sexual pleasure was considered a good thing. Men who God had made in His holy image lusted for impurity, praising a mixture of good and evil.

Satan promised Eve that she could be like God, knowing good and evil. This was more than a mental knowing, but a knowing of and by intercourse, one of the possible meanings of the Hebrew word for "know." She was going to have intercourse, an intimate relationship with evil (and probably literal intercourse with the evil one). She wanted more. She couldn't be filled up.

Girl's Gone Wild for Giants?

In our sex-saturated, Western world there's a series of films called "Girls Gone Wild." In the times of the giants, women went wild over the *nephilim*. Pre-Flood man wanted every perversion Satan could offer.

Why was that? They wanted to become high on the adrenalin rushes and drugs Satan could provide. Today people get high on sexual addictions, pornography, crack cocaine, marijuana, and even pharmaceuticals like codeine. These addictions produce their own drug rush. The drugs speed and ecstasy produce a sexual rush that attacks the sexual center of the brain.

Why am I speaking of these perversions? The reason is that the world is headed in the very same direction, and the voices of believers must be lifted up against evil, explaining the prophesied future of this burgeoning evil (Ps. 94:16; Isa. 58:1; 59:16; Ezek. 9:4).

Jesus' heart is again grieved today as He looks on the sexual perversion of the world, even the sexual looseness of His own people.

Whenever the heart of Jesus is grieved totally, He is forced to take action. He couldn't allow Satan to pollute mankind so effectively that He wouldn't be able to be his Redeemer.

Can you imagine a hurt so great as God's own sons and daughters openly hating their Creator, their own Father God, Jesus, and the Holy Spirit? Such a force of loss would be so great that God would have to take action to cleanse the earth of those whose only love was sin and sexual perversion. Everything that Satan and his watchers had touched would have to die as an offering for the penalty of sin.

Whatever sin had polluted would have to die. If Noah or Noah's sons had any *nephilim* material in them, they would have died; they would not have been taken into the ark.51 God could not have been

---

51 *The bloodlines were passed down through the dominant genes of the male. While the female genes influenced color, they did not alter the bloodline, so it was important for the males to be pure. It was the giants who corrupted the bloodlines before and after the flood, but the males*

able to fulfill His plan on the earth. He would have had to pick another solar system. That's why Genesis 6:6 says Jesus was sorry He "had made man *on the earth*." Read between the lines. God says much with few words. He would have had to choose another planet somewhere else in His universe.

Jesus is going to be forced to bring His wrath upon a sexually perverse and rebellious world for 390 days of a perfect, prolonged biblical year. This is exactly the same period of time that Noah and his family spent in the ark while Jesus brought His wrath on the pre-Flood world.

God's Grief over Pre-Flood World and Today

God knows the end from the beginning, just as Jesus knew the struggle He would go through in Gethsemane and on the cross. When Jesus had to actually go through these trials—even the Flood trial, as He saw His creation turn totally away from His love—He had a tough time dealing with it. His heart was greatly grieved. Later He would have to go through the same grief a man experiences in the flesh so He could bear all our sorrows.

Yet He sees a Christian world that has abandoned His Sabbaths and His new moons, designed so we could lay down our long-term grief and sorrows to Him on His cross (Isa. 53:4; 1 Pet. 5:7; Ps. 55:22).

Why was Jesus sorry that He made man?

Did they sin? Or was more involved? Were they part of the genetic material used by the watchers to make the *nephilim*? Both statements are correct. They were indeed cursed with the bad genes, but Jesus had a solution. He would end all air-breathing life on the earth. He would

---

of Noah's family were pure before the flood. Ham and Canaan's sexual sin allowed the giants to return about sixty years after the flood.

baptize the planet and thus wash away all the stench of sin, including the giants and their sons of renown.

This would become known as the first authorization of change and cleansing.

What's the first thing you have to do when the Father draws you to Jesus and you accept Him? God commands us to be baptized (Acts 2:38; Mark 16:16). In other words, open yourself up to change by burying the old self in a watery grave.

All God's commands have a purpose. Submitting yourself to baptism, for example, authorizes God to step into your life and start the purification process. Baptism is a starting point that begins in us the process of purification from giant DNA. The regressive genes are deactivated and the positive genes are activated, beginning with baptism.

Many Christians haven't even taken that first step, much less completed the process God created. Jesus gave us His body and blood to take for cleansing, not only annually at the Passover, but frequently so we could be purified on a regular basis.

Satan has deceived the Christian world about God's purification program because he wants to keep Christians polluted with bad DNA, as the men were before the Flood. Jesus gave us His Sabbaths, on which *Yahovah Makkadesh*, the Eternal Sanctifier, could cleanse us weekly. He also gave us the feast days, on which we could be cleansed throughout the year, and the new moons, so we could lay down our impurities from the past. But the Christian world has ignored His purification process.

Will you ignore it also? Will you allow yourself to be ruled by sexual perversion? A good beginning is finding the cause. What brings sexual perversion into one's life?

The Roots of Sexual Perversion

Sexual perversion seems to have no bounds today. The internet is full of opportunities to sin sexually. Swingers clubs and orgies aren't as uncommon as they used to be. Even at Christian schools, young people are encouraged to engage in sexual frolics before marriage. Adultery is on the rise, as is divorce.

What is the root of all this sexual perversion? In 2 Timothy 3, we see the terms "lovers of pleasure" and "irreconcilable." Unwillingness to forgive is one of the major roots of sexual perversion, notably when a child, especially a son, refuses to forgive a father who hurt him in any way. He falls into what our bloggers have called the C-S condition[52] that describes those who have not forgiven their fathers. This makes a son evaluate everyone and everything sexually, often leading him into sexual lust and perversion.

When we look at the root causes of sexual perversion in the general population, we see a correlation with the world of lies we live in today.

What is a lie? It's more often than not a twisted truth. It's a twist—a perversion.

Did you know that every time you believe a lie, speak a lie, or allow deception to speak through you, your eyes are open to sexual perversion? Nothing can stop it from entering your mind and heart. And with your heart and mind seduced, they set your will to allow perversion easy access in shaping your identity.

In the 1960s, a man named Chubby Checker made popular a new dance called the twist. Satan started singing his version of "Let's Do the Twist" many millennia ago in the Garden of Eden. It was the first

---

52 *Our bloggers coined this term when a poster named Colin (probably using a pseudonym) displayed what they began to call father-hating syndrome—or a "C-S condition."*

twist or perversion of the truth, and it opened up the world to the spirit of perversion, followed by sexual perversion.

Let's notice the very first word Satan said to Eve. It was a word that would introduce doubt, questioning God and the truth He had given Eve. He said, "Indeed, has God said, 'You shall not eat from any tree of the garden?'" (Gen. 3:1).

He was saying, "Did God *really* say that? Are you sure you haven't been lied to? Do you think He really meant that?" The irony is that Satan was lying by asking the question. He well knew what God had said, and so did Eve. But Satan knew that by introducing a small level of doubt, a little leaven of sin, he could leaven the whole lump and cause Adam and Eve to lose the garden and bring about the world the devil wanted.

When Eve accepted this twist, this lie, this perversion from Satan, the doors were opened wide for all kinds of perversion, including sexual perversion. And whether we realize it or not, the same thing has happened today.

If Isaiah lived in a world of lies and lived "among a people of unclean lips" (Isa. 6:5), how much more are we living today in a lying world? Almost everything we hear on the news, even on television as we watch TV evangelists, is laced with lies. The truth is twisted everywhere we look. Politicians make promises they don't keep. Press secretaries twist the truth to protect their bosses.

The Satanic Santa Lie

Most importantly, parents lie to their children. Yes, they lie to their little ones from a young age, at a time when they are completely dependent upon their parents and look to them as if they were God. When parents lie to their children, as most parents do, the child is faced with the "indeed" or "really" questions which start building perversion's hold on their young lives.

At a certain age, you begin to wonder about some of the things your parents have told you. They say Santa Claus comes down a chimney on Christmas Day to bring you toys. You wonder at this supernatural fellow, in reality a holdover from the pagan man-god Rah of Egypt, who brings toys to all the children in the world on the same night. And you see department store Santas that all look different, with different faces, some of them fat and others not so fat.

Then one fateful day you hear your peers laugh at anyone who's so dumb to believe in Santa Claus. You realize that your parents lied to you. I remember where I was and who told me the truth. I was older than most to learn about this lie at the age of nine, and when my older friend Pat told me, I was devastated. I felt betrayed. It was as if God had lied to me.

One boy said, "I found out there was no Santa Claus. Maybe I better look into this Jesus Christ business!"

The truth has been twisted, and so have our little psyches. Perversion now has a foothold. As we grow a bit older, we have greater independence and freedom of choice. At this point, Satan has legal right to send the demon of perversion to start controlling us. We begin to test barriers, limits, and our parents' love for us.

Even if our parents have shown only love to us, we make a choice as to whether or not we will obey the voice of perversion and receive the demon of defiance as a reward for our wrong choice.

If our parents respond in anger-rage, abuse, curses, or negative labeling ("You're a bad boy/girl!), then parental love is *always* in doubt thereafter; the test has been successful in proving doubt of a parent's love. Perversion has now established its hold. The door is now open for defiance to enter. This can happen at an early age to cause what can become the avoidable "terrible twos."

We are forced into a cycle of doubt and testing to find out when our parents love us and when they don't. This testing continues throughout our lives until we're certain where we stand on all fronts.

This pattern is established for testing God, teachers, grandparents, police, government, and future mates. This need for challenge so permeates our lives that we're attacked with lack of purpose, loss of identity, and erosion of barriers… and all of it leads to sexual perversion.

Looking for Love in All the Wrong Places

If the love test is constantly failed, all barriers are tested over and over, and we see no restraint on the testing of limits and laws. Nothing is ever certain, since the need to find love overwhelms the logic, reasoning, emotional, and evaluation centers of our brains.

If we've been sexually abused at an early age, the reasoning center of our brain is even shut down. All we have is the emotional center and the logic center, which can't figure out what to do with the emotions. When this sad state of affairs is turned over to Jesus at the new moon, we can call on His healing of our brains.

We will do, say, or think anything in order to fill this love gap and feel loved. Perversion opens the way to seek out every possibility for satisfying our need to be loved.

When rejection has set in at a very young age, fantasy, lust, rape, and "dreamscaping" are brought in by perversion and defiance. A lifelong gap opens in our identity that calls for seeking attention and self-gratification in sex. Love and empathy are replaced by lust, sex, and addictions.

Satan knows the power of the sexual urge God has placed in mankind. In our world of lies and troubles, people seek a way of escape.

One of the prime means of escape today is the world of sex fantasy and addictions. These addictions are the easiest means of escape, but also the most difficult to escape from. Sexual highs are connected to powerful hormones the body releases. Without Jesus, it's a losing battle.

Any thwarting of the quest for sexual satisfaction is viewed as further rejection and is an important trauma. The more often we face rejection's sting, the deeper into perversion we sink.

The acceptance of sexual perversions by society today makes it even easier to fall into these perversions. Speaking out against the powerful lobby of homosexuals, transsexuals, and other alternate lifestyles has become dangerous. A young lady who spoke out on YouTube against boys dressing like girls and being admitted to girls' restrooms and dressing rooms was met with threats and curses.

We have a perverted society as in Noah's day that is ready to persecute those who call their perversions sin.

Perversion Is Satan's Solution to Rejection's Pain

We need to make several important points about sexual perversions:

- They have a cause and effect. The effects touch everyone around you and contaminate everything you touch.
- They were designed by Satan to pollute mankind and create a mixed kind called humankind.
- All sexual perversions are addictions.
- No sexual perversion ever submits to control by common sense reasoning.
- All sexual perversions are promoted as normal by the media.
- All sexual perversions can be passed down from generation to generation.

- Even abuse, guilt, disease, or the threat of death won't stop you from seeking out sexual perversions.
- No sexual perversion is simply outgrown.
- Body mutilations do not stop the desire for involvement in sexual perversions.
- Only turning sexual perversions over to Jesus and allowing Him to work in your mind, will, and heart will ever get you rid of them.

What establishes sexual perversions?

1. What you allow your heart to hear and hold onto.

2. What you allow your eyes to see and dwell on.

3. When you speak out for what you have heard or seen.

4. When you add the perversions to your common speech.

5. When you allow your imagination to take you to where you should not go.

6. When you then seek opportunities to set your body into action.

7. When you then set your will to accept sexual perversion.

8. These then close the gates to logic, common sense, and reasoning in order to justify the lie of living in sin.

Sexual perversions are Satan's answer to rejection's pain. His hope is to lock you out of God's Kingdom. Then Satan ensures you're punished for using his methods. As with Eve, it's likely that the devil perverted what she saw and heard in order to have a sexual relationship with her and her children thereafter. Anything that's not one hundred percent true is a perversion of the truth and is therefore a door opener to sexual perversion.

God's Answer to Satan's Answer

Do you want Satan's answer to rejection, which is perversion, or do you want God's way out, His method of purification? A big step in the right direction would be to read a book I wrote called *Peace or Rejection—You Choose.*[53]

Properly dealing with sexual perversion involves immersing yourself in God's purification program, which begins with accepting Jesus and being literally immersed in water baptism, as we have explained.

Baptism is the first step to change, a step many Christians say isn't necessary. They speak of a spiritual baptism without hands, but they ignore Jesus' command to be baptized and to baptize believers. Mark writes, "He who has believed and has been *baptized* shall be saved"

53 *Peace or Rejection—You Choose is available online at www.freedomtruthseekers.com, www.freedomchurchofgod.com, or www.robertsmoreofjesus.com.*

(Mark 16:16). And Peter's words in Acts 2:28 don't sound like a mild suggestion.

If the pre-Flood world hadn't been baptized (in the Flood), you and I would not be alive today. Baptism isn't an option; it's a necessity. Jesus had to wash the stench of the *nephilim* off the face of the earth. If he hadn't done it, there would have been no way to save man from the giants. No other first step exists for us to be cleansed from a giant dose of pollution.

Keeping God's Sabbath, holy days, and using the powerful tool of the monthly new moon time of laying down long-term sins and burdens is essential. Turning over thoughts of perversion to Jesus on the cross starts the process of healing.

Taking the Passover, the body and blood of Jesus, is a powerful supernatural cleansing. Some problems cannot be resolved without the Passover being observed. The foot-washing ceremony is also an anointed washing away of all the unrecognized sins of the year.

Another necessity is being willing to seek God's empowerment (or grace) to obey all the laws He gave to keep us free from impurities. It all requires grace, since we cannot of ourselves keep the many laws God gave as boundaries of protection.

Few have utilized God's program of healing and sanctification. Even Christians have been so inundated by the flood of sexual perversion gushing into our modern world that they've submitted to the evil of our day.

Only one man stood against the evil of his day. His name was Noah.

Chapter Seventeen:
Noah Said No—Will You?

In the perverse world of pre-Flood times, only one man stayed pure both spiritually and genetically. Only he and his family were saved from the Flood. Will we be the Noahs of our evil generation?

Luke described and prophesied what our generation would look like: "And just as it happened in the days of Noah, so it will be also in the days of the Son of Man" (Luke 17:26).

Jesus is grieved with the perversion He sees in our world today, especially among the nations He calls His, the "believing" nations of Anglo-Saxon origin. He was greatly grieved at the rampant perversion of Noah's day. Sexual immorality was widespread, as epitomized by the lewdness of the giants and humanoids that were on the earth in those days.

The word evil and wickedness are basically the same word in Hebrew—*ra*. The word refers to something that is extremely bad or evil. Hebrew concordances and scholarly works hint at only a fraction of its conceptual meanings, of which we cite only a few: to think like the adversary (that is, adverse to the things of God); to bring afflictions or adhere to the ways and demands of the afflicter; to cause calamity to oneself and or to others; to do everything to bring displeasure from God; to distress the soul of God and one's self; to favor evil above anything good; to be totally submitted to worshipping the phallus; to be exceedingly caught up in seeking a man thing (What is a man thing? How about a humanoid that looks male?); to be great in phallus size; to cause harm to others when seeking sexual stimulation; to be ill in marking (this refers to an inability to claim the promises of God, being closed to any covenant of God, as evidenced by the mark of Cain); to be sexually mischievous; to be coyly naughty in order to attract sex; to cause no pleasure for another, always trying to get for yourself (the needs of others are of no concern); to be sadly sore after a sexual encounter or desire; to trouble others with one's sexual desires; to overpower or overshadow others, moving them into a weakened condition and taking advantage of them; to take out sexual pleasures on someone who is not willing (the nephilim released pheromones, and their erotic effect overwhelmed mankind); to rob another of his or her desired purpose; to choose the wrong sex for seeding, men with men and women with women; to affect another by rape.

Will You Be an End-Time Noah?

In a world of sin, perversion, and gross evil, Noah stood out as a righteous man. He resisted the evil expressed by this Hebrew word for wickedness.

Why? What set Noah apart? What kind of man was he?

Since Jesus said that these last days would be just like the days of Noah, perhaps we should learn some lessons from Noah. If the last days are going to be like his days, his example is important for us. He is an example for us to follow.

Genesis 6:17–21 explains that God could only establish a covenant with righteous Noah and his sons. They were still genetically pure in their line and had not corrupted themselves with the giants. But their wives needed covering, since they had been corrupted. Japheth's wife was the establisher of the Asian race. Ham's wife was the establisher of the Africans. Shem's wife was the establisher of the Caucasians, since she was the same genetic makeup as Shem.

God designated a certain time for the repentance of the pre-Flood world. He has also given us a period in which to repent. Pre-Flood man was like the church of God at Thyatira and its corresponding church era: "I gave her time to repent, and she does not want to repent of her immorality" (Rev. 2:21).

How many or how few will be those today who choose to change, to repent of their evil ways? Will you be among their number? Will you be "in the boat," or will you choose to drown in the coming calamities? Will you prepare for a rapture out of this mess, or will you follow along with the sexual depravity of this world?

God has shown us that the time for repentance of the nations has reached its term. Individuals can repent and turn to God, but not the nations as entities. Ezekiel prophesied about such a time and such a situation. He said at such a time the righteous could only save themselves, not the nation.

It is interesting to note the righteous men throughout history God gave us as examples in Ezekiel's prophecy, and who He mentioned first, ahead of Daniel and Job. "[Even] though these three men, Noah, Daniel and Job were in its midst, by their own righteousness they could only deliver themselves..." (Ezek. 14:14).

I preach a warning message as did Noah. We need the supernatural protection God gave him. God surrounds the righteous with favor as with a shield (Ps. 5:12). Noah's message, a very similar one to mine, could have caused him to be murdered. But God sends his angels to protect. Our common message of warning isn't popular, and it's as controversial as Noah's was.

Noah's message was similar to the message of those who come with a warning from Jesus and a hope in Him today. It is a message of judgment and of rapture, Noah's version involving a boat, and mine about a rapture to heaven, the best protection. Paul spoke of the rapture (1 Thes. 1:10) and said he spoke to them "the gospel of God amid much opposition" (1 Thes. 2:2). I have that fierce opposition in common with Paul and Noah. In these days, we must not compromise with the truth but set our standards high.

God sets a high standard for Christians in the last days. Jesus said in Matthew 11:11, "Truly I say to you, among those born of women there has not arisen anyone greater than John the Baptist!" God is calling those who have the same spirit that animated John the Baptist to prepare the way for the Messiah in this end time.

Elijah emphasized the reconciliation of families and the rapprochement of God's children to Father Love, and others are doing a similar work.[54] And as Elijah, we are being employed to turn the children of God away from Baal (or Lord worship) to the real Jesus. John called for the same kind of repentance in preparing the way of Jesus at His first coming.

God is calling us to look at the examples of these men of God as we seek to do His work in these last days. Noah becomes an important example to follow. After all, we are called not only to preach a message of warning of judgment to come, but also to be counted worthy to "get on the boat," so to speak (see Luke 21:36).

The question is: will you be in the boat? What puts you in the ark of supernatural protection?

---

54 I am presently working on a book about the principle of Malachi 4:6, of bringing the heart of children to their fathers, including Father God.

Noah's Name Says a Lot

Names are revealing. We shall get a clue as to why Noah was special in looking at his name. He found favor in the eyes of God (Gen. 6:8), and one reason is that he lived up to his name.

The name Noah means rest. The first mention of Noah in the Bible is important. In Genesis 5:29, we find that Noah was named as such because "[this] one will give us rest from our work and from the toil of our hands arising from the ground that [Jesus] has cursed."

The ground had been cursed, but now the whole earth will be cursed, except those who follow Noah's example, whose name meant rest. Only because Noah learned to rest in Jesus can we today follow his example and learn to rest in Jesus.

Because Noah was called righteous, we know he kept the Sabbath day. He walked with God for six days and then rested in Jesus on the Sabbath. Those who follow his example of rest in righteousness today will follow the example of Sabbath rest. Jesus said in Exodus 31:13 that He was *Yahovah Makkadesh*, the God who sanctified His people, employing mainly the Sabbath day to do so. We will only know that He is *Makkadesh*, who makes us holy, as we keep His holy day.

Noah found grace in God's eyes because He rested. He rested in God's promise and in God's day. In these last days, the only ones who are going to find the rest promised in Hebrews 3 and 4 are those who enter into God's Sabbath rest (Heb. 4:9).

It is only by resting in Jesus on the Sabbath day that we are given sanity amid the insanity of our times. Only Sabbath rest will give us peace in the face of the demonic rush fueled by computers, email, and television.

In the rat race of today's fast-forward society, who will be still and know that God is God? Who will come to the Good Shepherd and lie down in His green pastures and meditate beside His quiet waters?

The Sabbath-keepers will be the only ones who can truly cease striving and rushing through life. They will be able to "be still and know" that Jesus is God (not Lord!), that He will be "exalted in the earth" (Ps. 46:10). Yes, Jesus will be exalted on His Sabbath day among His people and in His millennial Sabbath day, the one-thousand-year reign of Jesus on earth.

We live in a harried, hurried, hectic world. We rush to and fro, doing five things at once, with cell phone in hand, wondering why we don't have time to enjoy life. God and family get put on the backburner of the sloppy stove of our frantic lives. We don't rest.

We especially need to rest and get away from the onslaught of perversion that assaults our eyes and ears during the week. We are refreshed with the pure Word of God to empower us for a new week, resisting by God's grace the impurity of the world that surrounds us and sometimes beckons us in weak moments.

The world in Noah's time was a fast-paced world like ours today. But Noah learned to rest in Jesus, as his name implies. He rested in the righteousness that comes by faith on the Sabbath day. His righteousness was a light to a world in utter darkness.

Pure in a Perverse World

"Noah was a righteous man, blameless in his time ['among his generations' (YLT)]; Noah walked with God" (Gen. 6:9). Here was a man who was morally upright, steadfast in his integrity.

The phrase "in his time" is quite revealing. The first few verses of Genesis 6 speak of the giants on the earth. We know that they were immoral to an extreme and tried to get all men and women involved sexually with them. Yet Noah said no. He was blameless in a world more blameworthy than ever.

We have, and soon to a greater extent, the same challenge today. Satan bombards us with sex, sex, and more sex on TV, the movies, and the internet. Billboards blast his not-so-subtle message of sexual debauchery, and the TV brings subtle, subliminal messages in the ads it diffuses. Satan is selling sex from all angles to prepare the world, and even Christians, for some giant size perversion which will begin a pollution to be completed by the giant *nephilim.* Will we allow ourselves to be polluted?

Noah didn't allow Satan's pollution to affect him. He kept God's days of purification, days that purify us from Satan's moral and genetic pollution. Keeping the false days that glorify sexual impurity in their origins only pollutes the church further.

On Freedom Blog, we enraged some and informed others when we produced a blog post entitled "Jesus Hates Christmas," followed by "Jesus Hates Valentine's Day." Is it possible that Jesus could hate a day that most Christians love, a day on which they believe they're celebrating His birth and worshipping Him?

While it comes as a shock to most Christians, Jesus never told us to keep December 25. He gave us the days He calls His in Leviticus 23. He kept them. The apostles kept them. The early church in Judea, composed of some Gentiles, kept them, as history and the Bible corroborate. But the church today chooses to compromise because… well, everybody's doing it, and why go against the flow?

The spotless Bride of Jesus cannot allow herself to eat of both tables—the table of demons and the table of God. God's people must be pure, blameless in these times of moral pollution and blameless in their generations. They must allow themselves to be cleansed from the *nephilim* DNA Satan has already programmed into their systems. Eating Jesus' body and drinking His blood in communion is the method God chose to replace the wrong DNA with the good, the DNA of Jesus.

Resisting the World's Influence

Will we walk with the world, or will we walk with Jesus as Noah did? He spent time with God. God was always on his mind. The minds of humankind were on sex and impurity. But Noah allowed his mind to be cleansed by the Word and the thoughts of God.

Noah said no to the world's ways. Will you?

Is the world "too much with us"? That's how William Wordsworth saw it. Too often we don't see the worth of God's Word in our thoughts and lives. Too often we meditate on sin, not on God's Word and ways.

John warns us in 1 John 2:15–17 to stay pure, that those who love the world do not have the love of the Father in them. How can we bring the hearts of God's children to Father Love if we don't have the Father's love in us?

Listen to the words of the apostle of love in 1 John 2:16–17: "For all that is in the world, the lust of the flesh and the lust of the eyes and the boastful pride of life, is not from the Father, but is from the world. The world is passing away…" How much more relevant is that statement today! This age of Satan and his rule is about to end, "and also its lusts; but the one who does the will of God lives forever."

Those who follow Noah's example of rest are resting in Jesus on the Sabbath day, the day that represents eternity, the government of the Eternal One over all the earth and the universe. The restful, righteous ones in these last days have an eternal focus. Their eyes aren't on what attracts worldly people, but rather on the Eternal One and His ways of love that last forever.

Now, Noah wasn't perfect. He did allow himself to get drunk on one occasion and thus became the victim of sexual perversion (Gen. 9:21), an act which allowed the giants legal right to return. Noah did, however, live a life of integrity. He didn't "practice" sin as a way of life (1 John 3:4, 8–9).

Americans have seen movies about men of integrity. One example is an old film, *Mr. Deeds Goes to Washington.* In this movie, one man stood up against the prevalent corruption in government. How hard would it be if the entire world was corrupt and you were the *only* one who said no to sin and perversion?

Noah knew. We need the strength Noah displayed to stand on God's principles as the world gets more and more corrupt around us.

Paul tells us not to follow the end-time example of evil men and impostors, deceiving and being deceived (2 Tim. 3:13–14). We have recently seen the phenomenon of criminals in high places of government, and frauds in even higher places. As they proceed from bad to worse, we need to be growing from glory to glory.

Obedience

Noah also set the example for us of being obedient in all things. Everything Jesus told him to do, he did (Gen. 6:22). The phrase is repeated for emphasis: "Noah did according to all that [Jesus] had commanded him" (Gen. 7:5). In this end time, two commandments become especially important. We can neglect them as the world does, and will do with greater and greater impunity, or we can obey them in the letter, spirit, and intent of the law of love.

Those two commandments are the commandments against adultery or sexual sin and the commandment to remember the Sabbath day. Since adultery is the same concept in Hebrew as idolatry, and since Sabbath-breaking is idolatry, the breaking of both commandments turns us away from the true God and our covenant with Him.

We actually have nine covenants with God at the present time, and one of those covenants is the covenant of Noah. How can we receive the promises of that covenant if we aren't following Noah's example?

Claiming God's Covenant with Noah as Ours

All mankind comes under the bow of God, the rainbow being the sign that He will never again destroy the earth by water. God saved all of Noah's family from the Flood, so we can claim this covenant for family salvation and protection. Noah's small family became a righteous seed that brought forth a harvest in the earth, so we can claim this covenant with any financial or other seed we sow.

Noah found favor with God, so we can claim favor under this covenant. As the world's sins and all the evil of the past were washed away in the Flood, we can claim the same for us in this covenant. All our sins are washed away. It's a new day!

The Flood symbolized our baptism (1 Pet. 3:21), washing away our evil conscience to give us a fresh, clean slate. God's grief at the pre-Flood evil caused Him to shorten man's lifespan to one hundred and twenty years (Gen. 6:3), a lifetime longer than most today and one we can claim in this covenant.

We can say, "Thank You, Father. I claim Your covenant with Noah as My covenant with You. I choose to walk with You, unpolluted by the world around me, doing all that You command. I declare that according to Genesis 6:18, I shall enter the ark of Your protection in these last days. Both my family and I will be protected from the Great Tribulation. I will be lifted up, not above the waters in a boat, but lifted up bodily to heaven to escape all these things and stand before the Son of Man (Luke 21:36). My family will be saved physically and spiritually, as was Noah's family. I have faithfully kept Your Sabbath day of rest, as Noah did, so I have found grace and favor in Your eyes. You will not forget my family and me. You have promised me in this covenant and in Psalm 91, 'With a long life I will satisfy him and let him see My salvation' (Ps. 91:16). This covenant and this psalm also promises that because I have solidly fastened my love on You in a time when love grows cold, You will deliver me. You will set me securely on high with Jesus in Your throne room because I have known Your name, Father Love, and the name of My God and Savior Jesus. You have said that when I call on You, You will answer me. You will be with me in trouble. You will rescue me and honor me (Ps. 91:14–15)."

I could say much more about Noah, but I'll now give additional insight into his name and an exhortation. Noah's name is *noon chet. Noon* means life. *Chet* is the word for fence or inner room. It implies the protection the ark provided, as we see in the root *navah,* "to rest," meaning "from the life that is secure." But we must ask why Noah was counted worthy to be in that inner room, or fenced-in enclosure of protection in the ark.

The answer is what will make us worthy to be raptured literally into heaven with Jesus. Unlike those around him who were walking dead men, Noah rested daily and especially on the Sabbath in the inner room, or throne room, of God in heaven.

As Cece Winans' song *Throne Room* suggests, those who dwell in that throne room are secure. In fact, the letter *chet* is the exact shape of the doorpost covered by the blood of the Lamb at the time of the Exodus. The blood of Jesus protects and shields us, allowing us access to the throne room.

The only real life is in the throne room. Jesus said that eternal life was to know the Father and know Him (John 17:3). When we are in fellowship with the One in the throne room, we have real life.

Cece's song *We Thirst for You,* and the popular song *As the Deer,* speak of a dry and barren land where we thirst for Jesus. The whole world was dry and barren, dwelling in death, but Noah thirsted for his God in the throne room. The world around us is getting more barren by the minute. Will we allow the world to lead us astray, or will we rest with our God in the throne room? Our answer will determine whether or not we'll be raptured up into a "heavenly boat."

So why don't we follow the example of this man who lived in a time like ours, fully embracing the covenant God made with him? We will thus see a spiritual rainbow in our lives, a promise that God gives us a future and the sure hope of real life—eternal life.

Jonathan Cahn's *The Harbinger* tells an amazing story, a story of unusual "coincidences" that are warnings to America of impending disaster, paralleling the history of ancient Israel. Now you have read the other part of that story, the full account of truth about the identity of nations, especially those God calls Israel.

You have read truth that has generally not been taught—hidden truth from Bible prophecy. This truth enables you to know the future and prepare for it. This is truth that can set you free. The question is, what will you do with it?

Chapter Eighteen:
What About You?

What about you? What will you do with what you've read?

You have read the good news of the glorious world to come under Jesus when He returns. You have also read a lot of bad news about cataclysms, conflicts, and unspeakable tragedies to come in the near future before Jesus comes back.

But what about you? Will you escape these perilous days ahead?

We all have been given an instinct of self-preservation. And we know God wants us to be protected in the time of the end, since He says He will rescue the faithful from the wrath to come (1 Thes. 1:10).

When we look at Paul's exhortations to the church that asked about a rapture, however, we see that the doorway to the rapture is not the "what about me" approach. The doorway to escape is love. It's growing in the love of our Father. Yes, it's reaching for the heart of love of our Father, whose name is Love.

If you're going to escape all these things, you need to know and practice the new moon turnover of problems to Jesus. Otherwise you won't be able to fully surrender your long-term burdens to Him, burdens that keep you from receiving the Father's love so you can give it to others.

Then you won't be asking, "What about me?" You'll be asking, "What about you?" You'll be seeking to show love to others, being the light of the world and the salt of the earth, interceding agents of preservation who open the door for Jesus to return to save the world.

Paul's letters to the Thessalonians are the most complete explanation of how to be ready for the rapture, the best rapture, to be caught up bodily to heaven to escape the calamities soon to come. The saints in the Thessalonian church asked Paul some important questions, some of which we have covered in this book: "What should we be doing now? What happens to those who are asleep in Christ? What are the signs of Jesus' return? Who is the son of perdition? Who will be in the rapture?"

Let's start as Paul did with what that word "rescues" or "delivers" (1 Thes. 1:10) means. The Greek word means to draw quickly away from imminent trouble, to draw up to oneself, to rescue alive, and to deliver from trouble while the blood still flows. The concept is to be saved and taken away from all dangers and troubles. The mention of wrath to come definitely refers to the end of this age.

These letters are all about the rapture and how to be ready for it. What are the conditions for being ready?

Be a Rapture-Ready Believer!

First of all, we must remind ourselves that it's not by our own might (or works) that we can be ready. Paul makes clear that the blamelessness we achieve will be by grace, by the power of Jesus in us (1 Thes. 5:23–24). We can't be ready by our strength, but we can submit to Jesus so He can prepare us.

Be sure of this: God is a God of infinite mercy. Were it not so, you wouldn't be reading this book, at least not from me. The Father of mercies will meet you where you are right now and make you ready if you are willing.

What Paul explains as the way to the rapture, especially in the first chapter of the first letter, is a life of thanksgiving. Instead of complaining about what Satan is doing, we should be in continual thanks for what God is doing in us and others.

Perhaps you haven't been given much reason to thank God for the brethren if they have hurt you. However, you can thank God in faith that the saints will exemplify God's love. Also, you can even start worshipping God on His Sabbath day in your own home, trusting Him to bring others into the fellowship. You can read our Freedom Blog and see the love exemplified by those who give praise reports of what God is doing for them and in them.

You can read what Paul says yourself. Paul tells us to give thanks to God…

1. For the brethren.

2. For their works of faith.

3. For their labors of love.

4. For their steadfastness in Jesus.

5. For their walk of hope.

6. For knowing they are the beloved of God.

7. That they are the ones chosen of God.

These are only seven of forty reasons for thanksgiving Paul gave. You can read the others in your Bible.

Paul gives these forty exhortations to thanksgiving so that our attitude may invite the rapture. Self-absorption and/or self-righteousness don't set the pattern for growth; thanksgiving does. We must see outside ourselves as distribution centers of the gifts and blessings of God. Givers are receivers of the rapture blessing.

Paul gives seven major exhortations to warn us about attitudes that could prevent us from being ready to be raptured.

By Jesus' Grace, You Can Be Ready

Be aware that Satan will try to thwart you (1 Thes. 2:17–18). When you begin to walk in love for the brethren and want to be with them, especially on the Sabbath day, Satan will try to hinder you. After all, you're coming to praise and give thanks for what Jesus did, for the gospel of the Kingdom, and for the love of the brethren. You're preparing for the rapture.

Build faith in order to endure afflictions and the moves of the tempter (1 Thes. 3:3–5). Jesus wants to find in the last days a faith-filled group who love and obey Him.

When we don't stand firm in Jesus, we affect those around us negatively (1 Thes. 3:8). Being united in faith and love makes it easier for all.

You must open the way for your heart to love God and be loved by Him and the brethren. It is our Father who must direct our hearts in love, not our pastor. Too many are into pastor worship today and look to their pastor more than Jesus.

Love never fails. Love opens the door to the rapture. God wants us to excel in love and not forget to love *all* men (1 Cor. 3:11–13). The rapture remains open to those whose hearts are open to growth in love, and who want to excel more and more in love.

Paul encouraged the brethren in that day to live a quiet, peaceful, and productive life as a light to others. And he told them not to be in any need. Fulfilling that last condition will be a challenge, but God is able to bring about this condition in our lives.

Being in need has a number of meanings: to be in lack; to be sick; to be without authority and power in prayer; to be deficient in faith, love, and confidence; to be in terror of the times; to be cursed with and affected by rejection; to be trapped in falseness; to live in selfishness; to be consumed by the devourer.

It's only in and through Jesus that we can be no longer in need. When we look to Him as our Source in all things, He is indeed all we need. I started my own person website (www.robertsmoreofjesus.com) because all believers, including me, need more of Jesus in these last days.

To be rapture-ready, we must not lose sight of the vision, purpose, and calling God has given us individually and collectively.

Paul gives a final, multifaceted warning (1 Thes. 4:28). He emphasizes obedience to all the commandments. The word *adonai* (or Greek *kurios*), in this context, implies the meaning of being more than Divine Master. It includes the concept of Jesus as Supreme Commander.

Paul is making sure the saints then and in these last days don't succumb to the increasing lawlessness Jesus prophesied. Paul is confirming that God is a God of law, that He demands obedience to express our love for Him. We cannot access the rapture if we believe the lie that the law is done away on the wings of grace. Grace is principally power to keep all of God's many laws of love. If we put aside any of the commandments, we are fighting God and cannot be ready for the rapture (Mat. 5:17–19; Mat. 19:17).

We have seen that sexual perversion was prophesied to abound in the last days, and it is already greatly on the rise. God wanted to know who would stay pure in a perverse world at the end. We see in these verses that rapture depends upon sanctification.

Sanctification, or becoming holy like God, isn't possible when sexual immorality exists in us, when we allow demons to affect us, when we believe in falseness, when we follow lustful passions and ways of impurity, defrauding our brothers, seeking our own revenge, and rejecting God.

Get Rid of Rejection

It is essential to do what is pleasing to our Father and allow our heavenly Father to be a Father to us. When we don't deal with rejection, such a state isn't possible. We need to understand the principles embodied in *Peace or Rejection—You Choose* and participate in communion to break off rejection.

The greatest blockage to sanctification is rejection. The spirit and curse of rejection will cause us to reject...

1. Those who teach the Word of God.

2. Ourselves as unworthy.

3. Others as unworthy.

4. The work of the Holy Spirit and the Holy Spirit Himself.

5. Correction.

6. The loss of our pet sin.

7. Sanctification.

8. The commandments of Jesus.

These eight targets of rejection will become the eight feet of betrayal that hold onto our lives. We'll be more easily led to accept the eight-pointed star of Cain that is to accompany the coming, evil beast power.

We're thankful that we serve a God of mercy. He doesn't demand absolute perfection in all the areas we have cited. He does, however, want us to call on Jesus, the Grace in us that does the works (2 Tim. 2:1). When we are weak, Jesus is strong. His grace is perfected in our weakness as we submit our weaknesses to Him.

A Foretaste of Whats to Come from the Hebrew

As believers, we tend to limit God and what He can do in and through us.

Years ago, my friend and colleague Gerald Budzinski told a pastor that his prayer was to have the Holy Spirit teach him a profound understanding of the Bible, a grasp of the original languages that would make the Word come alive to him. The pastor told him that this wasn't possible. He told Gerald that he had to go to Bible school and learn hermeneutics. "Hermewhat?" he thought.

Gerald would not be daunted. He believed what God said, that whatever we ask according to His will, He will give us. God fixes no limit on what He'll do for those with a childlike spirit.

God answered his prayer, showing him how even Bible scholars don't base their understanding on the amazingly conceptual Hebrew language as God inspired it in the original text. Gerald consults scholarly works and then asks the Holy Spirit to fill in the blanks.

The results are astounding. The Bible takes on added dimensions, truly becoming a diamond with multiple facets most have never seen. And one of the reasons God blessed Gerald in such a way is that he obeys the Sabbath commandment.

One of the revelations that came is that the Sabbath is the day for preparation for the rapture. This topic is one of the most misunderstood subjects among Christians today, and this short chapter is a foretaste of another exciting book I hope to publish, *The Days of the Rapture Are Here!*

The Hebrew Rapture Words and Their Sabbath Implication

The Hebrew words in Isaiah 26:20 reveal profound truths about the rapture. Many of these same words describe what happens on the Sabbath day: "Come, my people, enter your rooms and close your doors behind you; hide for a little while until indignation runs its course."

Being raptured, as indicated by these Hebrew words, is a matter of free will. God offers it, but we must choose to accept His offer.

Following are the meanings of these Hebrew words that can also apply to the Sabbath day, although in some cases only in a partial way, awaiting the final fulfillment:

Yalak (come)—God calling for His people to come to Him (on His day of convocation); to break out of troubles or tribulation (of the week);

to let down or drop one's hold on physical things (the routine things of the week); to let go or go elsewhere ("let go and let God" take care of things; to go into His holy presence).

Bow (enter; amplifier of *yalak*)—to attain safety, security, and/or peace (*Shabbat shalom,* or Sabbath rest, or peace); to call an assembly of true believers (holy, Sabbath convocation); to come into or enter into a sanctuary; to come out of what is dying or sick (the world); to enter a place of peace, rest, and celebration; to give of oneself (Sabbath being a time of giving); to be lifted up to heaven (the Holy of Holies in heaven); to put away the cares of the world (and of the week); to employ God's authority, using Jesus' name (in praise, prayer, and in healing on the Sabbath); to run down an enemy or worker of evil, putting Satan under your feet (terrorizing Satan the terrorist on the Sabbath, which is the meaning of one of the Hebrew words relating to the Sabbath and feast days); to stricken or end the age of evil (prophesied by the Sabbath); to expose the absolute truth; to take a time of refreshing (Sabbath is a time of refreshing which represents the millennial time of refreshing); to take away the foundations of deception (by learning the truth in Sabbath sermons); to agree with Jesus to leave the world behind, leaving everything that is of the flesh and that is not of heaven (if you take both worlds together); to agree to be in celebration and let Jesus celebrate over you; to celebrate our special home that is full of joy, light, and peace.

Enclosed in Peace and Protection

Cagar (close; one of several words that qualify *yalak*)—literally meaning to wrap tight (like the similar English word "cigar") so nothing else (but Jesus) can get in; close up access to Satan, the world, and those in rebellion (closing ourselves off in God's Sabbath sanctuary, away from the world); to deliver up oneself to God for provision and protection (give up a workday to receive double manna provision from Jesus, our

Manna and Provision); enclosed, wrapped up tight in the ways of peace and righteousness; to repair what was broken by Satan (during the week); to direct oneself away from fears and the way of fear (on God's day of love); to shut up Satan and his voice (by hearing God's Word and voice on the Sabbath); to be shut in together with those who walk with Jesus (congregating with other believers); to stop all influence of the world, flesh, and Satan (typified by the Sabbath); to allow oneself to be enclosed in love, peace, joy, glory, and righteousness (all part of the Sabbath); to close the doors to Satan and the world (by finding refuge in Jesus on the Sabbath).

Chabah (hide)—to cherish what God has given you (your body, allowing it to rest from the week's labor; cherishing His truth and fellowship); to reside under the wings of God (love is the shadow cast by His wings, and the Sabbath days are called shadows as well, *agapes* or feasts of love); to bind oneself to everything love is (on the day of Love where we meet with Love Himself); to be held away from evil's touch (by fellowshipping with the saints or holy ones—and with the Holy One Himself); to be held in a secret place (Psalm 91—the secret place or shadow of the Most High, protected and cherished in His love); to hide—spirit, soul, and body—in Jesus and without fear, where Satan and the world cannot get to you; to allow oneself by free will to be enclosed in love.

Abar (from *bar* or son; to "run its course; "overpast"; crossover—same word used in describing Passover; the concept is the son or seed of what was planted for a harvest)—to cover a road of sin or addiction with the blood of Jesus so you won't go back to it (the Sabbath is a day of freedom and celebrates freedom in the blood of Jesus); to live beyond the world; to bring over to another plane of existence while evil reigns (only typified by the Sabbath); to move outside the realm of time; to be conveyed past time and space, out of the current of evil (the Sabbath prophesies eternity); to do away with the confines of time (Sabbath is the day for taking it easy, taking your time); to escape the clutches of evil; to provoke Satan's anger by clinging to Jesus; to wait on Satan being put away (Sabbath prophesies his demise); to let rage run its course while you rest in safety (the world's system rages on while you rest away from it); to await the end of the reign of the taxing attacks of Satan and adversity; to remove all access to the promoters of sin; to set apart what is holy to God (like the holy time of the Sabbath) while evil is terminated (while evil is doing something down here, you are doing something much more important in heaven, in Sabbath fellowship with God); to shave off all of evil's hold; to cause one to make sounds of rejoicing away from evil's attack (singing songs of joy and celebration of the defeat of evil on the Sabbath); to cause a sweet-smelling aroma to fill heaven (our Sabbath prayers and songs rise as incense to God); to see the end of transgression (which the Sabbath represents); to depart evil bodily and let the soul depart from evil's control (the words here imply rapturing of the physical body as well as the spiritual part; on the Sabbath we depart bodily as well as spiritually from the world, in the sense that we move our bodies into God's earthly sanctuary and our spirits are lifted up in a special way into our Father's throne room); to fully cling to Jesus.

For two verses, that's a mouthful! And God did say, "Open your mouth wide and I will fill it" (Ps. 81:10). This mouthful is only a spoonful of what you'll learn when my book on the rapture comes out. While the English word "rapture" is not in most translations, the concept is abundantly present in the Bible—especially in the original words.

You Can Be Ready

I hope that after hearing how bad the world is going to become, and hearing in some detail the truth about the calamities to come ,you are motivated to make some changes in your life, the changes God calls repentance. My prayer is that you will heed the warnings in this book and be granted worthy to "hide for a little while" until the Great Tribulation and God's wrath run their course (Isa. 26:20).

Being raptured, as indicated by the Hebrew words in Isaiah 26:20–21, is a matter of free will. The choice is yours.

Please be encouraged, however. Thank God for His mercy. He doesn't require perfection to be raptured. He meets us where we are. He will rapture you if you're learning and willing to change when you find out how you need to change.

Sometimes, in fact, we aren't yet ready to hear about some things we need to change in our lives. For example, I just learned of some major problems in my young childhood that I was only able to receive at the age of sixty-one. These problems had to be lain down to Jesus on the new moon.

God wants us to have a willing heart and be in the process of change. We're all works in progress. We aren't where we want to be, but we aren't where we used to be. You don't have to be able to recite all the intricate prophecies explained in this book. You simply need to have a desire to obey Jesus and be the clay the Potter is transforming progressively into His image.

God is looking at your heart. He wants you to have a heart to love and obey His Word of love. Here is a prayer that will help you:

> Jesus (whose Hebrew name *Yashua* includes the rapture concept), I declare that I answer Your call as given in the conceptual Hebrew words of Isaiah 26:20–21: "My beloved brothers, allow

> Me to bring you out of trouble and tribulation so that you vanish from the eyes of the world and from Satan. Answer My call to be lifted up to heaven, to the assembly of believers, in the rooms made especially for you. Shut off the calls of Satan and the pressures of the world for a little while so that I may hide you—body, soul, and spirit—from all evil, disaster, death, or defeat. Allow indignation and the evil one their last vain efforts so that I will see you. Answer Me when I send for you to come into safety—a safety that is beyond time, beyond space, beyond evil's ability to touch you ever again, and beyond the effects of My punishment that will come upon the earth."

I hope you'll be able to make this declaration: "Thank You, Jesus, for Your call of love. I answer without hesitation, with joy and appreciation."

God has set before you the way of life and the way of death and destruction. His exhortation to all of us is written in Deuteronomy 30:19: "So choose life in order that you may live, you and your descendants."

The choice before you is one of literal life and death. I pray that by God's bountiful mercy and grace, you will choose life.

Appendix I:

The Saving Truth So Few Know

How do you sum up the truth a vast majority of Christians ignore, but truth that is proved by almost seven hundred Bible verses? That's a challenge I undertake by God's grace in this appendix. More on this subject is available in *Why Doesn't God Heal Me?* I have abridged this teaching by posting Scriptures that I invite you to read in your Bibles and meditate upon. I have given ten sermons on the subject, in which I didn't come close to citing the many verses that prove the truth so few have understood.

As I click the save button in this document, I save it all. And that's what God wants to do with all mankind, to save us all. But if we are to believe most evangelists, most people are burning in hell right now. They say, "If you die tonight without accepting Jesus, you will burn in hell!" They think they're doing God a service by cursing people to hell. Instead, they're spouting the popular doctrine of demons accepted without question by the majority of the Christian world.

Christians won't be ready to face the events beginning in late 2012 if they persist in this false doctrine, wasting their time and spinning their wheels by going against God's will and plan.

While God's desire is to save all mankind (2 Pet. 3:9), He has bound Himself by His words to grant Adam and thus mankind free will. Adam relinquished the authority Jesus gave him over the earth to Satan, who then became god of this world (2 Cor. 4:4). God foreknew that Satan would hold most of the world captive to do his will (2 Tim. 2:26; Rev. 12:9; Eph. 2:1–3). By respecting man's free will, which most would turn over to Satan, God had to wait until Jesus' return on the seventh-day Sabbath of a thousand years (Gen. 2:1–3; Ex. 20:8; 2 Pet. 3:8) to begin to bring Sabbath-like rest and peace to the world.

Jesus explained that a miracle was required to bring salvation to men in this age. No one could come to Jesus unless the Father drew them to Him (John 6:44), allowing Jesus to choose them (John 15:16), after which by the miracle of intercessory prayer they would be able to be free enough from Satan and teachable to accept the call of Jesus.

God foreknew that few would respond to the call and actually be chosen to be the first fruits in this age (Mat. 22:14). Matthew 13 explains what many pastors do not understand. Jesus gave the parables of the Kingdom of God to hide the truth from the majority only to reveal the mysteries of the Kingdom to His small number of disciples (Mat. 13:10–17; Isa. 28:9–13). You may be part of the few.

If Jesus had tried to save the world at His first coming, as many believe, He would have been a miserable failure. But He never said that was His goal. He knew that Satan had the authority over the world for six days of one thousand years, so He did not dispute that fact when Satan offered him the world in the desert temptation (Mat. 4:8–10). Jesus called the gate that leads to salvation in this age narrow (Mat. 7:13–14), evidence that the majority would have to wait until later.

That later time is prophesied in multiple Bible passages. The timing, however, is only clearly spelled out in this verse: "The rest of the dead did not come to life until the thousand years were completed" (Rev. 20:5). The second part of the verse referring to the first resurrection is parenthetical and refers back to the latter part of the previous verse.

God promises those who are guided by the Holy Spirit and walk in faith in this age "a better resurrection" (Heb. 11:35). Why call it better and call those who attain it "blessed and holy" (Rev. 20:6)? It is better than the second one because those called later will not be the Bride of Jesus (Rev. 19:7; 2 Cor. 11:2; Eph. 5:25–32).

The third resurrection, or raising up of the body to be thrown into a lake of fire, is obviously the worst resurrection of the three (God's first number of completion, exemplified by the Trinity and our triune nature of spirit, soul, and body). It is, however, one that comes from a deliberate, willful, and long-term choice of rejection of Jesus and the Holy Spirit (Heb. 10:26–27; Heb. 6:4–6). And that brings us to the most misunderstood Bible subject—hell.

Hell Yes or Hell No?

In the briefest of summaries, here is the truth about hell. By hell, we mean the Hebrew *sheol*, the place of the dead.[55] The Bible refers to various compartments of hell (Prov. 7:27), including "the depths" of hell (Deut. 32:22; Isa. 14:9–15; Ezek. 32:23), the lowest pit where the demons abide, or the bottom levels, the only levels where fire is mentioned. A middle compartment also exists (Ezek. 32:21).

The top compartment, before Jesus came, held the righteous dead. They couldn't become alive and be with Jesus until He paid the price for them (Eph. 4:8- 9; Ps. 68:18; 1 Pet. 3:18–19). The top levels of hell are holding places where the unconscious souls of the unsaved sleep until a future resurrection.

The souls and spirits of those who walked with Jesus but later committed the unpardonable sin are alive in the bottom levels of torment. They will be resurrected with their physical bodies to be thrown into the lake of fire in the same way that Satan is referred to as a "man" in Isaiah 14:16. God will give him the body he wished for in Job. In that

55 *Gehenna fire more often refers to the end-time lake of fire, especially the final one that encompasses the earth in Malachi 4:1–3*

book, Job made comments in conceptual Hebrew that prophesied the devil would have a body that could be destroyed by fire.

The Bible contradicts the popular belief that the wicked will burn in hell inside the earth forever. Hell is *not* forever! The Bible says so.

Hell itself is burned up at the end in the lake of fire (Rev. 20:14), which is a globe-girdling fire that destroys both the earth and the heavens that Satan has marred. God replaces them with new heavens and a new earth (2 Pet. 3:10–13). Satan and the demons and spirits of humankind or mankind that accepted Jesus but finally followed the evil one will be banished to a dimension of total darkness outside this universe—separated from God and from each other (Jude 1:13; 2 Pet. 2:17).

Probably less than one hundredth of one percent of all mankind who have ever lived will lose out on living as sons and daughters of God in the Family of Love forever. That's because God is indeed love with a capital L (1 John 4:8). He is not the cruel Father some make Him—the devilish Daddy who sends people willy-nilly to a fiery hell when He didn't even draw them to Jesus in this age.

That's how many portray the being who they think is the God of "that Old Testament," the one who loved to smite people. That's not God. That's not Love. Foreknowing what Satan and Adam would do, He devised the best plan to enable almost all mankind to be saved, while respecting the free will of everyone. God's wisdom is infinite.

If the Christian world had kept the days God calls holy rather than pagan holidays falsely baptized Christian, they would understand this concept. Jesus was the first of the first fruits by His resurrection just before sunset on a Saturday, three days and three nights after He was buried on the Wednesday Passover (Luke 23:54; Mat. 12:40; John 19:14). He offered Himself as the wave sheaf offering on the day after the Sabbath during the Feast of Unleavened Bread (Lev. 23:11), although that day was not a separate feast.

It was Pentecost, or the Feast of First Fruits, in which the small first harvest of souls in this age was depicted (Num. 28:26; Lev. 23:16–21). The larger harvest of Tabernacles and the Last Great Day signified the majority who come to Jesus in the Millennium and the much greater harvest when the book of life will be finally opened to all mankind through a second general resurrection (Rev. 20:11–12). Those who were blinded by Satan in this age (2 Cor. 4:3–4) will be given a second life and time of judgment (just as we who were called now have in this age, as seen in 1 Peter 4:17).

God tells us that "it is appointed for men to die *once* [no reincarnation here] and after this comes judgment" (Heb. 9:27). Judgment is simply a time period given in which we decide whether or not, and demonstrate how much we want Him. It's not a long line of people waiting before Jesus for sentencing to hell or entry into heaven. We are being judged now for the degree of our reward in the level of future service. We are thankful we can go before the mercy seat of Jesus and be washed in His blood.

The vast majority of Christians believe we should be on a frantic crusade to try to save all the nations today. But God said instead that the gospel of the Kingdom of God would be preached as a witness to all nations, not to save necessarily, because that's God's job, not ours (Mat. 24:14). And we would have understood this simple, saving truth if we had kept God's days, which show His plan of love to embrace all.

Instead, we have told God, as Cain did, that He must respect and go along with the way we choose to worship Him. After all, the majority keeps Sunday, Christmas, Easter, and other pagan days that God told the believers (Israel) not to mix with true worship (Deut. 12:30–32; John 4:24). We tried to force these days on God, all the while persecuting and at times in history murdering those who dared to keep all His commandments (Rev. 12:17; 14:12; Dan. 7:25).

Opportunity for Salvation for All Mankind

The major translations all render the following verse correctly, and this verse also correctly confirms the truth about few being called in this age: "When the Gentles heard this, they began rejoicing and glorifying the word of the [Divine Master Jesus]; and as many as had been appointed to eternal life believed" (Acts 13:48). Who appoints us to eternal life now? God, of course. He doesn't mandate us to go out and try to save those He is not drawing to Jesus. That's not *His* will (John 1:13).

God wrote the Bible as a puzzle, in a foreign conceptual tongue with doctrine established by reading verses that need to be put together. "A little here, a little there" is the way God expresses it (Isa. 28:13). In that way, only the teachable few, the weak of the world who recognize their need for God (1 Cor. 1:26–27), would be freed from Satan's captivity and understand. Only the even smaller group who kept the Sabbath and the holy days would accept the Sabbath rest in Jesus, in whom are hidden all knowledge and wisdom (Isa. 28:12; Heb. 4:9–11; Col. 2:3). Only they would fully grasp the Kingdom mysteries.

For those who accuse God of not being fair by giving people what they call a second chance, consider this. Satan is the one who complains about God not being fair. God is just, not fair. He shows mercy to those whom He chooses to show mercy (Ex. 33:19). Jesus is the perfect Judge because He lived as a man withstanding all the pressures of Satan, and He knows men's hearts.

For most, including all the deceived Muslims, Hindus, Buddhists, atheists, and agnostics who don't know Jesus is the only way to the Father (John 14:6), a second resurrection will be their very first chance. You can see why Joel Osteen and Billy Graham were less than clear to Larry King, a Jew, who asked them about all these people that are supposedly doomed to hell. How indeed could a God of love not give a chance of salvation in Jesus to those who died without knowing Him?

But what about those who were called and yet didn't fulfill what God requires to be the Bride of Jesus in the first resurrection? After all, Jesus said that he "who has believed and has been *baptized* shall be saved" (Mark 16:16), and only those who persevere in overcoming are granted the reward of the first resurrection (Rev. 3:21; Mat. 24:13).

If you are a believer, how many "chances" has God given you? How many times has He picked you up when you failed miserably? Those Christians who don't fulfill the conditions to be in the first resurrection will have to wait to be raised in the second one. God is just, and He is merciful. Who are we, the clay (Rom. 9:20), to judge the Potter? God is perfect and never makes mistakes in judgment. We make the mistake of judging Him.

Through many ministries that are endeavoring to do an end-time work in the spirit of Elijah, and I hope through this book, God is turning His children's hearts back to Him and preparing a people ready to be raptured and marry Jesus (Luke 1:17; Mal. 4:6; 1 Thes. 1:10; 5:9). Will we persist in thinking our job is to save everyone, or will we do the true work God has called us to do, preparing ourselves and others to marry Jesus, preaching the Kingdom message as a witness? Will we obey Jesus when He said to "make disciples *of* all the nations [not trying to save everyone in every nation]... teaching them to observe all that I commanded you..." (Mat. 28:19–20)?

Will we be doing His will when He calls us to heaven in a rapture? Will we be deceived by doctrines of demons that we teach others, or will we prove all things according to the Word (1 Thes. 5:21–24)? It's high time we became the light of the world to shine as examples of love, giving hope to a world that needs God's Kingdom to come.

Appendix II:

A Giant Oversight

In this appendix, before I tell you about the history you haven't read in your school books, I begin by giving you some places you can do further study on these fascinating subjects of giants and aliens. I don't necessarily agree with what all these sources say, yet I want you to be aware that much study has been done on these subjects, even though the mainstream media mocks this research. I follow these sources with a combination of factual evidence, ancient traditions, and divine revelation.

- http://www.thewatcherfiles.com/
- http://www.sidroth.org
- http://www.omegansareliars.com/
- http://www.orgoneblasters.com/
- http://stevequayle.com/
- http://www.mt.net/~watcher/about.html
- http://www.douglashamp.com/
- http://survivormall.com/longwalkersreturnofthenephilim.aspx
- http://www.raidersnewsupdate.com/
- http://enterprisemission.com/
- http://www.ancienttexts.org/library/ethiopian/enoch/1watchers/watchers.htm

- http://www.satansrapture.com/satanseed.htm56
- http://howcouldevehavesexwithaserpent.blogspot.ca/

A History of Mankind Not Taught in Schools—A Giant Oversight

I embark on a study of the history of mankind that isn't taught in schools, churches, and universities, even though it's in your Bible.

Have you ever wondered why people get sick, why we have cancer cells, birth deformities, flu, germs, and rare and weird diseases we don't even have names for yet? Why, when God made everything good for man, do we have plants and animals that are hostile to us? Something had to change them. God wouldn't have us be ignorant of what happened. He said that He grieves the fact that His people are dying for lack of knowledge, lack of understanding of His Word.

God established laws to ensure the health and prosperity of mankind. Everything was to produce after its kind. Mixing of kinds was an abomination to God. Variety within a kind could reproduce, but crossing kinds brought no increase.

The Creator God gave dominion of the earth to mankind, which means that in order to rule on the earth, you have to have an earth suit (a body). Satan didn't have an earth suit, did he? So he lost his ruling dominion over the earth.

As we saw in Chapters 12 and 14, Satan lost his throne to man because of his second rebellion. Nothing that existed prior to the devil's second rebellion had a right to live on the earth.

---

56 *This site has many errors, but I wanted to refer readers to it anyway to show how twins could have two fathers. Sex wasn't the forbidden fruit, but it is possible that Eve did have sex with Satan, which would explain many things and fits into a bigger picture.*

Satan wanted an earth suit, and he wanted to destroy God's plan for mankind. He lost his first estate (or kingdom) when he led with his evolved humanoids his rebellion about 12,600 years ago.

We know there were numerous types of humanoids that existed prior to that rebellion and that they were space travelers possessing computer technology. Amazing rings that made up discs have been found in Siberia and Mongolia. These rings vary in size, but specialists have put them together, finding that they form discs about seven inches across that contain astounding amounts of data.

Officials haven't found the code for reading them, but they can tell what they are made of and the way they are organized. Each molecule is organized in such a way that they had to be made in outer space in zero gravity, which means they had to be made at least 120,000 miles away from the earth.

They are made by magnesium that should burn up in the atmosphere. It's pure magnesium but it is crystallized in such a way that it will not oxidize. We can't do this today. We have never found a device to read these discs nor the code to break into them. The humanoids still out in space do know the codes, and they're waiting and watching for their time to return.

The *Nephilim*

Jude had a good understanding of the *nephilim* and Satan's estate. He says that some angels did not "keep their own domain [or estate]" (Jude 6). These angels didn't do what they were designed and required to do. They were to prepare the earth for mankind, not to create "strange flesh" (Jude 7) and/or any new kind of being... and they were definitely not to mate with women.

We see in Jude 7 that these same demons were the ones controlling events at Sodom and Gomorrah, inciting the gross immorality of those cities. These unspeakable perversions were similar to what happened before the Flood.

Before the Flood, parents sacrificed their firstborn to the demon Molech to be burnt as an offering. In a similar way, beginning in 1972, the legalized sacrifice of our children in the Western world began, beginning a forty-year period of the testing of man to see if repentance would come.

It didn't.

So beginning in late 2012, the consequences of our sins will start to come upon us. It seems Satan, who instigated these sins, knew of this timetable, and that's why the Mayans, inspired by aliens, fixed the end of their calendar on the winter solstice of 2012. But remember, God is in control, not Satan or the Mayans. Greater cataclysmic events would have been coming in late 2012 if the church had been made ready. The tests may still be substantial, but Jesus is giving the church more time to prepare.

The Hebrew word *nephilim* has many implications, among them giants, tyrants, part-trees (*ent* or *eant*, as in *The Lord of the Rings*, one form of gi-ent or gi-ant),[57] giant genitals, or fallen ones, as fallen from heaven like Satan (Luke 10:18)—or the giants and/or aliens who came down from "floating castles" or spaceships in the sky. Other meanings are: abortion, abomination, a mixed kind, a mixture of kinds from the false creator rather than from the Creator God, and genetically engineered beings from Satan's first estate.

While there is no biblical proof of the existence of Tolkien's talking trees, Sumerian writings talk of the great tree people, as do some Brazilian tribal legends. These giants were said to be the height of

---

57 *In English, the word giant was originally pronounced gi-gant (as in gigantic), the same root as in Latin and Greek. Gi refers to gene-spliced hybrids or mixed kinds. Eant or ent refers to something that is part-tree and part-flesh. Giant is a combo of the words "gi-eant."*

nineteen men, or about ninety feet tall. They were used as heavy burden builders on our planet, on Mars, on Titan (a moon of Jupiter), and on the planet Nabiru. It is also said that they were destroyed in a war from the heavens and that they were directed by metal men or robots. They were said to have to avoid too much sunlight, causing them to grow so huge that they would be unable to move.

The Bible speaks of giants, especially in the original Hebrew. Ancient cultures have traditions and writings that speak of human-eating giants or one-eyed destroyer giants.

The green giants were known as the giants of love. They had leaves for hair, highly green skin, and much plant DNA in them. But they were able to move.

Don't think Hollywood is all fantasy. Writers and producers know a great deal of the truth on which they base their movies. Tolkien, who wrote *The Lord of the Rings*, identified these giants as *ents*. They looked like trees that could move around and later became known as cave trolls. They didn't really need to eat, but they did eat. They were able to feed on the air.

These *ents* had to drink water. The more they drank and were out in the sun, the more they grew. Some of these giants were known as sex gods, although they also became known as manifesting principalities that ruled cities, states, banks, and governments.

On www.freedomtruthseekers.com, we have shown actual photos from NASA showing robot heads found on the moon. Many new movies feature robots that make war. This is nothing new. These interplanetary wars occurred before the rebellion that took place 12,600 years ago.

The pre-Flood giants seem to have fallen into two main groups: the area governors (star gate lords) that were twenty to thirty-five feet tall, and the herder-breeder group. This last group, of which Goliath was a descendant, was composed of giants who were ten to twenty feet tall.

They were quite sexually aggressive and always voraciously hungry. They were also quite protective of their area governors. Their purpose was to pollute bloodlines with their genomes, produced by transgenetics.

To be exact, it was the fallen angels (or demons) who controlled these giants. These fallen angels (*naphal*, thus called the *naphalim*) used these perverted giants to pollute the gene pool of mankind. Everyone wanted the *nephilim* because they let off great amounts of pheromones that addicted and overwhelmed people near them.

The shape-shifter group of giants is also referred to as genies, D-genes, or jennies. They were also sexually active and were worshipped as gods because of their ability to change people, grant wishes, and possess harems of about five hundred women. They were able to produce great amounts of sexually addictive pheromones that could control men and women for sexual perversions.

The Bible seems to make an oblique reference to these shape-shifters in the account in Exodus of Pharaoh's magicians who could transform rods to snakes. Middle Eastern traditions are full of information on this type of giants. The Hebrew word *nephilim* for giants, in Genesis 6, implies that different types, varieties, and numbers of giants existed before and after the Flood.

History Channel Blows Cover-Up

The History Channel's series *Ancient Aliens* has blown the lid of secrecy off what officialdom loves to cover up. Many cultures around the world show spaceship drawings with strange-looking humanoid creatures in them. You see them on caves. You see them etched into rock. You find them in Central America, even in the high Andes. You see signs left on top of mountains and runways for ships so the watchers could bring the *nephilim* back.

Temples were constructed high up in the mountains, so high up and with huge, 120-ton rocks, that it probably took the oxygen-independent giants to build them. Some of these temples required people eighteen feet tall to use them.

We find temples in Africa, India, and South America with statues and drawings of both the *guhr* (term originating in the Hebrew) or "gourish," and the ***nephlim***. The gourish were the teachers of science not based on God's Word, and they seemed to have developed and controlled the giants. These *guhr* were also space dwellers after they left the earth to attack God's throne about 12,600 years ago. They have been most interested in abducting humans for experimenting and making genetic alterations on humans.

In Genesis 2:18–23, God taught Adam a lesson that science needs to learn today: man was supposed to reproduce with the woman God had made for him (and of him) so that the blood would stay pure and unadulterated. A wrong planting of man's seed would be a donation to Satan for destroying mankind by claiming man's dominion power and access to eternal life as sons of God.

Satan wanted to get control of the tree of life. If he could get a body and control the tree of life, he wouldn't have to worry about the bottomless pit of eternal darkness. Satan couldn't use Adam and Eve to destroy God's plan unless he first got them to eat from the tree of the knowledge of good and evil.

He needed a legal opening to attack them. As long as they were covered with the glory of God, there was no legal opening to attack. He couldn't use their genetic material or their offspring. He couldn't use anything. And he had no legal right to be on the surface of the earth in the first place.

Adam knew and understood that to eat of the fruit of the tree of the knowledge of good and evil meant death, disease, pain, and suffering.

He knew that an unseen enemy would be able to bring in genetic changes to himself, his wife, and their children thereafter.

These genetic changes would cause death by poisoning, by viruses, by germs, and by genetic dysfunction. The nature and function of plants and animals could be changed, twisted, or intertwined to make new kinds of things that God had not created. Satan lusted after man's blessing and the estate that man now controlled.

Biblical Star Wars?

When God made man in His image, Satan was irked. Satan had been the ruler over the earth since its creation. As we have seen, he caused the first rebellion against God's rule about sixty-six million years ago (more probably 66.6 million years ago) and caused one-third of the angels to fall from heaven (Isa. 14:12; Luke 10:18; Rev. 12:4). A second rebellion about 12,600 years ago caused Satan to lose his dominion over the earth. With each rebellion, he has lost certain powers and privileges.

Satan had to use genetic aberrations for his second attempt at dethroning God the Father. Because these beings were of the earth, they needed spaceships to travel in space. Satan could translate them to the throne of God, but they needed spaceships to get there, as well as special gateways to catapult them through wormholes directly into parts of the universe.

Their earthbound flesh wasn't strong enough to withstand the rigors of space travel, however. These became operators of the UFOS we most commonly see today. There has been a dramatic increase in UFO sightings since 1996, the end of the six-thousand-year reign of man on this planet (to be followed by an extension of no less than nineteen years).

It's interesting that all the pre-Flood drawings and the current drawings match. They're so alike that we know there are at least six forms of *guhr*. They wait and watch for their time of return to lead the battle against the returning Jesus with His saints.

Eve's taking of the forbidden fruit was Satan's breakthrough moment. Yet he heard what Jesus told Eve in Genesis 3:15, that the seed of the woman would crush his head (or destroy him). He knew that unless he polluted the seed, a woman would come and give birth to a man-child who would take everything he had just stolen away.

We can only understand Genesis 4:1 with the above in mind. The "Eve having sex with Satan" theory is indeed a theory. However, it's not unlikely when we understand the full scope of the conceptual Hebrew. Were it true, it would answer many questions and cause the Bible story to fit together and make greater sense.[58]

---

58 *Eve declared she had gotten a man-child, the Eternal. Some translations also say "with the Eternal." The conceptual Hebrew is so flexible that both are probably intended.*
Satan was the false creator god who often appears as an angel of light (2 Cor. 11:14). The Hebrew does not waste its words. God said "the man" had relations with his wife Eve. He didn't say "Adam," but the man. In biblical parlance, when a man has sex with a woman, they become one flesh and it is the same as a marriage, albeit unholy.
While it may sound strange to say, it looks like Eve had sex with Satan! The indication is that Satan transformed himself into a physical being that closely resembled Jesus, whom Eve had seen face to face. She thought Satan was Jesus, "the Eternal," so she said she had her "manchild" with the man she thought was Jesus, but who was rather the false creator, Satan.
When Cain was born, she thought she had the promised seed that would be a Messiah (Gen. 3:15). She spoiled him because she thought he was going to deliver her from her toil and bring her back into the Garden of Eden.

Raising Cain as Savior

Some of the following information is based on the possibility that the "Eve having sex with Satan" theory is plausible from the context of the original Hebrew. I share this teaching because, if true, it would explain much of the Bible story and cause the facts to fit together to establish the whole truth. I admit that it's not possible to prove this theory beyond the shadow of a doubt, but I believe the theory is based solidly enough on the conceptual Hebrew and the rest of the Bible that it merits telling.

Because of his fear of what this future man-child would do to him, Satan put all his effort into controlling Cain. The devil inspired Eve to direct her anger, betrayal, and rejection into raising Cain as her savior and provider of her needs.

Tradition and the Hebrew wording indicate that Cain and Abel were twins, and the conceiving of twins by different fathers if impregnations occur within days of each other has been proven to be a scientific possibility. Eve would thus have taught Cain, but would have rejected Abel and turned him over to Adam.

Abel knew that God required blood offerings for the covering of sin. Cain was determined to tell God who was boss and how God was going to be worshipped. He gave God the defective products of the ground.

This gave Satan greater and greater access to Cain's will and the ability to tempt him to do whatever the devil suggested. As Eve fell by looking, Cain opened himself up to the evil one by the offerings he gave to God. Jesus even warned Cain that sin was crouching at the door (Gen. 4:7). The power of sin was moving to get control of Cain and his children.

Cain rose up (*quwm*, in Hebrew) against Abel, his brother, and killed him (Gen. 4:8). Because of its context, the word has a number of additional meanings that would substantiate the theory that rape preceded the murder and would thus allow Satan to use Abel's DNA (presumed to be from Adam, unlike Cain, if the "Eve having sex with Satan" theory is true).[59]

Cain Opened a Door to Evil

As our footnotes explain, we believe we have evidence of probable cause that the rape-murder of Abel by his brother occurred. This event would have opened the door for cancer, all forms of nerve disease, immune disease, digestive problems, and deformities in man's offspring. Animals could be used after that to mutate diseases and infect mankind. Now Satan and his demons were able to possess mankind. They could actually take over human bodies and/or attack them with multiple personalities.

---

59 *These meanings include: to accomplish a hidden desire or lust; to enjoy as in intercourse; to hold against another's will; and to perform an indecent act upon. These meanings are supported by other clues.*
If Cain were Satan's son, he would already have legal right to use Cain's DNA for evil purposes. He would have needed, however, to have Abel become unclean in some way to use his DNA. Otherwise the devil couldn't produce a different kind than the race of mankind created by God. Without this sinful uncleanness, Satan couldn't pollute the bloodlines, causing these new kinds to help him fight God and His plan.
When Jesus asked Cain where his brother Abel was, Cain said he didn't know and that he wasn't his brother's keeper. The original Hebrew in this phrase (supported by the meaning of "rose up," as explained previously) can imply illicit sexual behavior. The indication is that Cain raped and murdered his brother.
When Satan lost his creative powers, he had to have something to work with in order to "create." He had to manipulate genes, but he first needed an open door—the sin of rape-murder. Then he could use the unclean seed of Cain and the body of Abel to produce the abominations of a new kind.
When Jesus asked Cain what he had done, he meant much more than having sex with Abel and killing him, since Jesus knew all that, and so did Cain. The inference is that Jesus was saying, "Do you know you have now opened a door to Satan that will be extremely difficult to shut?"
Jesus already knew that Abel was dead and all the events relating around it. His question was to let Cain know that he had just offered his brother as a blood seed offering to open a gate for the humanoid watchers and the coming of the nephilim to attack mankind and bring great evil into the earth. Cain didn't initially realize that his donation of Abel plus his own sperm authorized Satan to do that.

Sexual sin caused men to have their will bound to Satan. Paul tells us that when we sin sexually, we sin against our own bodies (1 Cor. 6:18).

Satan was given the right to inspire people to use plants, with their musk and pheromones, to drive men mad with lust and erotic desires. Perfumes and colognes attract the opposite sex in an effort to reproduce the pheromones that these *nephilim* gave off, which could be smelled for miles. Our bodies give off a foul odor when sweating because of the genetic material from the *nephilim*.

We were made to attract only the one with whom we have intercourse, and when it is our marriage partner, the bond grows greater and the light given off during intercourse, as photographed with special methods, is much brighter and more powerful than with any illicit union. Giant DNA allows changes in these intended holy relationships.

Jesus then declared to Cain, "Now you are cursed from the ground, which has opened its mouth to receive your brother's blood from your hand" (Gen. 4:11). This is a curse of failure, futility, and forfeiture. We come under this curse when we wish someone dead or accept the mark of Cain. God gave us 120 years of healthy, productive life (Gen. 6:3). Sin causes forfeiture, a cutting back of that time. And Satan is able to use mental flashcards to remind us of our failures.

It finally dawned on Cain what punishment this presumed rape-murder was going to cost him. He told Jesus, "My punishment is too great to bear! Behold, You have driven me this day from the face of the ground; and from Your face I will be hidden, and I will be a vagrant and a wanderer…" (Gen. 4:13–14). Cain would have no rest and be hidden from Jesus, meaning He would have *no Sabbath rest* and would not be able to meet with Jesus on the only day that represented a door to Him after Adam's sin.

Whether or not rape preceded the murder, Cain became the eighth-day (or Sunday) worshipper of strange gods. His children were cut off from finding Jesus until the eighth-day (or Last Great Day) of God's plan of salvation. The unsaved are raised in the eighth millennium, whereas the Bride of Jesus is raised to rule with Jesus on the Sabbath, or seventh day of a thousand years. Cain's children would be ruled by the mark of the beast and seek a false security in it.

It's important to step back for a moment and realize what Adam and Eve did when they ate of the fruit. They gave Satan and his demons legal right to walk on the earth, to manifest, and to be worshipped. They also gave Satan full legal right to alter plant and animal DNA, and to alter genes and mutate and evolve new kinds. Scientists are even beginning to follow in Satan's footsteps in trying to produce new kinds.

One of my colleagues spoke in 1978 to an East German scientist who had been involved in a project that combined different animal DNA codes with humans. They implanted an altered embryo into a woman. She gave birth to a beautiful, extremely intelligent child, but he had the worst evil attitude you could ever find. He went out of his way to cause pain and suffering in everyone else, and he was totally fixated on sex, especially on male genitalia, from the time he could crawl.

The scientist changed his identity and had plastic surgery. He said, "This child is the end of the world." That child is still alive and is a man now. Will this "other kind" be the son of perdition? Time will tell.

Satan is continuing the pollution program he started with Cain. The righteous line, however, continued to prosper.

The implication of Genesis 5:3 is that Seth was the only son among many who was in Adam's likeness, looking like him and doing things the way he did them. Seth's line began to have children at a younger and younger age (Gen. 5:21), until Lamech's father had Lamech at the age of 187 (Gen. 5:25) and Noah had his three sons at the age of five hundred. The indications are that the advent of the giants blocked the reproductive process.

The recording of Lamech's words regarding Noah is further evidence: "This one will give us rest from our work and from the toil of our hands…" (Gen. 5:29). With the giants impregnating the women before passive males, who allowed these *nephilim* to take their wives, men had to toil overtime to feed their wives, their children, and the voracious giants.

Art throughout the span of human history has depicted UFO encounters and abductions into space, so when God says "men began to multiply on the face of the land" (Gen. 6:1), we believe He may be saying more than is written.[60]

Close Encounters Too Close for the Government's Comfort

We live in such a world of lies and don't know what to believe. It is more than evident that the government squashes any seeming credibility given to alien encounters. The government wants us to believe that only kooks have alien encounters, which is far from the case.

More and more films about aliens and giants are coming out, preparing us to be in fear when we do see them. We don't read much about giants and aliens in our newspapers, because governments, under the pretext of avoiding panic among the population, cover up encounters with giants (usually much smaller ones, about ten feet tall) and aliens. We receive quite credible accounts on Freedom Blog, in great numbers,

60 *We believe the implication is that some were not on the earth; they were either in space or under the earth. Those taken elsewhere were not multiplying, and men on the earth were rendered passive by the giants' pheromones, which drew their wives to the giants rather than to their husbands.*

from hurting people who need help and healing and who wouldn't be making up their experiences.

Governments don't want these things to be known, leaving us to read about them from a new source that tells yesterday's, today's, and tomorrow's news stories—that amazing book of prophecy called the Bible. Yes, the book of the beginnings, Genesis, tells us what will happen in the end.

The children of the unholy unions between the sons of Satan[61] and women were "the mighty men who were of old, men of renown" (Gen. 6:4), taller and stronger than most men but smaller and weaker than the giants.

That which characterized them has permeated our world today. They were immoral and selfish, displaying a macho mentality. Their charisma caused them to be slaves to their lusts, gratifying their sexual desires in public, taking for themselves and trampling on others' rights. They were competitive, boastful, unappreciative, vulgar, and ruled by the flesh.

Our leaders today fit this mode and our society has followed in the degenerate lifestyle of the giants and men of renown. God calls us out of this society, but sadly, even Christians haven't been set free from these end-time perversions (2 Tim. 3:5).

---

61 *While the book of Enoch speaks of "angels" having sex with women, we must remember that angels are simply messengers. They can be spirit being messengers—in this case, fallen angels—or evil physical messengers, such as the humanoids Satan genetically produced, but not the holy angels. It is probable that both demons who manifested as men and humanoids are included in these "sons of [elohim]" (Gen. 6:2), in this case referring to the false creator, Satan.*

Our society is headed on fast-forward to the evil that permeated the world God had to destroy by water. God's grief was overwhelming as He saw the continual evil (*ra*, meaning in Hebrew "a man sees") in the world. In this case, men only saw evil in everything, and the conceptual meanings of the word are full of every kind of evil.

One of the giants who escaped Shem's wrath against them in the area that later became Rome was named *Ra* or *Rah*. Long before Rome was founded, that area was a center for the worship of the sun god Mithra. This evil giant fled to the land of evil (or sin), Egypt, where Satan had the watchers coordinate the building of the pyramids, one which pointed to the constellation Orion in its position about 12,600 years ago at Satan's second rebellion.

Satan used the Great Pyramid and those surrounding it for his plan. Apparently, Satan had giants and humanoids herded into it during his second rebellion 12,600 years ago so they could be translated instantly into spaceships in the constellation of Orion. The combined three-pyramid formation pointed to Orion at that moment in time.

It appears that Satan will also use this method in his end-time rebellion. After all, while many rebellions have taken place, the "war in heaven, Michael and his angels waging war with the dragon" (Rev. 12:7) is a prophesied future event.

Evil (or *ra*, in Hebrew) will have to run its course before it is fully defeated at the hands of Jesus, who will exert His wrath on the growing evil in this earth. God calls His people to come out of the evil of what He calls Babylon (Rev. 18:4), in the same manner that He called His physical people out of the land of sin, Egypt, many years ago, a land in which *ra* and *Rah* ruled.

Rah was raw in every sense of the word, a crude and perverted descendant of Cain, pictured in an eight-pointed sun crest with a hawklike head reflecting his flight from Rome. He made the three pyramids in the shape of Orion's belt in order to call back the watchers. Rah is referred to obliquely in Isaiah 51:9 in the word Rahab. This Egyptian *nephilim* ruler symbolized pride, arrogance, and defiance.

The Holy Spirit has inspired us in Freedom Church of God in these last days to speak out His Word. He instructed us to quote verses especially from Isaiah 49:11 to the end of chapter, and from Isaiah 50–52 on each Sabbath during this time of tribulation. This will build our faith as we celebrate what God has done throughout the ages to defeat our enemies, including the giants. We must be awake from spiritual sleep to call on God to awake "as in the days of old" (Isa. 51:9–10).

In Isaiah 49:24–26, God prophesies the defeat of the *nephilim* that Satan will release just before the wrath of God at the very end. We believe that the Hebrew has some amazing implications.[62]

Giant Purple People Eaters and Endowed Lords

Stories of giants exist in over 146 societies. We even find them in seemingly innocent children's stories like *Jack and the Beanstalk*. Years ago, a popular song spoke of a one-eyed, one-horned, giant purple people eater. Songs from pop culture often reveal realities. We sing about giants that did indeed exist.

More importantly, we call them forth with our pious but in reality irreverent titles taken from a King James mistranslation, "Lord." This famous mistranslation set the course for a significant polluting of

62 *The Hebrew could imply that God will supernaturally translate humans (who have been polluted with giant DNA, and are called Jacob in Isaiah 49:26 for that reason) from the caverns in which the giants will have trapped these victims. These giants will descend from the dark cold they cannot bear, as verse Isaiah 49:3 and other scriptures explain. Isaiah 49:26 indicates that these giants will attack each other after this translation, which causes them to go insane and eat each other. All flesh will know the power of God and know who His chosen are. The humans rescued by God will then realize that God loves them too, and will give glory to the "Mighty One of Jacob [unbelievers and/or humans]."*

Christianity in the last days, paving the way for the return of the evil giants.

The information I provide next may be graphic, but remember that God often uses quite graphic examples in the Bible. I don't share this revelation without a purpose or to be gratuitously salacious; I am simply exposing the deeds of darkness (Eph. 5:11). I don't intend to dwell on the works of darkness, but a certain amount of description is necessary to expose the blatantly pagan and sexual roots of modern churchianity. "To the pure, all things are pure" (Titus 1:15).

The Bible speaks of incestuous rape, gang rapes, and even gives us laws about rape. God uses a Hebrew word for penis, *shopka* (Deut. 23:1), and He speaks openly of genitals (Deut. 25:11). God records Solomon's son Rehoboam mocking the size of his father's penis (1 Kings 12:10). So why should it be shocking when we point out that the typical church steeple is in reality a pagan holdover representing Nimrod's male organ?

It's time we realized that when Jesus forbade His people to mix paganism into their worship of Him (Deut. 12:29–32), He was also talking to the modern church, which has done exactly the same thing, albeit a bit more subtly. When will we begin to believe Jesus meant what He said when He declared that we are to live by every word of God? (Mat. 4:4) The "Old Testament" was all that existed when He said those words.

The truth is, the church has committed spiritual whoredom by mixing sexual emblems and pagan practices into its liturgy. If someone doesn't tell it like it is, the church will neither be warned nor know of its need to repent.

The Baals (or lords) were chosen by the size of their genitalia, so we are inadvertently giving a sexual title to Jesus, and yet that word doesn't call on Him. Instead it calls on the return of the false gods (or Baals) that came in the form of men of renown and giants.

Should it be surprising that the holidays Christians celebrate today to "the Lord" come right out of pagan sexual rites dedicated originally to Baal? The word Baal, written and pronounced one way, can mean loving husband, but when pronounced another way it puts the emphasis on the "rod" of man, and you can guess what that means.

We choose to allow the Holy Spirit to lead us into all truth (John 16:13), even truth that isn't always spelled out in our English translations. A number of strong believers on our Freedom Blog, who in some cases have spent fifty years in the "dark arts," have confirmed what we are saying. They even add that "lord" is the name used to identify a demon named Quagmire. Is it any wonder then that Christians who use the term Lord rather than Jesus almost exclusively find themselves in a spiritual quagmire?

God's people are indeed destroyed for lack of knowledge (Hos. 4:6), but He is moving in these last days to remove the names of false gods out of the mouths of His people (Hos. 2:16–17). Shouldn't the end-time spotless bride be calling on the name of her Bridegroom, Jesus (Acts 4:12)?

Think about that. His name is Jesus. It isn't Lord. It isn't even Christ. Christ was not Jesus' last name. He was called Jesus of Nazareth. He was indeed the *Christos* (or Messiah), the Anointed One. But there are others who are false anointed ones.

The giants' anointing was a bodily fluid emitted through sexual activity and spread in perversion. Anointing can be physical or spiritual. Anointed and charismatic leaders will arise in the end time, but their anointings will be false, leading us away from the truth of the real Anointed One, Jesus.

The term "Christ" is tame compared to Lord. Lord is an unacceptable term when translated back into the original Hebrew. Why are we so naïve to the significance and origin of the steeples on the churches in which we worship? What is different from the Masonic symbols "hidden in plain view" in the capital of the Israelite nation of the United States? What does the Washington monument truly depict? What does the maypole signify? Oh, and here I'll be stepping on many toes… what does the Christmas tree represent?

You may not think you're worshipping the sexual prowess of Nimrod, and you may revolt at the very mention of that possibility, but in our churches today we worship what we know not. We're not worshipping in spirit and in truth. We're mixing our worship with pagan sex symbols that beckon false gods and giants, but God wants us to wake up to the truth: we aren't worshipping Jesus by these methods.

God is merciful, of course. He knows when we don't know the truth but are trying in all sincerity to worship Him, and He meets us in His mercy where we are. He answers our prayers and wants to lead us into all truth (John 16:13). But a Christian world that rejects what it, not God, calls the "Old Testament" will one day have a rude awakening: the prophecies condemning Israel for worshipping the Ashtoreth, the Baals, and other false gods apply to the Israelite, Anglo-Saxon peoples, and they apply to spiritual Israel, the church (Gal. 3:29; 6:16).

It's time for a wake-up call. Sometimes we need a little shock to wake us up. I hope this hard-hitting revelation will do just that.

Appendix III:
Fascinating Q&A You Won't Read Anywhere Else

Freedom Blog is a rare reservoir of godly wisdom and answers to some amazing and unusual questions. I believe you will learn from these questions and answers so as not to be surprised by strange events that have occurred and continue to occur, events that will increase in intensity in the near future. We have basically left the blog posts as they appeared with only minimal editing.

Comments on Freedom Blog Regarding Giants, Aliens, and UFOs

Annetta: Our pastor also told us to expect spaceships to come and save the believers. He said it was what burned Mount Sinai and what is talked about in Ezekiel. If we are not to expect spaceships, what are we to expect when Jesus comes to collect his saints and gather them into the clouds?

Annetta,

Much confusion surrounds the rapture teaching, and a whole book is necessary to explain it. In the first and best rapture, which depends on how believers prepare, Jesus does not come to gather the saints (that is the third rapture, or first resurrection, of 1 Thes. 4:17). They are translated instantaneously and supernaturally in spirit, soul, and body to heaven (1 Thes. 5:23) for a marriage supper that will last for a number of earth years while those involved are outside of time. They won't stay forever in heaven as most preachers falsely teach, but they will descend with Jesus to rule the earth with Him for a thousand years (Rev. 5:10). The TV series *Ancient Aliens* gets far afield of your pastor in putting UFOs into Ezekiel. The presence of Jesus burned Sinai, not an alien presence.

Wenton: I had a dream that I somehow got transported to Mars and was inside a great stone structure. Inside these huge, glass humidity cases were about 170 giants that must have been thirty to thirty-five feet tall. They wanted me to cut some cords that were tying up their hands and feet so that they could eat me. How do I get such vivid dreams and what do they mean?

Wenton ,

Your dream may not have been a dream; it may be astral projection or soul traveling. The giants were said to have the power to pull a person to them in their sleep. If their soul agreed to do something for them or was sexually attracted to a giant, the giant could cause that person's body to be translated to them. It is said that Ra and a group of his evil giants were sent to Mars and bound with bands that they cannot break, but a man can. And they do eat their slaves. I suggest that you learn to pray protection over your soul before going to sleep at night.

Troy: Can prayers be a defense against giants, aliens, and watchers? If the blood of Jesus can be a defense against demons, could it be a defense against giants and UFO aliens?

Troy,

Faith-filled prayers are defense against giants and UFOs. The blood of Jesus is a defense against the controlling demons. The Word of God is a defense against all weapons, especially when you quote Isaiah 54:17.

Norm: I find this a very interesting blog. You seem to be implying that these ships are on the way back with aliens, alien watchers, and giants? Is there any biblical scripture that would indicate that could happen?

Norm and Craig (who thought we were preoccupied with aliens and giants),

A number of verses speak of the return of these aliens, not always in the English translation. We have little written up about them... Jesus' warning not to be deceived in the last days is part of our mission: to tell the truth from the Bible and other writings about Satan's use of giants and humanoids to come against the Kingdom of God, and the proclamation of the gospel of that Kingdom as a witness or warning (Mat. 24:14). These missions involve Satan's effort both to destroy that Kingdom and to try to deceive even the elect. We do not center our message on aliens. We center it on the Kingdom and Jesus, the King of that Kingdom, but we cannot neglect to tell what is going to happen, for Amos says that God does nothing without first revealing it to His servants(Amos 3:7). We must reveal as well the schemes of the devil, and the aliens and giants are a big part of His end-time schemes. Not all our readers may like that part of our message, but we are called of God to warn of these events that are like those in the days of Noah (Mat. 24:37). Giving one post on giants to answer questions about them from our readers and having a series on the subject do not constitute being "preoccupied" with aliens and giants...

The good news is that Jesus is soon going to return and He is going to bring peace to a world torn apart by those who destroy the earth. Only ten percent of today's population is going to be saved alive. *What happened to the other ninety percent* who did not make it? Everything has a cause and every cause produces a result. What happened in Noah's day that caused billions to die? Why did God have the giants mentioned in Genesis 6 and the hosts of the universe to watch what He is doing on the earth? If Jesus caused it to be written for our time, then we should know about it so that we are prepared and at peace in our souls. Otherwise all you can do is fear when you refuse to understand how great our God really is.

Craig: Thank you for your replies. Isn't the goal of a Christian to be raptured OUT of the end time? And if I WAS left to suffer through the tribulation, how I meet my demise is somewhat irrelevant. It is human nature to want ALL the answers; however, maybe there are some things we are not meant to understand yet. After all, Genesis 1:1 says "In the beginning God created the heavens and the earth." …He doesn't tell us exactly HOW He did it. Would it not be a better use of our time to strive to become more like Jesus than being distracted by theories and speculations of what happens to the other ninety percent of today's population? After all, I'm pretty sure there will not be a Tribulation "pop quiz" when we stand before God in the final judgment.

Craig,

The Word of God says to prove all things, holding fast that which is proven true. Even Paul told the brethren that he didn't want them to be uninformed or ignorant about certain subjects (1 Thes. 4:13). Focusing ourselves to be like Jesus is our number one priority, but it does not mean we should be ignorant of everything else that is in the Bible. Believers are promised a destiny beyond the average person's imagination, but that does not mean we don't glean whatever information we can from God's Word and from the Holy Spirit in order to increase our hope and understanding. Peace be with you, Craig. Enjoy the day and every opportunity you have to learn more about our God.

Marsha: Can a fear of giants or being eaten by them cause one to be disqualified from the kingdom of God? Our pastor said that if a giant ate you, your soul would be bound to the giant's controlling demon forever? He said anyone who sins is food for giants. Can you help me understand?

Marsha,

Fear, when taken to an extreme, and an unwillingness to fight it could in the long term conceivably keep us out of the Kingdom, but being eaten by a giant will not. You will simply be resurrected, most probably in the second resurrection after the Millennium (Rev. 20:5). Jesus is the Judge, and He is a merciful Judge. Your pastor seems to know a lot more than most about the giants, but being perfectly free from sin is not a God-prescribed giant repellent. The best thing is to grow by Jesus' grace and be ready for a rapture that will allow us to escape the time of the giants. The faith you build will enable you to face giants without fear if they should come before a rapture. No need to fear being bound to the demons that control giants forever. That's going too far.

Marsha,

There are stories from ancient times that say if a giant eats you or kills you that a demon controlling the giant can claim your soul and use it as a shield against God's wrath. I believe this is what your pastor may have been referring to. Many kings of old used to say that you keep the souls of whomever you kill; they are your slaves forever. It should also be noted that many ancient kings were giants. If you have turned your life over to Jesus and been baptized with water and the Holy Spirit, your soul and spirit belong to Jesus and cannot ever belong to a demon. So stay right with God and you can have no fear of any giant controlling your soul.

Troy: I have been trying to study into giants and these humanoid watchers. If the humanoid watchers were the designers of the genetic structure that the giants had, would they be calling the humanoid watchers dad? Where they programed by demons or the humanoid watchers to be the way they are? Could their instinctive behaviors be reprogramed to work for mankind instead of eating them?

Troy,

The giants could call the watchers their dads, but more likely they would call them their bosses, since Satan hates family relationships. The humanoid watchers programmed animal instincts into the giants. This is a very interesting question for the following reasons: until cell phone technology, what you write would not be possible, but now it would be possible to control them with microwave technology. Even the humanoid watchers could be controlled and reprogrammed.

Troy: Could viral and bacterial warfare be used on these giants and humanoid aliens? If their skin is supposed to be almost impervious to bullets, would lasers work to blind them and stop their attacks?

Troy,

These giants are genetic mutations and already have antibodies in them that defeat viruses, unless a new one is engineered that wouldn't affect them. Lasers would blind them, but their animal instinct would lead them nonetheless to their prey.

They should not be a danger to anyone who escapes the Great Tribulation or who has God's seal on them, since they only appear a short time before the wrath of God. They are part of the locusts and scorpions that come out of a bottomless pit, which in this case includes star gates, from which these giants will emerge (Rev. 9:1–12). They have power for only five months, and those who have the seal of God, even though they did not qualify to escape the Great Tribulation, are protected (Rev. 9:4).

Zoe: Are giants dangerous to just non-believers, or Christians, or those who have been marked by UFOs? Do we have ways to destroy them before they get us?

Zoe,

Giants are dangerous to everyone because:

- They work for the destroyers.
- They are quickly motivated by demons full of wrath.
- They run on instinct to eat and have sex.
- They have no moral conscience of right and wrong.

As far as we can tell, the only things that can really injure them are armor-piercing bullets. And only the removal of their head actually kills them.

The demons that control them are in fear of the Word of God. Now is the time to build our faith by reading and studying the Word and speaking it out against the mountains (or "giants") in our lives.

Here are some examples of powerful words based on God's Word that will keep giants from having any effect on believers:

- "No weapon that is formed against you will prosper" (Isa. 54:17).
- Giant, the hand of God is against you!
- We are shielded by the blood of Jesus.

Anonymous: I have heard that Adam and Eve did not have sex for forty years, and then only after Satan had sex with her. I think that this was a type of Passover that never brought any joy. I also hear that for a thousand years after Jesus returns, there will not be any sex. So why would anyone want to enter this type of joy that passes over sex?

You have an interesting comment and question. The forty-year no-sex idea regarding Adam and Eve is quite possible, but we have no proof of it. However, Genesis 4:1 has certain implications in the Hebrew. Answers to the first part of this question can be found in Appendix II.

As far as the typically masculine comments on sex, yes, there will be sex in the Millennium among physical people. The church is the Bride of Jesus and those saints will have glorified physical bodies like Jesus, with flesh and bone and no blood, sustained by the life of God, with inherent eternal life.

The indications are that they will have a unifying experience with their Bridegroom that is far more pleasurable than physical sex. It's hard, especially for men it seems, to envision anything that could surpass the pleasure of sex, but God says at His right hand are pleasures forevermore, and He only gives good things.

Don't you think the good God who gave us in marriage the wonderful blessing of sex and mutual sexual satisfaction would create a much greater equivalent in His future plan of ecstasy between Jesus and His bride?

Young people especially who may miss out on the joys of marital sex will not be deprived of a similar and more fulfilling and pleasurable experience forever, according to the indications of the original languages. This makes sense because God wants His children to have the best of pleasures. He does not want them to be deprived of any good thing. It is only as we are willing to put Him first that He says He will add all things to us and give us richly all things to enjoy.

We men especially need to realize, in this sex-crazed society that surrounds and beckons us, that sex is not everything, and that sex is not a need like food and water, even though some men may think it is. Jesus lived over thirty-three years without physical sex, and He was the most joyous and happy man who ever lived, even though He endured His share of sorrows, which He laid down to His Father. He was looking forward to the intimacy and ecstasy of love with His future bride, a mystery we have not yet fully unraveled.

As a fulfillment of Genesis 3:15, Satan has used poisonous snakes to attack people, especially women, and to cause seeds of fear to be planted into mankind, causing fear, and subsequently rebellion, to manifest…

Rita: I know from God's Word that perfect love casts out fear; if we show love to the giants, does that mean they would just up and go away?

Rita,

It is likely that those who are ready for an imminent rapture out of the Great Tribulation will not even have to deal with the giants, but those who will be obliged to do so can remember David's experience. He spoke the Word of God at the giant and used a weapon. Weapons may not be necessary when we speak the powerful Word of Love.

No, Rita, giants run on instinct, feeding, and having sex. They even eat their sexual servants. Getting close to Jesus and learning how to use the Word of God against enemies will help much, much more.

Do not fear giants, demons, or people. There are more angels with a believer than with a person in fear.

Lydia: I saw a program where giants were used to fight in robot wars about twenty thousand years before the coming of man. Was Satan somehow responsible for the robots also? And if not, where did they come from and who would have controlled them? These wars were said to have been fought on Earth, the moon, and Mars, yet no one seems to know who or what was behind these wars. It was claimed that NASA brought back robot parts from the moon, yet NASA declined to comment on this. Does the Bible indicate anything like this that could have happened?

Thank you, Lydia. It has been estimated that the war took place twenty-five thousand to twenty-six thousand years ago, so that is when the granite became irradiated and is now at one-half shelf life. We are not sure who was responsible for the robots and what the rush was about. Speculation is that aliens from elsewhere in the galaxy reprogrammed Satan's robots, forcing Satan to destroy them or have the robots destroy his fleet of spacecraft.

NASA's policies are a mystery to them and everyone. Carvings on Mars are shown, but they are quickly removed as soon as they show up. We do not believe NASA knows what their real program is. Some have speculated that the U.S. government has secured the robot heads for technological development and other purposes.

David: I have always believed that there was a vast number of aliens in the universe. Are you saying that Satan created them, or did God? And what would all the hosts of the heavens be waiting for man to do? This host must live a very long time to be able to cross the galaxies to come to earth.

Thanks, David, for your questions. We would probably understand better if we called the aliens Satan created by genetic manipulation "humanoids," or perhaps "alien humanoids."

If you read closely Genesis 2:1–3, you will realize that God completed all *He* created at that time, including all the hosts, which include inanimate stars as well as beings alien to our earth, which was to be the center of God's government forever, heaven being transferred down to earth after God's plan is completed on the planet. From there, Jesus and the saints with glorified physical bodies will be qualified not only to rule on earth but to travel in the same manner that certain ancient writings say the "father of man" (or Adam) did, walking throughout the universe and strolling on the sun.

The good or neutral "hosts" or "aliens" that were created by God (Gen. 2:1; Isa. 1:2) are waiting for us sons of God to come to maturity (Rom. 8:19–22) so we can teach and help them come to wherever God wants them to grow and understand. We don't have all the answers yet, but these are the indications we can perceive.

God's repetitive Hebraic use of the word "He" in these verses shows that He knew a false creator would come to try to emulate and counterfeit what God had done, and that's where the humanoid aliens come in. Satan created them to mock God and to use them to defeat God, mounting up to His throne through "star gates" or gateways opened by certain forces at certain times to allow them to attack and try to defeat God, which of course never did and never will happen.

Yes, it seems the hosts God created can live quite a long time, just as God created Adam to live forever, but he blew it, as we know. It seems these hosts are waiting for man to transform the void and emptiness Satan placed the earth in, just as Jesus did in "re-creating" the earth by His Word. God has given authority to His Sons to help Him re-create the universe, for we are to inherit all things (Heb. 2:8)—and all means all. Sure, God could do it Himself, but because He is love, He allows us to help, and He gives us His power, especially the power of the spoken word.

First of all, God has a plan to bring back from the heavens the men and humans who have been abducted by aliens. We see such an event intimated in Nehemiah 1:9, that those who turn back to God will be gathered by Him back to earth. He says that even "though those of you who have been scattered were in the *most remote part of the heavens,* I will gather them from there and will bring them to the place where I have chosen to cause My name to dwell."

In the movie *Close Encounters of the Third Kind* (which is based on a *true* story!), humanoid watchers brought back the people they had kidnapped in return for others they called to come. In the above verses, God is saying that He will gather those who have been scattered to the most remote part of the heavens, including those who have been abducted by aliens and reside in outer space.

Furthermore, because of the words of a righteous king, God will be required to show mercy to those Satan has caused to come into existence—the humanoid watchers. Most people do not understand the power of the manifold meanings of one conceptual Hebrew word. In this case, the word "foreigner" in 1 Kings 8:41 means not only a literal foreigner who is not of Israel but also an alien or humanoid watcher. Because of Solomon's prayer, God must show mercy to such a being who seeks Him and answer his prayer.

After all, God had placed porpoise skins as a part of the tabernacle covering, intimating such a plan for even the aliens. Porpoises and dolphins are humanlike creatures in their abilities and capacity to befriend mankind. They could symbolize the humanoids whom Satan produced by genetic manipulation. These verses open a door for them to be sons of God if they so desire.

Anonymous: Could Satan repent and change God's plans?

No. Satan chose a permanent path of rebellion and his fate is sealed, as shows Revelation 20. He has committed the unpardonable sin and wants others to follow his example, although very few will. While God's plan allows for human and demonic error, He knows what will happen, knowing the end from the beginning, so nothing surprises Him and nothing can defeat His purpose. That being said, He allows for several outcomes in prophecy in His Word because of free will, but He knows what will ultimately occur.

Bunny: If a person were to marry a humanoid, would they be in rebellion to God? Would God hate the child that came from such a union?

Bunny,

God made us after His kind (Gen. 1:26–27) and He told us not to mix kinds. Nor are we to eat at the table of demons and the table of God. Humanoids are a creation of Satan. We would be in rebellion to God if we had sex with or married a humanoid. Being forced to do so when kidnapped by aliens, which has been documented, is another story. We are not absolutely sure if a child would result from such a union, but we know that God is merciful, and He would not hate such a child.

On Freedom Blog, we often discuss strange things that few know about, yet some of our readers are quite familiar with these mysteries. Steve asked a question about "shape-shifters." This was one of those strange questions we sometimes refer to our apostle Gerald Budzinski, who has gotten a reputation, especially among youth on Facebook, for answering seemingly impossible-to-answer questions. He gets calls from around the world and he asks for God's revelation knowledge to answer the questions about situations that are sometimes unspeakable in their nature.

Gerald was once in a church service when the lady behind him began to change into a hyena. God gave him the knowledge of what to bind and declare, so she stopped the horrid transformation. Some of these things don't sound believable, like the $8000 we received miraculously at a church service years ago to pay for a car. But when you see it, you believe it. As Jesus said, blessed are those who have not seen and believe—although we realize that may be a stretch when talking about demonic activity of women turning into hyenas. Nevertheless, it is important in these last days to know Satan's schemes, and shape-shifting is one of them. So here is the answer in full...

Steve: I would like to know what a shape-shifter is and how any living thing can change shapes. Do you know of any shape-shifters that exist today?

In regards to giants, shape-shifting is the ability to change in order to look like an animal, allowing them to get closer to their prey (people). Certain types of shaman are able to change themselves for very short periods of time to look like predatory animals. In South America, they claim to be able to attach their souls to birds or snakes.

In India, there are humans who claim their bones can become or have become cartilage so they can adjust them to look like someone else for short periods of time. In Africa, witchdoctors can make themselves look like trees or even become invisible.

Shape-shifters, or shifter-changers, either have demons attached to them or are able to speak to the body and soul and change what they look like.

In Western society, people practice different kinds of shape-shifting, including plastic surgery, amputation, and exercising at "fat farms" in order to change their shape.

Believers change their soul by their choices and the building of integrity to shift their shape. We rely on Jesus and His Word, the Holy Spirit, and the body and blood of Jesus to permanently change who we are in order to be more like our Father in heaven. We change into being sons of God.[63]

Korban: I believe people in the U.S. change shapes by putting on costumes and by playing roles about being religious. I also think that their character changes with what holyday they decide to play a part of. Could you ask your apostle what he thinks of this?

Korban,

Gerald's answer: People can change physically and spiritually by role-playing and costumes. Church people often have one face for Sunday and several others for the rest of the week. They are not fixed on being in the shape of Jesus. Thanks for the conceptually-based question.

Anonymous: When I was about nine years old, my friends and I decided to test the Word of God as to see if man could be made of dirt. We made a man-like figure, then just before 11:11 p.m. on the Feast of Trumpets, we spoke the words of life into it. The goyim chased us frightfully for nearly an hour before crumbling. Those who want to have sex with demons and giants do not know what they are doing. They need to cut off their head before they bring great disaster to the earth.

Russel: Were all the giants saved by pre-Adamic spacecraft or was it just a few? If Satan's heart is set only on destruction, how did he become so creative as to evolve humanoids and develop spaceships?

Russel,

Not all giants were saved in spaceships. Some were saved in caverns and some in underwater vaults. Some of Satan's demons are imaginative and had plans for how to defeat God. A demon named Mockery was one of them. God was able to witness what was going on elsewhere

63 *If you want to know more about this subject, visit www.robertsmoreofjesus.com.*

in the universe as far as spacecraft are concerned. However, Mockery developed humanoids to fight God with invading ships right into the throne of God.

Aaron: While reading your blog on giants, it brought another question to mind. If believers are gathered together in prayer, would they be able to stop the giants from attacking them by their prayers in unity? Thanks for the great response to my previous question; it really makes things very clear.

Aaron, you are most welcome. Prayers in unity would definitely protect from giants, and as we grow, we thank God that the prayer of even one righteous man or woman will avail much. Speaking out the Word can be even more powerful since angels are released to defend us (James 5:16; Ps. 103:20). Isaiah 49:25 is another verse that is good against giants, who are tyrants: "And the prey of the tyrant will be rescued; for I will contend with the one who contends with you..."

Rudy: While I was visiting Nova Scotia last fall, I heard of similar situations to the ones experienced by Monty (who had a comment about zombies). The question I have is how do you stop this, how do you make sure that they are no longer walking around?

Rudy, when we encounter a dead body walking, we must realize that the body is being controlled by demons, usually a familiar spirit (a demon that basically followed the person from cradle to grave and knows exactly how he or she thinks, talks, and acts). These curses are sometimes put on people before they die to become "after death" curses. As a believer, you can reject the curses in Jesus' name, bind and send the demons to the pit, and send the soul of the person, which has no will because of the demonic control, back to *sheol*, the place of the dead, to await the call of Jesus at the time of their resurrection.

Response to a question about zombies: Stacy, I was given a verbal report from a high government official that said that they estimate more than a million zombie-like bodies were documented last year in North America alone. I believe that this was a ten-year summary of reports that was released in 2010. But it is a very large number. Brazil apparently has the largest number per capita in the world.

George: If a demon enters your mate and is able to change her shape, would that mean that the demon in her could change you as well, if you had sex with her. I think my wife has more than one demon in her and she has now started trying to have sex with everyone and everything.

Yes, George, since you are one flesh, the demons could change you as well. She is affected by the combo of siccibus and iccibus. You have authority over her spiritually, so you can bind those demons by name, in Jesus' name, and send them to the pit. Call for her healing by Jesus' stripes and ask her to consult a physician, since it seems these demons have caused a hormonal imbalance, judging from your last sentence.

Randy: Was Jesus a shape-shifter? When the women at the tomb could not recognize Him or His apostles, did he have an angel overshadowing Him or was HE just covering his person?

Randy,

Yes, Jesus was a shape-shifter in the best sense of the word. Transfiguration is the word used to describe His change. He can move from man-like to God-kind instantly. When He arose from the dead, He was not recognizable because of the damage that had been done to His body. No angel covered His real shape and features. He only received His glorified physical body when He ascended to His Father in heaven the day after His resurrection to be accepted as the first of the first fruits.

Lloyd: Do you think that the spirit of Nimrod causes people to hate the things of God? To call what is evil good and good evil? Could that spirit be responsible for the building hatred for believers that we see growing so strong in the U.S.?

Thank you, Lloyd, for the great question. Yes, your speculations seem to be right on all counts. Nimrod was a mighty hunter and destroyer of those who would seek the things of God. He hated anything to do with righteousness, and he loved cruelty. Traditions say that because he had one arm longer than the other, he was in constant pain in serving the genie Gilgamesh. The hatred, pain, and cruelty formed a combination principality that is constantly gaining in power and authority over the human race. Many feel the effects since this principality now controls all governmental departments and courts.

Miss Fateesma: If angels cannot marry humans and have children, how come demons can manifest as humans and have children? Do children of demons have eternal souls, or are they immortal, like the demons? Is it okay to have sex with a demon even if you don't get pregnant? Can a demon rape you against your will? If you have sex with a demon, does that mean you are married to him? If yes, should you get a divorce? And would that divorce be legal and acceptable to God, who hates divorce?

Fateesma,

Thank you for your question. Jesus said in Mark 12:25 that at the resurrection people will "neither marry nor are given in marriage, but are like angels in heaven." Angels are not to marry or have sex with people because God commanded it to be so. Angels are free to rebel like the demons did and go against that order, but they have chosen to obey. Cain was "of the evil one" (1 John 3:12) in more ways than one, since in Genesis 4:1 Eve said upon the birth of Cain: "I have gotten a manchild with… the Eternal" ("the help of" is in italics and is not in the original).

So Satan actually appeared as an angel of light, as he often does, appearing as Jesus to have sex with Eve and bring forth Cain. As with Satan, demons can manifest as people and have sex with women. Some demons specialize in this. The children born of such unions are evil, but they are physical, not immortal. It is definitely not okay to have sex with a demon. We are called to resist the devil and the demons so they will flee from us (James 4:7). A demon cannot rape someone against his or her will unless that person has opened a door of sexual sin for that to happen. If you have sex with a demon, yes, you're married to that demon and must speak out a divorce. God does not hate divorces from demons. Malachi 2:16 is referring to divorce between a man and a woman God has joined together.

Mose: I saw a UFO just south of the Bow River. It followed me about three miles towards Calgary. Very scary. I didn't sleep for two days after the event.

Munice

When I was about eight years old, I went camping with several friends near a deep crater lake not far from my dad's place. We saw four different ships within two days go into the lake and then come out about an hour later. We were convinced never to go camping there again.

In response to a question by Munice about the harvesting of humans by giants as part of Northern Alberta tradition, one of our bloggers wrote the following response.

Thank you, Munice. The UFOs are indeed a sort of advance to that harvest by the man-eating giants to come just before the wrath of God. It is helpful in the writing of our prophecy book to know that this period of great darkness, beginning at the winter solstice of 2012, is supported by the traditions of Northern Alberta.

Renne: Is it the DNA from giants that makes us susceptible to sicknesses and diseases or is it the viruses that are leftover parts of gene splicing that causes sicknesses, because they can mimic the cell key?

Renne, we become susceptible to sicknesses because of sin, both original sin and current sins. The viruses we see today are leftovers from the original gene splicing. They attach themselves to our genomes and force our cells to duplicate them over and over. They were originally developed by genies to alter and mutate mankind into humanoid hybrids.

What these genies did is the active cause of all weaknesses, diseases, and defects we see in the human race today. Many scientists are specializing in doing the same thing so that new and different defects will develop.

Angie: I know this sounds odd, but do the different sizes in women's [breasts] reflect interference by the watcher humanoids, the aliens, or is it the result of these giant DNA?

Angie, the answer is all of the above, as well as diet in preteen years, amount of exercise, and the amount of pheromones from the father and male influence in the early teens. All contribute to the level of growth and functionality.

Edna: Regarding star constellations, why did you pick out certain constellations as being sources of evil humanoids and giants? The Pleiades are supposed to be sisters, not covens of evil.

Edna, when God called Abraham out of the tent, He pointed him to the stars to see if he could count them, saying that He had caused the constellations to declare His plan and timing. Satan caused people to look at the stars as astrological signs. God identified the Pleiades, Orion, and the Great Bear as star groups that had decided to back Satan against God carrying out His purpose (see Job). The sisters you speak of were witches of seduction, not leaders of love and truth.

John: Something has bothered me about this blog since I first read it. Are the demons that control the giants going to be punished or just the giants themselves? If a giant is under the control of a demon, does a giant have free will? Could they repent?

John, giants do not have free will and they cannot repent. All indications are that they run by instinct. The giants will die. All demons will be sent for all eternity to the bottomless pit. There would be no purpose or results in praying for their repentance.

Raj: In India, we have many good gods that were giants. Some owned both sexes. How can you imply our giants were bad? Even their sex was good and our land prospered.

Raj,

There is no God but the Creator God, *Yahovah*, the Father, Jesus, and the Holy Spirit. Giants may be worshipped as gods, as money and sex are in the Western world. It is all idolatry, but only the true God can open your mind to understand that.

You need to understand that Eastern gods were giants and noted for their large sexual equipment and were worshipped based on feelings, not understanding. The Western world takes on the worship of Eastern gods because they also prefer ignorance to understanding. Everyone judges facts and truth based on feelings nowadays, which is the reason our world is so messed up.

Blayne: I would not believe in UFOs or aliens until I was in one of their ships. The U.S. government has said that they do not exist and I believe them.

Blayne,

If you believe everything the government says, we pray God will give you the spirit of discernment.

Terry: Alien abductions happen daily and only a fool would deny it.

Daisy: You have never been abducted. Therefore, you are talking about your own personal theory—not fact or truth. I have a sister who I saw being abducted. I know what it did to her when we finally got her back. Please consider the suffering of those abducted and their families before you condemn without knowledge.

Ken: I have been reading and checking into alien abductions and I think that, with this much material available from so many people and so many areas of the world, they have been abducted. These people need support and acknowledgement, not condemnation and ridicule. I, for one, will be praying for them.

Edward: For fifty years, I have been having bad dreams about a UFO that chased my dad's car for over ten miles. In these dreams, I see the ship catching the car and then some reptile-like thing grabbing me from out of the car and eating me alive. I seem to remain alive with other people inside its belly, even though my body was in pieces and being dissolved. I think that whatever was in the craft put that dream in my head. Do you know what it means?

Edward,

Having dreams of such events are very common and are often a warning that an abduction has occurred in your past. Because of the trauma involved, such experiences often allow the aliens the opportunity to plant nightmare-type dreams in your mind to rehash what happened. The fear involved energizes a device that they imbed in the skull. Accepting the peace of Jesus and the cleansing of the blood will neutralize the dreams, the device, and the uncleanness they left upon you. After that, you need to read up on the trauma communion and do that. We thank God for your freedom.

CPSIA information can be obtained at www.ICGtesting.com
Printed in the USA
LVOW100226201112

308038LV00002B/3/P